THE VIEW FROM
NASHVILLE

ALSO BY RALPH EMERY

Memories
More Memories

THE VIEW FROM NASHVILLE

Ralph Emery

WITH PATSI BALE COX

WILLIAM MORROW AND COMPANY, INC. / NEW YORK

It is the policy of William Morrow and Company, Inc., and its imprints and affiliates, recognizing the importance of preserving what has been written, to print the books we publish on acid-free paper, and we exert our best efforts to that end.

Library of Congress Cataloging-in-Publication Data

Emery, Ralph.
   The view from Nashville / Ralph Emery.
      p.   cm.
   Includes index.
   ISBN 0-688-15150-7
    1. Country music—History and criticism.   2. Country musicians—
Biography.   I. Title.
ML3524.E45   1998
781.642'092'273—dc21
[b]   98-19588
                                                      CIP
                                                     MN

Printed in the United States of America

First Edition

2   3   4   5   6   7   8   9   10

BOOK DESIGN BY JO ANNE METSCH

www.williammorrow.com

To Chet Atkins and Owen Bradley,
whose leadership made Nashville
one of the most important
music centers in the world

CONTENTS

PREFACE

I believe I had the best seat in the house as country music grew up over the past four decades, and it all started in 1957 when I got fired from a job at WMAK radio in Nashville. It was the luckiest break I ever had because it led me to WSM. I'll admit that applying for a job at the mighty WSM, with its roster of legendary broadcasters, was one of the most fearsome ideas I'd ever had. But I was desperate for a job, and figured I didn't have anything to lose. The station interviewed a lot of people that week, but by a stroke of luck, I was the only one with both straight announcing and disc jockey experience.

I went on the air in November 1957, hosting the all-night show. It was the perfect place to get to know the stars of country music, because so many of them stopped by when their buses rolled into town after a tour, following a long recording session, and, yes, after a few hours of barhopping many stopped by feeling the effects of what Tex Ritter called "a touch of the grape."

I was named Country Disc Jockey of the Year six times, and ultimately inducted into the Disc Jockey Hall of Fame. And no matter what twists and turns my career in country music has taken, I think of myself first and foremost as a broadcaster. That is what introduced me to the best seat in the house, after all. Over a quarter of a century later, after years of working in radio and television, I began hosting *Nashville Now* on a new country music cable channel called The Nashville Network.

Nashville Now started in 1983 and was the bellwether show on TNN for the first ten years the network was in existence.

We went on the air on March 7, 1983, and signed off the third week of October 1993. A lot had happened during those ten years. *Music City News* readers had named *Nashville Now* their Favorite TV Series five times and *Cable Guide* magazine even voted me the favorite cable television personality in 1987. I wrote two autobiographical books, *Memories* and *More Memories,* that sold nearly a half million copies combined; *Memories* hit #2 on the *New York Times* Best Seller list. But the biggest thrill of all was the night Barbara Mandrell surprised me with the *All Star Salute to Ralph Emery,* when most of the big names in country music came together for a special tribute. I've never known whether they came because of me or because they were afraid to say "no" to Barbara, who called them all personally.

In 1993, with *Nashville Now* winding down, I was ready to embark on a new path and retained a contract to continue with TNN, exploring some other programming opportunities.

In order to allow my successors, *Crook & Chase,* to build their own set, we did the last week's shows in San Antonio at Fiesta Texas. At that time, TNN's parent company, Gaylord, had some ownership in the theme park, so we were dealing with a lot of our old friends and acquaintances. During some of our conversations I mentioned that among the "other opportunities" I was exploring was long form interviews, which I would produce through my new company, Ralph Emery Television Productions.

On the Record wasn't a new idea. I'd done several extensive interview shows while at the helm of *Nashville Now.* The first was with my old friend Merle Haggard. Bayron Binkley had phoned me one day back in 1986 and asked me to shoot some interview footage with the Hag so they could intersperse him talking with concert footage. All they needed for the special they were doing was some comments about his hit songs, but once we sat down to talk, Merle and I started talking about his entire life and career in country music. It was as if the cameras and crew members didn't exist.

When I took a look at the raw footage, I saw that the piece could stand on its own; after they pulled the scenes they needed for the concert video, we reedited and aired a second special titled *An Inside Look: Poet of the Common Man.* Later that year I was in London when an American tourist stopped me in Harrod's department store. "I don't know who you are," she said apologetically. "But I loved the show you did with Merle Haggard!"

It's funny how some of the best ideas happen by accident. We never set out to do a long form interview, but we ended up with one. And I hadn't planned on doing another one until Johnny Cash saw Merle's interview, called me and said, "You know, Ralph, I've got a few things to say, too." Well, how could I turn down a chance to talk to the Man in Black? Once we did Cash, the network decided to do one on Eddy Arnold, and then on Dick Clark.

We tried something different with Dick's interview. I traveled to California to interview him, then he interviewed me. I wrote at length about the Dick Clark interview in my second book, *More Memories,* and I remain very proud of that show. Rac Clark, Dick's son, and the producer of *Prime Time Country* on The Nashville Network, told me that one Christmas Dick gave all his children copies of the interview and told them it was the best one he'd ever done. "Dad told me that in this interview we'd learn more about him than in any other," Rac said. "He's done a lot of interviews, and I'd never heard him say anything like that before."

My debut *On the Record* was shot in the spring of 1994, and since I wanted to come out of the chute with a winner, I asked my good friend Reba McEntire to be my first guest. The numbers were good, and *On the Record* was on its way. Over the next year we taped Vince Gill, Dolly Parton and Tammy Wynette. In Dolly's case we got so much good footage that we made two versions, an hour-long show and a ninety-minute show. Since then we've done shows on so many more people: Lorrie Morgan, Barbara Mandrell, Mel Tillis, Tanya Tucker, Olivia Newton John, Travis Tritt, Johnny Cash, Randy Travis . . . the list goes on. I traveled to Houston, Texas, to interview the former President and First Lady, George and Barbara Bush, and to North Carolina to interview television icon Andy Griffith.

The experience is vastly different than when I was doing a ninety-minute early morning show, as well as a ninety-minute evening edition of *Nashville Now.* Those hours will burn you out. If you ever had an ad lib in your brain, the grind of two live shows a day will kill it. With *On the Record*, I have the opportunity to do research like I never had before, and I find I love doing it.

I want to single out three guests from the *On the Record* lineup who are real troupers. Tanya Tucker had a bad cold and Tammy Wynette was so sick that she had to go to the rest room and heave just before the show. I don't think anyone realized just how sick she was. Her health problems finally caused her death in 1998. Johnny Cash's health was fragile to the point that following our show to celebrate his newest book, he did only a few more days on the road, a few more book signings, and he was admitted to the hospital where he almost died. I appreciated the effort they gave me to make sure that I got the interview.

I know I've been fortunate to be here in Nashville and witness the growth of this wonderful industry called country music. And as I read through my two previous books, I realized there was a wealth of material left out. There were so many more stories to share that when my agent, Mel Berger, spoke with me about a third book, I agreed.

A View from Nashville is not as autobiographical as *Memories* and *More Memories*, but more of a behind-the-scenes reflection on the people and times that shaped this town. As he did in Nashville during his life, Decca's Owen Bradley looms large on the pages. He was the man who, perhaps more than anyone, turned Nashville into a major recording center. The contributions of other recording visionaries are chronicled, too: Capitol's Ken Nelson, RCA's Chet Atkins, Columbia's Don Law and Monument's Fred Foster.

Many of my friends are included: Barbara Mandrell, Dolly Parton, Conway Twitty, Loretta Lynn, Brenda Lee and Faron Young. Nashville represents more than country music: rockabilly king Carl Perkins recorded here, and Brenda Lee proved that Nashville could launch a rock 'n' roll star. Fred Foster and Monument Records brought us Roy Orbison, certainly one of popular music's greatest voices—the man Elvis Presley called the "greatest singer in the world."

Country music has long run the gamut from traditional to pop-flavored to rock-inspired; just listen to the very traditional Loretta Lynn, the pop stylings of Patsy Cline and the rock-edge of Waylon

Jennings. Today's Nashville reflects those styles too, with traditionalists like Alan Jackson, balladeers like Vince Gill and Southern rockers like Travis Tritt.

I was fortunate to get one of the few interviews that Colonel Tom
Parker ever gave, thanks to my friend Buddy Lee and the fact that
the Colonel was a big fan of *Nashville Now*. Sadly, the interviews with
the Colonel, Owen Bradley and Carl Perkins were among their last.

The stories included in *A View from Nashville* are often funny, often
poignant, and sometimes heartbreaking. And it starts with the death
of a friend, Conway Twitty. Ironically, Mel Berger was in Nashville
waiting to meet with Conway about writing an autobiography when
the star died. Mel attended the funeral with me, and as we were
leaving, he said: "If you write another book, you should begin
right here."

So that's where I began writing back in January 1997. I just had
no idea there would be so many more funerals of dear friends to
report by the time I finished in the winter of 1998.

Don't feel you have to read this book front to back. We've included vignettes throughout—some funny, some sad. This was just
one of the great ideas from the book's editor, Henry Ferris.

1

CONWAY TWITTY:

THE UNCROWNED KING

OF COUNTRY MUSIC

onway, are you all right?'' Dee Jenkins called through the door of the bathroom. There was no answer.

"Conway?'' she called again. With a tight feeling in her stomach, Dee pushed the door open. There, sprawled on the floor, lay one of country music's most legendary stars, her husband, Conway Twitty.

It was 6:42 P.M. on Friday, June 4, 1993. The two had been in Branson, Missouri, where Conway was playing a series of matinees at Jim Stafford's Theater. Just before an intense afternoon show, Conway packed up the car and drove to his bus. Since his schedule called for a hundred dates in Branson that year, Conway had brought his favorite vehicle to drive, a 1980 Pacer station wagon. It wasn't what anybody would call a "star vehicle" at first glance, but Conway loved it and drove it everywhere. He loved that car so much, in fact, that he'd just had a coat of classic car paint applied and replaced the vinyl seats with leather. He unpacked the Pacer and loaded up the bus for the trip back to Nashville.

Shortly after they were on the road, Conway turned to Dee and said he was experiencing an odd sensation in his side.

"I feel a kind of pressure," he said. "I just don't know how to explain the feeling to you."

"Well, I'm going to get the driver to stop," Dee said. "Let's go into Springfield and get it checked."

"No, it's not that bad," Conway answered. His lack of concern worried Dee, since earlier that day, before his show, he'd mentioned having a slight feeling of discomfort. It didn't stop him from performing, though. With Conway, almost nothing stopped him from fulfilling a concert date.

Dee usually kept the bus stocked with food, but this particular run had been a long one and the refrigerator was bare. When it was time for dinner, they stopped at a food mart so the band and crew could eat. Conway didn't feel hungry, so he and Dee stayed behind. He hadn't complained, but Dee knew he wasn't feeling well. When he went into the bathroom and didn't come back out for some time, she became concerned and called in to him. Conway didn't answer. She opened the door and screamed for help.

The band and crew scrambled back on the bus, and called 911. By the time the ambulance and paramedic team arrived, Conway was conscious and trying to reassure Dee. Cox Medical Center in Springfield, Missouri, was alerted that Conway Twitty was being rushed to their emergency room.

Dee felt more confident after the emergency room doctor finished his examination, because he said Conway appeared to have a textbook case of kidney stones. Several years earlier, Conway had suffered problems with kidney crystals that caused him to cancel several shows. He could be in for a painful night, but he would be all right. The ER personnel continued routine procedure. Conway's blood was checked for allergies, then he was wheeled into X-ray to be injected with the dye that could confirm the preliminary diagnosis.

Conway insisted Dee accompany him to X-ray, and once there, her confidence was short-lived. The doctor soon gave her terrifying news: Conway had an abdominal aortic aneurysm and had already lost a dangerously large amount of blood. Dee's first reaction was disbelief. Conway had recently undergone an extensive physical for a new life insurance policy and been pronounced fine. And although he was taking blood pressure medicine, it was down to just a half a pill a day. Conway had developed high blood pressure ten years earlier and since that time he had taken pains to stay in shape. He was watching what he ate, working out and walking. His weight was down to 168 pounds, the least he'd weighed in years. Their strategy seemed to be working, because until the episode on the bus, Conway appeared to be in excellent health.

Frantically, she attempted to locate their family doctor in Nashville so he could consult with the Springfield doctors. Failing that, there was nothing she could do but wait. When they wheeled Conway into emergency surgery, one of the band members began phoning Conway's children to alert them.

Dee knew how dangerous this condition could be. Aneurysms form when pressure from the blood flow causes a weak artery wall to distend. If that distention bursts, the condition becomes life-threatening in minutes. And she realized that in Conway's case, the condition was probably genetic, since a few years earlier Conway's brother Howard had been diagnosed with the same condition. "Don't even sneeze," his doctors had told Howard as they rushed him to surgery. Dee also knew that her husband had that day performed his usual intense, hard-hitting show, a show that obviously would strain his abdomen.

Ironically, Conway's friend and duet partner, Loretta Lynn, was also at the Springfield hospital, where her husband, Mooney, was a patient. Loretta was sitting with Mooney when a local newscast reported that Conway Twitty was undergoing emergency surgery at Cox Medical Center. She sat up straight in her chair, wondering if she'd fallen asleep and dreamed such a thing. Just then the hospital chaplain walked in and confirmed the news. Loretta stumbled out of Mooney's room to find Dee. Loretta's nerves were already on edge from a sleepless bedside vigil with Mooney. She stayed with Dee until Conway was out of surgery, then finally went back to Mooney's room to try and sleep. Loretta remembers a chaplain rushing into Mooney's room to tell her that Conway was gone.

"I'd always heard that the spirit stays right there above the body for a while," Loretta says. "So when I went back to intensive care, I stood beside Conway's body and tried to talk him back down. I said, 'Conway, don't you die on me! You know you don't want to go!' I cut such a shine they had to take me out of the room."

"I was lucky she was there because Loretta is the strongest woman I know," Dee later acknowledged.

Subsequent events proved to me that Dee Jenkins is herself an unusually strong woman. Her husband didn't make it through the surgery, and June 5, 1993, the final day of my friend Conway Twitty's life, marked the beginning of a nightmare for his widow.

Problems arose immediately. Because Conway had died in a state other than Tennessee, there was a short-lived legal snarl about releasing his body for transportation home. Once that was untangled, Dee phoned her uncle, Dennis Sprouse, in Nashville, and he began to make burial arrangements. Reba McEntire had sent her private plane to Springfield with Conway's sister and son Michael the night of the surgery. After Conway's death, Reba sent a second plane to bring some of the family home. That return flight carried a somber group of passengers.

By the time Dee's uncle picked her up at the airport in Gallatin, she says she didn't want to live.

"When I got back to Tennessee, I felt I had no reason to go on. I couldn't imagine facing a world without Conway. The doctors in Springfield had given me pills for my nerves, and I was ready to take all of them. But when I walked into my uncle Dennis's house, my little nine-month-old godson, Nicholas, came into my arms and patted me on the back, as if he somehow understood and wanted to help me. It was instinctive and protective and something changed inside me at that moment. That little pat saved my life."

It was a life, however, that was forever changed. For the next year, every Friday was the same. She replayed June 4 throughout the day, remembering when they awakened, when Conway began to pack the car, right up to when they wheeled him into surgery. "I couldn't get that day out of my mind," she confesses. "If I tried to go out and do something to take my mind off of it, I'd end up running back home and collapsing in the kitchen, crying and looking at the clock as the minutes ticked by."

On the advice of her doctor, Dee went to a grief counselor, sometimes seeing the therapist on a daily basis. "I asked myself all the usual questions," Dee says. "Had I done something awful in my life to cause this tragedy? Was God mad at me? I knew I was mad at Him." One thing she learned: healing the wounds of grief is much like healing a burn. The wound must be reopened and cleansed. It can't remain closed to fester underneath the surface.

But on that first day home, the initial concern was the question of his burial. Conway never wanted a funeral service. Earlier that year, Roy Acuff had been buried before the public even knew of his death. Conway said that was how he'd want it if something happened to him. "He'd been through my mother's illness and death with me," Dee says. "And he frequently said he didn't want a big fuss or people crying over him. He said he wanted to be like Roy, buried before anybody knew he was gone." But as much as she would have liked to comply with his wishes, Dee understood that funerals and memorial services are for the living, not the dead. There were too many grieving family members, friends and fans; although Conway was the most private of celebrities, private arrangements were impossible.

I don't think Conway ever really felt comfortable in the role of a celebrity. The public versus the private Conway was a bit of an enigma. I had a chance to see that side of him once when we were taping a segment of *Pop Goes the Country*. While the cameras rolled, he seemed so relaxed that I'm sure the audiences believed television was a natural medium for Conway Twitty. Then we had a little downtime while the crew readjusted the lighting, and we just had to sit there with nothing to do in front of an audience of several hundred people.

Conway looked out at everyone and tucked his head down so no one could see what he was saying. "I don't know how you stand this," he whispered. He was most comfortable when he was singing. He didn't have a lot of stage talk. Just that voice and those songs. He didn't like to be called a legend, either. On one radio show we taped out at Twitty City, he told me that words like "legend" usually were used when the active years of someone's career were over. So he tried to avoid it.

His intensely private nature made what happened in the wake of his death all the more tragic.

I don't remember where I was when I heard that Conway was dead. But I do remember being shocked that a freak occurrence like a burst blood vessel in his stomach could have done this. Conway Twitty was in as good a shape as anyone I knew. He had looked like a million bucks the last time I'd seen him.

Conway was buried on Sunday, June 6, in Memory Mausoleum in Sumner Memorial Gardens in Gallatin, Tennessee. Dee called me soon after the private service and asked me to host his public memorial, scheduled for Wednesday, June 9, at the First Baptist Church in Hendersonville. She said I was the person she first thought of, because I had always been there for Conway, and I appreciated that.

Conway and I went back a long way, phone-friends before we actually met. Back in the early 1960s, when Conway was a rock 'n' roll singer, he used to call me on my late night show at WSM. Conway had one of the most important pop/rock hits of 1958 with "It's Only Make Believe," and by the early '60s he was one of the nation's biggest rock 'n' roll stars. I always thought it was strange, a rock celebrity out on the road, calling me up at WSM to request Webb Pierce and George Jones records.

But when you work the late shift at a radio station, you get a lot of weird calls, and you never know what you might play that would encourage a seemingly unlikely individual to call. One night I heard from Woody Herman, the bandleader, who had finished playing a show in Indianapolis, and just checked into his hotel room. He had turned the radio on and heard Pee Wee King's western swing version of "The Woodchopper's Ball" on my show. He'd missed my introduction of the song, but heard me identify the station: WSM in Nashville. So he phoned in to ask who had just played the song.

The first time Conway and I actually met was when one of country music's songwriting greats, Harlan Howard, brought him to the WSM studio one night in 1964. When he introduced us, I responded with, "Are you that guy who's been calling me and requesting country songs?" He said he was that guy, and he not only loved to hear country songs, he liked to sing them. I didn't know whether he was for real or not, so I called him on it and asked him to sing me something.

"Well, if you've got a guitar I will," Conway answered.

Johnny Russell was there that night so he went out and got his guitar, and Conway sat down and sang "The Window Up Above."

"I believe this old boy really does like country music," I said into the microphone.

It made a believer of me, and Johnny Russell, and the listening audience, too, because the phones lit up with people from all over the country wanting to know about this great country singer who'd just performed live on WSM.

Harlan gave Conway his big break in this business. They both played shows in Canada during the early '6os, and Harlan started making a point of attending Conway's performances. Back then the country and rock performers frequently ran into each other at venues, since many clubs booked both kinds of acts. Conway told about Faron Young approaching him one night in 1956 and asking him his name. Conway had changed his name from Harold Jenkins, hoping that an unusual name would give him an edge at radio. And when he said to Faron, "It's Conway Twitty," Faron reared back and said, "Well, hell. You can't help that!" Faron didn't know that Harold Jenkins had spent months searching through maps for stage name ideas before he found Conway, Arkansas, and Twitty, Texas.

One night at a ballroom in Ontario, Conway sang Harlan some of the country songs he'd written. Harlan said, "I don't know why you're out here singing rock 'n' roll. You're a country singer."

It wasn't easy to get out of rock and into country. Harlan helped Conway extricate himself from the managers and agents who controlled his career and didn't want him moving to country music. Rock was big money even in those days, and it was sure to put a dent in his earnings, at least for a few years. And the only person in his organization who didn't care about the money was Conway. It took courage to walk away.

The next step was to secure a recording contract.

Harlan used a little reverse psychology on Owen Bradley at Decca to help Conway get a record deal. He simply pitched some of Conway's songs to the record executive, knowing that the vocals would impress Owen. Sure enough, Owen listened and said, "Well, I like these songs, but who's that singer?" Harlan kept up his game, responding, "Oh, it doesn't matter who's singing the demo."

"Well, it does matter because I like his voice," Owen protested. So Harlan told him it was Conway Twitty, the rock star, and that he was looking for a deal in country music.

"You send him to see me," Owen replied. Harlan must have grinned all the way home.

What most people, even in the industry, don't know is that Conway hoped to have parallel careers in rock and country. When I recently spoke with Owen about Conway's signing, Owen explained: "When I first met with Conway, he told me he wanted to continue recording rock as Conway Twitty, and release country records under his real name, Harold Jenkins. I believed strongly in his ability to sing country, but wasn't sure how he could balance the two recording careers. I called my boss in New York, Paul Cohen, and Paul said he didn't think it would work. So Conway gave up rock and focused on country.''

When Conway signed with Decca in August 1965, it turned out that one of his labelmates was already a big fan. Loretta Lynn told me she had known about Conway since she was fifteen, and someone gave her a poster of him. She immediately put it on the wall of her bedroom. And, she laughed, "It was a good thing the poster was big, because the wallpaper we had wasn't much!" Evidently Mooney Lynn didn't mind, because she kept that poster for years, even after she was a big star.

Owen Bradley knew Loretta was a big Conway Twitty fan, so he arranged for the two to meet. One day when she came to the Bradley Barn studio, Owen said, "Loretta, you told me you love Conway Twitty, didn't you? How would you like to meet him?" Loretta said she'd love to meet him, but she probably wouldn't ever get to do it.

"Just turn around," Owen told her.

Loretta said she almost fainted, because there stood the man she'd only heard on records and seen on a poster on her bedroom wall, Conway Twitty. They felt an immediate rapport, but it wasn't until 1967, when Conway, Loretta and Mooney traveled to England for the Wembley Festival, that the two started talking about singing duets together.

Conway said Owen Bradley was against it at first, afraid the two might end up fighting each other, possibly like Dolly and Porter had done. Of course, that never happened, and the two remained fast friends until the day he died. And both Conway and Loretta liked the idea of a former rock singer dueting with one of the most country women in the industry. Conway always loved Loretta because it never occurred to her to question the fact that he'd never had a country hit when they first talked of recording together. Some country stars might have shied away from the connection to a rock artist trying to break into country music. Not Loretta Lynn.

By the time Conway and Loretta released their 1971 debut single, "After the Fire Is Gone," Conway had more than established himself in country music, with six #1 releases, including his signature song, "Hello Darlin'." "After the Fire Is Gone" confirmed their belief that the two voices were a magical match, because the song went straight to the top and stayed there two weeks. They became one of the top duos in the history of country music, having twelve top-10 hits and winning twenty-two major industry performance awards.

His four Duet-of-the-Year awards with Loretta were the only Country Music Association awards Conway ever won. He was named Top Male Vocalist at the fan-voted *Music City News* awards four times, and he once took home honors as both the Academy of Country Music's Male Vocalist and the American Music Award's Favorite Male Artist in the country category. Considering his huge career, with fifty-five #1 singles, it is strange that he didn't win more CMA awards. Jim Foglesong, who headed MCA during some of Conway's biggest years, told me he believed the award problem had to do with the fact that Conway didn't have a big management team playing politics in Nashville. Conway liked to do things himself, and he was never an in-your-face kind of guy; his industry presence may have suffered some from it. Another factor, according to Jim, was Conway's low-key nature. Some of the folks on the television board at the CMA thought Conway wasn't too exciting in front of the cameras. I never felt that way, even though I knew he wasn't comfortable on television. His fans watched him for his repertoire, not his repartee.

I always wondered if that hurt Conway, and I asked Dee about it.

"I don't think the lack of industry awards bothered him," she said. "He won a lot of fan-voted awards, and those meant the world to him. I do think he wished that when some of the newer artists were coming along they'd have named him as an influence, though. I think he'd have liked that."

One of the fan-voted awards that Dee said mattered most to him was one I'd had a hand in. The first year we came on the air with *Nashville Now,* I held a secret viewers' poll to discover the audience's favorites. I say secret, because we spent weeks polling our studio audience, tracking letters and phone calls about specific performers without letting it out that we were keeping score, because I knew fan clubs would begin to call and write, and we wouldn't get a fair accounting. When the thousands of "votes" were tallied, Conway

Twitty had won Top Male Performer and Barbara Mandrell was the Top Female. But all that seemed very far away as I tried to think what I would say the day we buried Conway.

I was uneasy about hosting his memorial. No matter what you called it, when all was said and done the service was a funeral, and I'd certainly never emceed a funeral before. I thought a long time, and one thing I decided was that I would try to keep the tone positive. Conway would never want the memorial to turn maudlin.

I looked out over the crowd while the First Baptist pastor, Glenn Weekley, spoke, and while Conway's daughter Kathy addressed the crowd in a shaky voice. I saw so many stars there to pay their personal respects. Among the entertainers present were Naomi Judd, Barbara Mandrell, Vince Gill, Reba McEntire, the Oak Ridge Boys, William Lee Golden, Mickey Gilley, Roger Murrah, Harlan Howard, Don Cook, Donna Hilley, Buddy Killen, George Jones, Johnny Russell, Tammy Wynette, Jeanne Pruett, The Statlers, Tony Brown, Connie Smith, Bill Anderson, Porter Wagoner, Ricky Skaggs, Sharon White, Garth Brooks and Jimmy Dickens. Many more would have been there were it not for their tight summer concert schedules. And there were fans who had come to Nashville for Fan Fair, many of them expecting to attend Conway's annual star-studded events. He loved Fan Fair and wanted to make sure no fan left feeling like they hadn't got their money's worth.

So when I took the podium, I said: "I recall for a number of years in conjunction with Fan Fair, Conway presented a Fan Fair Explosion. Conway, today this is your Fan Fair Explosion." I read a letter Conway's daughter Joni had written to commemorate her father, then introduced another of Conway's close friends, Vince Gill.

Vince walked to the microphone and said: "When I first moved to Nashville, my first gig was at Twitty City with Steve Wariner. I went on to work with Conway on records, and even after I had some success as an artist Conway called me to sing harmony on his records. After I had a big enough hit, I went on tour with him. A lot of people talk about the old school and the new school, referring to folks like Conway and George Jones as the old school. I'm just here to say that the old school was best and I'm glad I got to be a student of it." And then he dedicated a song to Conway: "When I Call Your Name."

A great many people spoke that day, including George Jones, who had been on tour with Conway and Merle Haggard that year. George talked about the fact that he and Conway started out at the same time back in the '50s, and ended up by saying, "I love him and I'll miss him very much. And I'm speechless." The Statler Brothers sang "Rock of Ages," prefacing it by describing Conway as ". . . the kind of guy that as soon as you turn your back on him, he'll say something nice about you."

Ronnie McDowell told a story that was a wonderful and typical Conway Twitty tale.

"On my twenty-ninth birthday, Conway brought me a forty-five-record and said, 'Ronnie, I know this is a hit. I want you to take it home and I want you to listen to it. It's a smash.' I took it home and listened to it. I brought it back the next day and said, 'Conway, I don't really like that song.' Conway said, 'Okay, well, then, I'm gonna record it and you watch. It'll do good.' He did and it went to number one. It was 'Happy Birthday Darlin'.' That same day he told me he'd make a deal with me. He said, 'If I find a song that I think is a hit, I'm gonna give you first shot at it.' So next he brought me 'I May Never Get to Heaven,' and I told him I didn't like that one either. It went to number one. He also gave me 'In a Letter to You.' I sat on that for two years. Eddie Raven cut it and it went number one. I want you to know that not long after that, Conway pulled up in his Pacer at Center Point B-B-Que, and I said, 'What's up, Conway?' He said, 'I've got a song for you.' I didn't hesitate."

At this point, Ronnie's voice broke.

"He was an introvert and so am I. He hated speeches and so do I. He was the best friend a song ever had."

Ever since Dee had asked me to host the memorial, I'd been thinking about a poem I'd often heard Tennessee Ernie Ford quote. It's about overcoming adversity, poverty, climbing the ladder of success and being successful despite yourself.

> I asked God for strength, that I might achieve;
> I was made weak, that I might learn to humbly obey.
> I asked for health, that I might do greater things;
> I was given infirmity, that I might do better things.
> I asked for riches, that I might be happy;

I was given poverty, that I might learn to be wise.
I asked for power, that I might have the praise of men;
I was given weakness, that I might feel the need of God.
I asked for all things, that I might enjoy life;
I was given life, that I might enjoy all things.
I got nothing that I asked for
But everything I had hoped for.
Almost despite myself, my unspoken prayers were answered.
I am, among all men, most richly blessed.

I read the poem, saying, "Conway, if you were here today, with friends being the most valuable possessions a man can have, this particular poem speaks to the occasion and to your life."

Following the Oak Ridge Boys' performance of "Farther Along," Porter Wagoner paid insightful homage to Conway, the person and the entertainer: "I met Conway in 1956. He told me then, 'I'm gonna be a country singer like you.' He was a man of his fans, not a politician. He didn't hype his music. He didn't move in political circles to promote his career, he left that up to his fans to determine. I think that's probably why he had more hits than anyone in the history of country music. He left enough memories and music to last us forever."

Tammy Wynette sang "Precious Memories," and her husband, George Richey, stayed on stage long enough to play piano while Connie Smith sang "How Great Thou Art."

When Connie handed the microphone back to me I said, "Well, Conway, your Fan Fair Explosion had Vince Gill, George Jones, Ronnie McDowell, The Statlers, the Oak Ridge Boys, Tammy Wynette, Barbara Mandrell, Bill Anderson, Porter Wagoner, Mae Axton, Connie Smith and now for your big finish, here's Miss Reba McEntire."

Reba stepped up to the microphone and said: "My mama and daddy taught me early in life, if you start a project, you finish it. Give it one hundred and ten percent. Well, when you are a kid that goes in one ear and out the other. You probably keep about fifty percent of it. It wasn't until I started working with Conway that I realized how that applied to your everyday life. When you work for a living you give one hundred and ten percent. You start a project and you finish it. Conway did that. I've worked with him when he had a huge temperature, the flu. He went to soundcheck. I thought, 'My goodness, he's a superstar and he's going to soundcheck.' That showed me to work harder because Conway did. I never did get to tell Conway how much a big fan I was of him and how he instilled in me what my mama and daddy started. I wish I had. They planted the seed and he set it a little bit deeper. If Dolly was here I'd tell her too. But Barbara, and The Statlers—you all helped me tremendously. It was your determination and hard work.

"Conway was a legend. He'll always be a legend. He wasn't a renegade. He plugged right along steadily. And if I can be one-fourth the role model he was to some little kid, then I will be doing the job God sent me down here to do. I opened shows for Conway. He was my big tour after The Statlers let me open for them. I loved opening for Conway because I loved for him to close the show with that audience reaction. Well, I'm not ready for Conway to close the show yet."

None of us were ready for Conway to close the show yet. And none of us were ready for what was about to happen to his image. As the family backlash against Dee began, I was reminded of the words Joni Jenkins had written in the letter I read for her at her father's memorial:

"Daddy, I know you are with us today and that gives me great comfort. You are the most unselfish and forgiving man I've ever known in my life. You told us all to turn the other cheek and to forgive one another in times of trouble. And I'm thankful for each special person you have brought into our family. Rest assured that we will remain one big happy family."

ONE BIG

HAPPY FAMILY

Was Dee one of those special people to which Joni re-ferred? Did "one big happy family" include the woman he loved? In the years since Conway's death Dee has spent much of her time in court, trying to get her rightful share of Conway's estate. She has never asked for more. Yet she has been portrayed as a scheming gold digger at best and a possible poisoner at worst. The word "bitch" is scratched across her name on the tomb she hoped to one day share with Conway. She can no longer decorate his grave, since the flowers will be destroyed by the following morning. She repeatedly receives hang-up phone calls. Her life has been threatened.

On June 22, 1993, headlines in the Nashville *Tennessean* read: TWITTY WILLS HIS CITY TO KIDS, OMITS WIVES. People who knew the close relationship between Conway and Dee had were stunned. How could he cut her out of his will? More importantly, why? The will in question was an old one, written in 1982, later amended in 1984 when Conway and his second wife, Mickey, divorced. Why after all those years hadn't Conway written a new will?

Some speculated that Conway and Dee hadn't been quite the happy couple they appeared. Others believed he knew Dee would be provided for anyway. Under Tennessee law, Dee was eligible for a third of the estate whether she was in the will or not. She was additionally provided for through insurance policies and personal property.

The fact is, Conway had begun work on a trust in 1988 with attorney Gary Spicer. The trust was a long and complicated document, since Conway's sources of income included many and varied interests. The trust begins thus:

> This agreement is entered into (date) by and between Harold L. Jenkins (P/K/A Conway Twitty), of Hendersonville, Tennessee, as "Settlor" and as the "Initial Trustee."
> Article 1.2 identifies Delores V. Jenkins as "Settlor's spouse."

As the Settlor's Spouse, Dee would have immediately received, free of trust, one and a half million dollars in cash, plus one third of the Settlor's gross estate.

> Article 10.1 [reads]: Upon the Settlor's death, resignation or incapacity, the following persons are hereby nominated, in priority of the order enlisted, to serve as successor, trustee of the Trust: (i) Settlor's spouse. [Author's note: *Additional names had not been decided upon, but Conway indicated he planned to include at least one bank as a secondary trustee.*]

As the Trustee, Dee would have been in complete control of the remainder of his estate, including what funds would be transferred to his children and when.

Given that Conway planned to leave his wife Dee in complete charge of his entire estate, it is telling that he made the following provisions:

> Article 9.7: Determination of support. In determining whether to make discretionary distributions of net income or principal to a beneficiary [Author's note: *Conway's four children*], the Trustee [Author's note: *Dee Jenkins*] may take into account:
> (A) The beneficiary's demonstrated ability to handle money usefully and prudently and to assume the responsibilities of adult life and self-support,
> (B) The standard of living to which the beneficiary is accustomed,

(C) The obligation, if any, and the ability of others to support the beneficiary,

(D) The beneficiary's educational expenses,

(E) The beneficiary's health care expenses,

(F) The stability of the beneficiary's marriage,

(G) Other income, resources, and assets known to the trustee to be available to the beneficiary, and

(H) The affect [sic] of such distribution on the beneficiary's ability to qualify for or to receive governmental benefits or assistance (including social security, Medicare, Medicaid, and supplementary security income benefits).

Conway realized his children might fight Dee following his death, possibly contesting the Trust, so he made provisions to stop any such action:

Article 22.5: Incontestability: The beneficial provisions of this instrument (and of Settlor's last will and testament) are intended to be in lieu of any other rights, claims, or interests of whatsoever nature, whether statutory or otherwise, except bona fide predeath debts, which any beneficiary hereunder may have against or in Settlor's estate or the properties in trust hereunder. Accordingly, if any beneficiary hereunder acting without probable cause asserts any claim whatsoever (except a legally enforceable debt), statutory election, or other right or interest against or in Settlor's estate, Settlor's will, or any properties of the Trust, other than pursuant to the express terms hereof or of said will, or directly or indirectly contests, disputes or calls into question, or conspires to do any of the aforesaid, before any tribunal, the validity of this instrument or of said will or the validity of any provisions of this instrument or said will, then (i) All costs related to any such assertion by such beneficiary shall be directly charged to and borne by such beneficiary's interests hereunder, and (ii) Such beneficiary shall absolutely forfeit any and all beneficial interests.

Clearly, Conway meant to protect Dee in the strongest terms possible. But the document, which had taken four years to produce, had been sitting in his accountant's office for about a year being reviewed for tax consequences. The document was still without the signatures it needed, one of them that of Dee Jenkins, whom he'd named trustee. "I told Conway I didn't think the children would accept me being in charge of their trust funds," Dee told me. "Conway suggested also naming his son Jimmy as an additional trustee, but that worried me, too. I told him that Jimmy would then find himself in a terrible position between me and his sisters, as well as his mother, Mickey, whom I was sure would reemerge should Conway die. And of course, I never believed God would take Conway without taking me with him. I believed that when we went, we would go together."

When it came time to read the will, his children wanted to see the Living Trust, thinking that Jimmy was named a trustee. But once they read the sixty-page document, it was never mentioned again. And so, Conway's earlier will stood, and the public believed the star had made no provisions for Dee, who would simply receive the third due a surviving spouse under Tennessee law.

In the existing signed will, Conway had appointed two close friends and longtime business associates as the estate executors, Hugh Carden and Donald Garis. Hugh had worked for Conway for twenty-five years, and Donald, twenty-one. Days after Conway died, the two men called the family together and explained the importance of working together in the coming months. Without cooperation, the estate would be sold to the highest bidder. "And that would be a shame," Hugh Carden said. Everyone agreed. It would be a shame.

Dee was entitled to a year's support as well as her third of the estate. She and the executors came up with what they thought was a fair arrangement. "I suggested that the estate pay me three million dollars over a period of five years, interest free," Dee says. "But I offered to work for the money over the next two years. At the end of this period it would have all been theirs."

That seemed reasonable. After all, Dee had been Conway's right hand since 1977. She understood the intellectual property, and how to increase the estate's value. She coproduced his albums. She also was the person who dealt with the record label and she had the respect of the music business community. And even though Dee was owed the money, she was willing to continue working for it. The press had a field day on learning the amount of her monthly payments: $19,500. She was criticized for the amount she spent on cosmetics, on landscaping, on clothing. Even Dee's $400-a-month payment to her grief counselor came under attack. People were left with the impression that the entire amount was her so-called "consultant's fee," but of the $19,500, only $3,000 was a salary. The additional $16,500 was due her by state law.

Kathy Jenkins objected to Dee's payments and to her continued involvement in the business. When Kathy asked the Sumner County Court to remove the estate's executors, Joni and Jimmy sided with their sister. Conway's oldest son, Michael, stuck by his father's old friends, Carden and Garis. Part of Kathy's objection may have been that executors had suspended the Twitty children's salaries until the estate could be settled. Conway had always supported his children: he built them homes at Twitty City, and kept them on salaries between $45,000 and $55,000. But unlike Dee's spousal payments, the children's salaries were not dictated by state law.

The children further questioned a 5 percent raise Carden and Garis had recently given themselves. The executors, who were Twitty employees prior to Conway's death, countered that the raises were a token amount and justified because of the additional duties now thrust upon them. Kathy, Joni and Jimmy were also angered that the executors had sold one of Conway's buses to alleviate a cash shortfall that left only $63,000 in the business and petty cash accounts. However, they had signed the agreement to sell the bus.

The executors were simply trying to keep the business running and, with Dee's help, continue to turn a profit. But the judge granted the children a temporary restraining order preventing Carden and Garis from hiring employees, making any purchases or entering into any business deals. When media coverage threatened to turn the entire affair into a circus, Dee asked for a gag order. The judge refused and it became a media circus. Even though she was under no obligation to do so, she returned to the estate the $36,000 she'd been paid.

"Conway was such a private person," she says. "He would have hated the publicity so much. I prayed the children would keep the differences confidential." It was not to be. Business deals couldn't be consummated and with no one in charge, Conway's estate appeared to be dangerously close to crumbling. Hugh Carden saw his worst fear coming true, and announced that if agreements couldn't be reached, the estate would have to be sold, its debts paid and the remaining moneys distributed among the five heirs.

The estate's attorney, Rose Palermo, explained it this way: "In order for the estate to enter any long-term business agreements to make money from Twitty's musical legacy, Kathy, Jimmy, Joni, Michael and Dee must be in agreement over the estate's future. Since they cannot agree, the estate must be liquidated so all heirs and creditors receive their shares." The estate included Twitty City, record and song royalties, licensing agreements and property in both Tennessee and Oklahoma.

Kathy Jenkins wanted to play an integral role in the Twitty businesses, and on December 29, 1993, Palermo went to court to question Kathy's abilities and expertise. "The heart of this lawsuit is her [Kathy's] hurt and hatred and resentment toward the widow, and it has caught these poor executors in the middle," Palermo said. During questioning Kathy admitted that she had experienced substance abuse problems and had two drug overdoses, according to the Nashville *Tennessean* on December 30, 1993.

TWITTY HEIRS SAY WIDOW RICH ENOUGH the headline blasted on April 5, 1994. "I'm surprised the heavens don't open up and Daddy doesn't come down and knock her in the head," Kathy Jenkins told the *Tennessean*. "When he [Conway] died, I said 'No more Daddy's little girl,' " Kathy added. "It's time to grow up."

Still, no agreements about the division of properties could be reached. A year later Twitty City was sold to Trinity Broadcasting Network, with the California conglomerate planning to turn the complex into a country and gospel music attraction and television production center. In August of '94 it was announced that the entire estate would go on the auction block. Items were removed from Twitty City, as well as from Dee and Conway's home. One of the first things the court took from Dee was Conway's beloved old Pacer, with a book value of $625. Much more would be taken, including many of the couple's personal possessions.

"My father draped her in diamonds," Kathy Jenkins told the *Tennessean*. "She was lucky to have known him."

Three years later, Dee Jenkins shakes her head sadly when she rereads Kathy's comments. "That's the sad part," Dee says. "Of course I was incredibly lucky to have known Conway. But not because of money. I was lucky because he was the love of my life. And he was the finest human being I ever met.''

DEE SAYS THAT she doesn't remember the first time she actually met Conway Twitty, but that she does know the first time she heard him sing. She was a teenager living in Laurel, Maryland, and had just gotten her first driver's license. While she was driving around town, Conway's "Together Forever" came on the radio. Years later the two were sitting in a Baltimore airport, and Conway mentioned to Dee that while he was in the military, he'd once been stationed at nearby Fort Belvoir, Virginia.

"It's funny to think about you being here then," he admitted.

"Well, what year would that have been?" Dee asked.

"Nineteen fifty-four," he said.

"Uh, what month in 1954?" Dee asked.

"Oh, no!" Conway laughed. "It was June. Were you even born yet?"

"Just barely," she said.

Despite the twenty-five-year difference in their ages, Dee and Conway were close emotionally and mentally. "They say opposites attract, but that wasn't the way it was with us," she says. "We were friends for years before we started dating, and during that time we learned that we had many of the same beliefs. We were both spiritual, religious people. Neither of us drank and although Conway smoked at the time, he later gave that up. Neither one of us liked to go to parties or go out carousing. Neither of us liked listening to the dirty jokes people sometimes told in the studio. We were both very 'straight' people. And we were both very private people.''

It's hard to imagine a happier couple than Conway and Dee. They called themselves soulmates, and I believe they were. Dee told me that she thinks part of the reason she took Conway's death so hard, and is still taking it hard, is that she was so dependent on him. "When Conway died I lost my best friend, my husband and my job," she says. "Because everything I did professionally was tied to Conway and had been for seventeen years. I miss him more now than a year ago. And more a year ago than the year before.'' But I believe that Conway was also very dependent on Dee.

In light of the press Dee received as Conway's widow, I thought it might be of interest to tell a little of how these two met and how their relationship developed. Dee moved from Maryland to Tennessee in 1974 and took a job at Marty Robbins's company, Entertainment Exclusive. Dee worked there for about a year before accepting a receptionist job at Woodland Recording Studios.

Conway was in and out of Woodland a lot back then, since he owned a production company and recorded there with both Nat Stuckey and Cal Smith. He had recently moved from Oklahoma to Nashville, bringing his family and his business adviser, childhood friend Hugh Carden. It was Hugh who was helping Conway set up his businesses here, and Hugh offered Dee a job with the company in 1977.

"For two years I answered phones and paid bills, things like that," Dee recalls. "But in a couple of years I got a little bored doing those things. I very much wanted a career. I honestly didn't think I'd ever get married. In my life I'd run into so few really good relationships, ones where the two people absolutely loved and trusted one another. Marriage wasn't one of my early goals. I felt lucky to be living in a time when women didn't feel pressured to find a husband.

"I didn't think I would really find a career with Conway's company, so I started sending out some résumés. Conway found out about it. When he asked me about it, I wasn't afraid he'd fire me or think I'd been disloyal. He was one of the easiest people to work for in the world. For someone to get fired by Conway, they'd have to do something pretty bad! I was honest with him about my wanting a career, and he asked me to stay, promising me that I'd get the opportunity to take on more responsibility. So I took him at his word and stayed put."

Conway lived up to his promise to Dee. He had been working on a feasibility study for Twitty City, an entertainment and tourist complex he hoped to build. There he wanted to build homes for himself, his mother and his children. Later, during a 1989 radio interview, Conway told me he'd always worried that tourists coming to Nashville might go away feeling a little shortchanged. He wanted them to feel like they'd really been close to the entertainment world, and to that end, he started planning Twitty City. He was also getting ready to sign with Elektra Records, and knew he was going to need a production assistant. Because of Dee's experience at Woodland Studios, he believed she'd be an asset. When he flew to Los Angeles to meet with Elektra executives, Conway took Dee and other staff members with him. He explained that she would be the label's contact in his office. There was still no hint of a romance between the two. For one thing, Conway was still married to his second wife, Mickey. After the two divorced in 1984, Mickey remarried and moved to Texas.

"Conway started working in the studio with [Elektra label head] Jimmy Bowen, and I went to the sessions with him," Dee says. "Those sessions were where Conway and I really got to know each other. There is where we both learned that our religious beliefs were so similar, and that we had so many other values and ideals that were alike. We both believed in taking care of our families. He kept all his children and his mother close to him, and I'd had to take care of my mother. Conway later told me that he believed I knew him better than anyone in the world, because he opened up to me about so much.

"We had plenty of time to talk. There's a lot of downtime at recording sessions, and that's especially true with Bowen, since he didn't want people leaving to get their meals. He always said that mealtime was when the musicians would go out and drink beer. So he shrewdly had food sent in."

Jimmy Bowen, who has run half the labels in Nashville at one time or another, does have a shrewd mind and he looks at things differently than a lot of people. Dee's observations reminded me of a conversation I'd once had with Bowen. I brought him a tape of a duet I'd heard that I liked, and explained to him that one of the principals was a veteran singer, and the other was a fifteen-year-old girl. Bowen said, "Oh, I never sign kids." When I asked him why not, he said: "Because you can't sue them. You can make all the deals with their parents you want, but it's the kid who has to deliver, and if they decide they don't want to work, you can't make them do it." In Nashville we call those things "Bowenisms."

Bowen also changed Conway's mind about his song selection. Conway Twitty has often been called "the best friend a song ever had." He listened to over three thousand songs before going in to record every album, and until he started working with Bowen he listened for ten songs that could be radio hits.

"I've always looked for songs that say things a woman wants to hear, and a man would like to say," Conway told me. "I still do that, but Bowen changed how I approached an entire album of material. He said, 'Look, you're at a point in your career where you can make some changes, and stretch out some. Find me four songs to release to radio, and six songs that you like, but might have been afraid to cut because they might not get airplay.' "

Conway said he thought about that and realized he had heard a lot of songs over the years that were either too long or not commercial enough. But they were great songs.

"I went out and looked for those great songs," Conway said. "I looked for those songs where the writer bleeds on the paper." And interestingly enough, those songs sometimes did get radio airplay. "That's My Job" on his *Borderline* album was one he probably wouldn't have recorded several years earlier.

During the years after Conway's divorce, Conway and Dee began to think their relationship might be more than platonic. They began dating, and in 1987, ten years after Dee had started working for Conway, the two wed. They went to Las Vegas to be married. No one stood up with them, and in true Conway fashion, they were dressed very casually. Conway wore slacks, a T-shirt and a Members Only jacket. Dee's bridal attire was a long sweater and leggings.

That was Conway. He had one persona on stage, and a completely different one in person. He hated to get dressed up.

Conway called me up one time and asked me to come to Grand Cayman Island. He said, "Ralph, I want you to cut the ribbon and help me open this new hotel I've invested in." So I went out and bought a white tuxedo jacket for the tropics, and I got there and was wearing my finery. Nashville Mayor Richard Fulton and his wife, Sandra, who was the Commissioner of Tourism, attended. The Governor General of the island was there wearing his tuxedo while we waited for the ceremonies to begin. We were painfully overdressed standing among all the tourists. Then I looked up the steps and noticed Conway standing up on the balcony, where he was watching it all. He was laughing and looking at me standing there in a tux, while he was wearing a baseball cap, a short-sleeved shirt, bathing trunks, long socks and Nikes! That was the Conway I knew.

In their seven years of marriage, Dee and Conway never spent a night apart. They used to laugh and say the only time they weren't joined at the hip was when he was on the stage singing. Like many couples who have been married much longer than Dee and Conway, people started saying they resembled each other. Dee recalls times after shows, when Conway would be signing autographs, someone would comment that they looked alike. "Say thank you, Henry," Conway would wisecrack. That's what he called her: "Henry."

She recalls times when she'd go to a department store to buy makeup, and Conway would sit and sign autographs at the counter while she tried to find the right shade of lipstick. Conway even went with his wife to grocery shop; he pushed the cart and tried to slip in some of his favorite non-health-food items like potato chips. In fact, Conway loved to shop. He once told me that shopping malls were some of his favorite places. "It's where America is," he said. That was especially true in California, where even though he was recognized, few people made an issue of the fact that he was a celebrity. And in California, Conway himself turned into a fan, buying maps of the celebrities' homes and, with Dee navigating, cruising around Beverly Hills checking out movie stars' mansions.

One thing that concerned Conway was the fact that so many people depended on him for a living. It wasn't just Dee and his children that concerned him, either. Conway worried about his band, road crew and all his employees. He was constantly trying to find ways to provide an outside income, one that didn't depend on him being on the stage singing. That led him to many business ventures, and while some were profitable, others had disastrous financial consequences.

Some investments were simply for the fun of it. He was an original investor in the Nashville Sounds baseball team, and minor league teams in eight other cities. Conway had considered playing professional baseball as a young man. He was such a good player that he was set to sign with the Philadelphia Phillies when the army drafted him to serve in the Korean war. His love of the sport never waned.

Some of his ideas were simply ahead of their time. For example,

Conway foresaw the need for more entertainment complexes in Nashville long before Branson cut into the city's tourist trade. He invested in Music Village, which he envisioned as a large entertainment complex. He also knew that artists and record labels would need to find alternative ways to market their music. Several years before his death he conceived of and developed the Direct Entertainment Corporation, set up similar to Amway, where music, videos and other entertainment-related items could be sold at home parties. This company, Conway believed, could reach out to rural America, to small towns where no record stores might exist.

Still, Dee says she hates the word "entrepreneur." Conway not only lost money on many of these ventures, she believed they took valuable time away from his music. During one of my last radio interviews with Conway, he said he had cut back on his investments. "I don't want to have anything to do with things that need to be mowed, fed or hauled," he laughed. "Or anything that needs accountants or lawyers."

Conway wanted the time to enjoy his life, his music and his wife, Dee. Sadly, Conway and Dee didn't have much time left, and the money that has gone to accountants and lawyers since his death is now in the millions.

IN THE SUMMER of 1994 Dee began sorting through Conway's possessions, preparing them for the auction. For her, every item had a history. She found a playbill from the Broadway production of *The Bells Are Ringing*. When the two had gone to New York to see *Phantom of the Opera*, Conway told her *The Bells Are Ringing* had been the first Broadway play he'd ever seen, and he was embarrassed to say that he fell asleep during the second act.

Although Kathy, Joni and Jimmy fought it all the way to the Tennessee Supreme Court, Conway's belongings went on the block on October 14, 1994. The children insisted the items rightfully belonged to them anyway, and refused to buy anything except Conway and Mickey's marriage certificate. Early that day, authorities had detained Mickey for attempting to steal the marriage license and divorce decree. Dee bought the things that meant the most to her: the Pacer, for $27,500; a wristwatch she'd given him several years earlier, for $19,000; and Conway's trademark "CT" necklace, for $19,000. The sale brought in over a million dollars.

That might have been the end of it. But on February 2, 1996, Nashville newspapers reported what appeared to be a bizarre request from Dee. She wanted Conway's body exhumed and cremated. Music Row tongues wagged incessantly about the strange request. Some people thought it was proof that Conway's widow had gone over the edge. Others speculated she was just being evil toward the children.

What had happened was that Conway's grave had been desecrated once too often. As far back as June, Dee had filed reports with the police. "Bitch" had been scratched across her name on the tomb. The flowers she'd left were torn apart. When she removed the flowers and replaced them with a fresh bouquet, those too were scattered and stomped upon. Slanderous notes were left beside the grave. The request for cremation even caused one old friend of Conway's, songwriter L. E. White, to circulate a petition against the proposed act. Letters were written to the editors of the *Tennessean* expressing disgust with Dee. She withdrew her request.

In 1997 the battle for Conway's intellectual properties heated up. At issue were the rights to Conway's song catalog, his name and likeness, and the Twitty Bird trademark. They were valued at $3.8 million. After a short bidding process, Dee backed away from that fight, too, leaving Conway's children to purchase it all. "I'm a businesswoman," Dee said. "I can't go broke fighting." I don't think Conway would want his widow to hand over everything to accountants and lawyers. Those were the folks he was trying to remove from his life when he died.

But I believe the worst blow of all for my friend Conway Twitty would have been the headline in the Nashville *Tennessean* on February 26, 1997: TWITTY'S DAUGHTERS SUE LAWYER OVER STORY. The tale told was a sordid one. Kathy and Joni had allegedly paid a Georgia attorney named Edwin Marger a $25,000 retainer to represent them in the fight to keep Conway from being cremated. Marger told the *National Enquirer* that the girls were also trying to find $80 million they believed Conway had stashed away in overseas accounts. According to Marger, Kathy and Joni also wanted him to find out if

Conway could be exhumed in an effort to prove Dee had poisoned him.

On June 8, Marger and the Twitty children were back in the *Tennessean* when court reporter Kirk Loggins filed an article titled LAWYER: TWITTY DAUGHTERS LACK BASE FOR CLAIMS. The article noted:

> He [lawyer Marger] said Twitty's daughters provided him with "innumerable leads" to investigate, but they all "came to nought."
>
> "I could find no indication that Dee Jenkins killed her husband. I found no smoking gun that indicated that anybody had secreted funds."
>
> Marger said Twitty's daughters referred him last year to a witness—supposedly a nurse at the Springfield, Mo., hospital where Twitty died—whom they expected to provide evidence of misconduct by Dee Jenkins and the hospital.
>
> "I traveled to meet with the witness and took notarized statements from the witness, only to be advised shortly thereafter that they had made a mistake and the witness was not who she purported to be and that none of the statements were accurate."
>
> Marger said he decided, after a lengthy investigation, "that the only thing that there was to this case was the vivid imagination and vituperative attitude of the sisters and their mother [Twitty's second wife, Temple Maxine (Mickey) Jenkins] toward the widow. . . ."
>
> The lawyer said that Twitty's daughters and his ex-wife "need to realize that Conway Twitty made a choice and that Dee Jenkins was his choice."

"I know it'll be hard for you to believe, but I truly feel sorry for Conway's children," Dee told me early in 1998. "I pity them, and I pray for them because they've turned miserable in their hatred. I don't like what they've become."

When I think about all that has happened, I'm reminded of something Conway once asked Dee: "When you were a little kid, did you ever wake up on Christmas morning and find that one special thing you'd always wanted but never dreamed you'd really get?" Dee thought a few minutes and said, "I once got a television set. I didn't think I'd ever get one of my own." Conway grinned at her. "That's how I feel about you," he said. "I feel like I woke up on Christmas morning, and found you there."

*   *   *

DEE BELIEVES THAT as hard as the last few years have been, it is possible that the court battles strengthened her.

"I had to appear in court right after Christmas the first year after Conway died. If I hadn't had to worry about that through the holidays, I don't know how I'd have made it. Christmas was Conway's favorite time of the year. He'd go shopping for tree lights and ornaments. He decorated our house. I didn't have the luxury of thinking about Christmas that year.

"In some ways, these legal problems have kept me from the normal grieving process. My grief counselor says I'm still several years behind. But in other ways, they have been a gift from God. I guess it's true, whatever doesn't kill you makes you stronger."

I asked Dee if she believed God left her behind for a purpose, if possibly there was some mission she had to fulfill. "Well, people tell you that," she said quietly. "And I do believe I've made a difference in my little godson's life. And I want to continue to do that. One thing I do is make sure he has responsibilities. And I'll encourage him to go to school, to work and to never start thinking people owe him anything. There, maybe I will make a difference to someone."

If Conway's widow had been a rose garden, or a house, or any "thing" that Conway held as dear, his family would have cherished and protected her after his death. And I think her mission is something else. Of all things Conway believed sacred, his personal integrity was paramount. And when all of these legal battles shake down, maybe people will understand just how much Dee Henry Jenkins tried to keep others from violating her husband's principles. She didn't retain the rights to his intellectual properties, but I think she is still here to help Conway Twitty retain his integrity.

"TELL THEM KIDS TO SHUT UP!"

IN NOVEMBER 1957 I went to work on the all-night shift at WSM, the biggest fifty-thousand-watt, clear-channel country station in the South. During my decades at WSM I had the opportunity to meet countless country music stars, songwriters, producers and other public figures, a ringside seat from which to view Nashville. The job also allowed me the opportunity to work side by side with one of my heroes, Tex Ritter.

In 1966 the station wanted to shore up ratings, and decided to offer the listening audience two for the price of one, teaming me with Tex, the legendary singer and film star. Tex's family lived in Los Angeles at the time, but because most of the profitable concert jobs were in the South or on the Eastern seaboard, Tex stayed in Nashville a good part of the year. I think Tex took the job just to give him something to do when he wasn't touring and it was too far to commute to California each week. Tex Ritter was an imposing figure: tall, deep-voiced, happy and warm. But because Tex took his music very seriously, he could also be formidable, as one little girl learned.

Lorrie Morgan was a child of the Opry. Her father, George Morgan, had been taking her with him for his Opry performances for as long as Lorrie can remember. One night Lorrie decided to start collecting autographs of the stars, and got more than she bargained for. "I was very excited that night," Lorrie recalls. "I took a girlfriend with me and we ran all through the backstage area collecting signatures. I got the Four Guys, Jeannie Seely, Jeanne Pruett and Grandpa Jones. Then I saw Tex Ritter standing back stage. I was just amazed to see a real movie star there at the Opry, so I ran right over and got his autograph."

Back in those days, the Opry had benches across one side of the stage where family members could sit. When Tex took the stage, Lorrie and her girlfriend went over and sat down. As young girls are prone to do, the two started cutting up, giggling and talking. They didn't catch the sour glances Tex was throwing them while he sang.

"Then, during one of the turnarounds, the musical breaks, Tex turned to the folks sitting on the benches," Lorrie laughs. "He growled out in that big voice, 'Tell them kids to shut up while I'm singing!' I shut up, and then ripped his autograph from my book and tore it up!"

Lorrie looked at me as though the story was finished. Then she rolled her eyes, shook her head, frowned and sighed.

"I'd give anything to have it today."

3

LORETTA LYNN:

KEEPING COUNTRY HONEST

When Johnny Cash introduced Loretta Lynn as a 1988 inductee to the Country Music Hall of Fame, he said: "This year the Country Music Hall of Fame honors one of the most admired women of our time. She was born in humble surroundings in a tiny coal mining town in Kentucky. She married before she was fourteen, but used her God-given gifts—as a writer of songs, as a singer of songs, plus her courage, determination and plain guts—to rise above the poverty she had always known and to make a better life for herself and her family. Because her music comes from the heart she touched our very deepest and most personal emotions and became an inspiration for millions. She was born a coal miner's daughter, but she has become a country music legend."

Loretta says she used to listen to my radio show on WSM religiously, no matter where she was playing out on the road. If she could tune to WSM, she listened. I'd like to think it was because she was a big fan, but according to her, she had an ulterior motive. "I'd listen to your show all the time and call in to request my songs," she says with a wicked twinkle in her eyes. "I'd try to disguise my voice and pretend to be somebody else every time I called. Sometimes I'd stay up all night when I was on the road so I could say I was callin' you from different states. Shoot, that's the only way I could get my records played! You have to do all sorts of things you don't want to do to make it, and that's the truth.''

Loretta Lynn is one of my favorite people in show business, partly due to her plainspoken honesty, which stands in contrast to many public figures who stop and mull over their real thoughts, picking and choosing how they present their beliefs depending on who they're around. Not Loretta Lynn. If Loretta thinks it, you'll hear about it, whether you are friend or foe.

A few years ago, when my wife, Joy, and I were attending a gala event in Nashville honoring a Miss U.S.A., I saw firsthand just how candid Loretta can be about her personal standards. Loretta and Mooney were also in attendance, and I noticed her giving me the evil eye several times from across the room. I was shocked, since I considered Loretta a good friend. Joy and I continued to mingle, with me keeping an eye on Loretta, who seemed to be keeping me under close scrutiny as well.

Finally I couldn't stand it any longer. I walked over to her and said, "Loretta, have I done something wrong? You act like you're mad at me.''

Her eyes flared, and she squared her shoulders. "Well, Ralph, I think it's just terrible that you're here with another woman!''

It took me a few seconds to recover from that comment, then I looked across the room and realized that this was Joy's first time out in public after adding blond highlights to her dark hair.

"Loretta,'' I said, laughing. "That is my wife! Joy 'blondeened' her hair!''

The beauty of being Loretta is that she treats everyone the same, whether it be a radio and television host like myself, or the President of the United States. Take, for example, her experience in Washington, D.C., where she was helping raise money for United Way. Speaking from the stage, she referred to then-President Nixon as "Richard.'' Later a newsman stuck a microphone in her face and asked, "Mrs. Lynn, why did you refer to the President of the United States as 'Richard'?'' Loretta didn't miss a beat. "They called Jesus 'Jesus' didn't they?''

Or consider the time she played the Palladium in London with a group of country stars including Conway Twitty, Tex Ritter and Bill

Anderson. "There was this writer over there, named Peter Hines, who gave us a terrible write-up before the show," Loretta says. "He called me the 'toothy' Loretta Lynn, 'cause I got buck teeth, and it's just a good thing for him that he didn't mention my bow legs, 'cause then I would 'a really whupped him. He called Conway 'fat and fortyish' and Tex Ritter a 'tinhorn cowboy.' I tried to talk myself outta sayin' anything, and Conway and Bill Anderson tried to talk me out of it, too. I even promised them I would be nice, but then when I got out on stage, I changed my mind. I sang four songs and the more I sang the madder I got. Finally I put my arms up and said, 'Is Pet-ah Hines out there?' See, I thought I had to talk in an English accent or they wouldn't understand me. Nobody said a word. I said, 'If you're out there, Pet-ah, you come backstage, because I'm 'a gonna whup you all over the state of England.' " Loretta's eyes twinkled and she added, "He never came backstage, and all I did was look stupid, because I didn't even know there wasn't states over there!"

Unlike so many who work years to upscale their speech patterns, Loretta takes pride in her authentic mountain-style pronunciation. She recently reminded me that when she was first introduced to one of her film idols, Gregory Peck, he corrected her after she addressed him as "Gra-gary Peck."

"I was excited to meet him," she says. "Then him and Doo sat there and talked about huntin' the whole time. The next time I saw him, I was in Los Angeles, on my way to meet Doo, who was huntin' up in Idee-ho. He says, 'Loretta, it's Idaho.' I said 'That's right, Gra-gary, Idee-ho.' "

Her personality carried through when working professionally with superstars from other music genres, too. Take, for example, her appearance on the *Frank Sinatra and Friends* special. "You never saw Frank at the rehearsals," she told me. "So I was by myself and tryin' to learn the song we was gonna sing, 'All or Nothing at All.' I never even heard of that song before. The piano player kept goin' over it with me, and over it with me. I just couldn't sing it, and told the piano player it was the worst song I ever heard in my life! When I finally run into Frank, I told him I'd rather sing the song Conway and I had on the charts right then, 'Louisiana Woman/Mississippi Man.' He said, 'Well, little girl, when you have a show called *Loretta*

Lynn and Friends, you can sing that song. But this is *Frank Sinatra and Friends,* and 'All or Nothing at All' was my first hit record!' When we went out there to sing I was so scared I didn't dare miss any notes!''

Dean Martin was another Rat-Packer who hated to rehearse his show, and in fact, whether out of indifference or assurance, *would* not rehearse. So when Loretta found herself rehearsing alone for their segment on *The Dean Martin Show* she was dismayed to find that any questions she had about production must be addressed to someone other than the star. She learned that after the two performed a duet, Dean would twirl her around and down onto his lap. Loretta's mouth dropped open.

"On his lap?"

The director nodded distractedly.

"Well, that ain't gonna happen," Loretta said.

That got his attention. "Well, it's got to happen," he said.

Loretta got that Coal Miner's Daughter fire in her eyes and set to her jaw, one that I'm sure her husband Mooney had seen many times over the years. "My mama taught me to never sit in no man's lap," she said firmly. "I never even saw my mama sit in my daddy's lap, and I ain't 'a gonna sit in Dean Martin's lap."

The next day Loretta's dressing room was filled with roses from the show's producer—so many roses she could barely squeeze past them to get through the door. When she went back into the hall, a man was waiting for her. "Have you ever seen so many flowers?" Loretta asked.

"Are you the little girl who won't sit in Dino's lap?" the man asked.

"Yes, I am," she said.

"Well, I'm this show's producer," he admitted. "And with all the millions of women in the world who'd love to sit in Dean Martin's lap, I just wanted to come and meet the one who wouldn't."

IT WAS A staunch country upbringing that wouldn't allow Loretta to sit on a man's lap. She was born on April 14, 1935, in the now-famous "Butcher Holler" Kentucky, located close to the Van Leer Coal Mines where her beloved father, Ted Webb, worked. Loretta's mother, Clara, named her for a favorite movie star, Loretta Young, and as Loretta told me in a 1971 radio interview, she gave herself a middle name. "I got mad at Mama because she didn't give me a middle name, and all the other kids had one," she said. "So I named myself Loretta Mae Webb. Of course, it didn't go nowhere. They called me Lettie for short."

Loretta was just short of fourteen years old when she married Oliver Vanetta "Doolittle" Lynn, the man she called Doo and most other people called Mooney. Ironically, Loretta didn't realize that his last name wasn't "Little" until the day she married him and he signed the marriage license as O. V. Lynn Jr. Loretta looked down and stunned the preacher by asking her new husband the identity of Mr. O. V. Lynn Jr.!

"Well, that's my name," Mooney said.

"What's your name?" Loretta demanded to know.

"Oliver Vanetta Lynn Junior," Mooney laughed.

"I guess that preacher thought we was crazy," Loretta said looking back on the day.

I'd always heard that O. V. Lynn Jr. had received the nickname "Mooney" because of his early moonshining activities, and "Doolittle" because of an aversion to work. But when Mooney and I spent some time together on the *Mississippi Queen* riverboat while Loretta and I worked on a Conway Twitty special, Mooney corrected the misconception. "I love to work. I've worked all my life," he said. "The nickname Doolittle came from my uncle, because I was a short, chubby little boy. It just stuck with me."

But Mooney was no longer a chubby little boy when he returned to Butcher's Hollow, Kentucky, in 1948, following a stint in the army. Everyone who read *Coal Miner's Daughter* knows the story of his buying Loretta's pie at a pie supper and marrying the naive young girl months later. "I didn't know anything about boys, let alone sex," she now laughs. "The only thing I ever done was throw a little note across the school room to my first cousin. I was stuck on him. Then I got whipped for it, you know." Even when Loretta became pregnant with her first child, she made no connection to having sex and having babies.

"My daddy always said he picked up a cabbage leaf and found me," Loretta says. "When I was pregnant with my first kid, I was getting fat but I never thought a thing about it. Doo said, 'Loretta, I think you ought to go to the doctor. You're getting fat.' I thought, 'Well, big deal. I've seen a lot of fat people.' So he said it again: 'I think you ought to go to the doctor.' So I went to Doctor Turner and he said I was pregnant. He put me up on this table and set my feet in those stirrups. Then he draped a sheet over me and I covered up my head with it because my whole bottom end was stickin' out and I was too embarrassed to show my face. I really didn't want him to see no part of me, but what could I do? He said, 'Loretta, you are going to have a baby,' I said, 'There ain't no way I could have a baby!' And he said, 'You got married, Loretta. Don't you sleep with Doo?' I said, 'Yeah.' And he said, 'Well, you are going to have a baby.' I was about four and a half months pregnant and didn't know it.''

The highly acclaimed movie made from *Coal Miner's Daughter* won actress Sissy Spacek an Academy Award, and she has Loretta's dogged determination to thank, since many Hollywood insiders, including Sissy's manager, felt she'd be miscast in the part.

''The Universal people gave me some pictures of different actresses they thought could play me,'' Loretta recalls. ''They were flying in a lot of women singers, too, for the auditions. But once I saw Sissy's picture, I told 'em they was just 'a wastin' their money. She was the one to play me—she *was* me. I started goin' on all the television shows sayin' Sissy Spacek was playin' me, and she started seein' me do it even though she hadn't said she would or she wouldn't. But her manager told her it'd hurt her reputation to play a country singer, and of course that made me mad. Then one night Sissy prayed over it, and asked God to give her a sign. She got up the next morning, and turned on the radio to the pop station she usually listened to, and there I was singin' 'Coal Miner's Daughter.' That was the sign she needed.''

Sissy Spacek played the role to perfection, so much so that when I had lunch with her during filming, she stayed in character the whole time. Loretta says it's still hard for Sissy to visit Hurricane Mills and not revert to the character of Coal Miner's Daughter, and she insists it's because Sissy somehow had the ability to get inside her mind, the sign of a truly great talent.

The casting, which included Levon Helm as Ted Webb and

Tommy Lee Jones as Mooney Lynn, certainly added to the authenticity of the picture. Sissy's performance in particular was singled out on Oscar night. "Sissy didn't think she was gonna win that year," Loretta recalls. "I went out to Los Angeles a few nights before the awards, and called her up. She was cryin'! I said, 'Sissy, ain't you ready?' She said, 'Loretta, Mary Tyler Moore is gonna get the award, not me.' So I said, 'You go out and get you a new dress. You better be ready, 'cause you are gonna win!' Later she told me she did go out and get a new dress, and it made her feel better. Then she won, and that made her feel a *lot* better!"

LORETTA WAS NOTHING if not naive when she married Mooney. "The first time I ever went inside a public restroom was after I married Doo. We was in Paintsville, Kentucky, and he stopped to let me go to the bathroom at the bus station. Well, they had them toilets that start flushin' when you sit down on the seat, and the minute I sat down, I jumped right back up! I run outta there 'a leavin' a trail all the way from the stall to the street! Doo said, 'What happened, Loretta?' And I said, 'Doo, that toilet was gonna suck me right down into it!' "

In her book, she openly discussed her husband's fondness for liquor and their early marital ups and downs, one of the lowest points being when Mooney decided to move to Washington State, where his father, Oliver "Red" Lynn, was living. For Loretta it meant leaving her family, something that her father had feared might happen once she wed, but that she'd never dreamed of doing.

Doo and Loretta lived in Washington thirteen years, with Doo working as a heavy machinery operator, and Loretta working as a housekeeper for their landlords. Her days were long and hard. She arose at 5 A.M., cooked breakfast for Doo and the four children, got him off to work and then walked to her landlord's ranch where she spent the rest of the day cleaning, washing, ironing, canning and cooking for their twenty-six field hands. One year Doo estimated that Loretta had canned two thousand quarts of food for her employer and two thousand quarts for her own family. Her canning was a great source of pride for Loretta, especially when she took home an extensive collection of ribbons and other prizes, including a set of dishes and a barrel of Crisco, at the local county fair. When they finally made the move to Nashville, Loretta's biggest regret was leaving thousands of jars of canned food behind.

I once asked Loretta if she'd ever got over being poor. "I don't think much about it, 'cause I don't live high," she said. "I shop at Wal-Mart myself. I got my garden, and I still can vegetables. I got my chickens. I know how to survive—I did it for years before I started singin'."

I mentioned Loretta's frugal side to Faron Young one time, telling him about calling her at home one day and finding out that she was busy painting her house. "What in the world is a big star doing painting her house?" I asked Loretta. "Well, if you want to get something done right, do it yourself," she said.

"Loretta has got to be the sweetest, kindest, most gentle person that the good Lord ever set on this earth," Faron replied. "And it is funny how down-home she is. Here is a woman probably worth millions, yet she bakes just like any other old country gal."

LORETTA ALWAYS SANG around the house, and when Mooney bought her a seventeen-dollar Harmony guitar at Sears Roebuck for her eighteenth birthday, she learned to accompany herself on the instrument. While many people associate the famous Wilburn Brothers with Loretta's ultimate success, it was a less well-known pair of brothers who gave her a start in the business. In the early months of 1960 Mooney took his young wife to the local Grange Hall, to hear the house band, the Westerners, play. In that band were the Penn brothers, John and Marshall, and following an audition, the two added her to the Westerners lineup. Loretta loved the singing, but the spotlight made her physically ill. "I'd start to get a migraine on Thursday just thinkin' about havin' to sing for people on Friday and Saturday, then it wouldn't start to ease up until the next Tuesday. And on Thursday, it'd start all over again." Despite her nervousness about performing, Mooney Lynn decided his wife could make it on her own, and within a few months helped her form a band, which they called Loretta's Trail Blazers.

Buck Owens was singing in Tacoma at what Loretta describes as ". . . the loudest and orneriest bar you ever seen." When Doo heard that Buck had a talent show at the club, he took Loretta to Tacoma for an audition, only to have Buck tell him they were booked solid. "We came all the way from Custer, Washington," Doo said. "Loretta ought to get to sing."

Sing she did, and although uncomfortable about the way she looked, Loretta won first prize. "Doo'd got me a new black-and-white dotted dress," she explains. "But my slip was too long for the dress, and it worried me to death, knowin' it was showin' all the time I was singing 'My Shoes Keep Walking Back to You.' " The prize was either a man's or a woman's watch, so I picked the man's watch for Doo. Then we walked right down the street to another club and I sang and won a woman's watch for me!"

On the following day, Loretta learned how quickly music's material rewards can vanish, when Mooney was working on his car and the watch fell apart. True to form, the next time Loretta saw Buck she confronted him about the shoddiness of what she believed to have been a prize worth at least four hundred dollars. "Well, Loretta, what'd you expect from a three-dollar watch?" Buck asked.

In 1997, when I interviewed Loretta for *On the Record*, I decided to surprise her with a satellite feed from Bakersfield, California, with her old friend Buck Owens. It turned out that both Loretta and I were taken by surprise. Buck reminisced about the old days, when the two of them were struggling to get their music heard on the West Coast. They laughed about the time Mooney Lynn dressed up like a woman for a New Year's Eve show Loretta played. Loretta recalled being stunned from the stage as she watched her impish husband, in full drag, allowing an unsuspecting—and very drunk—cowboy to buy him drinks all evening. Buck reminded Loretta that it had only seemed like minutes between the time they were unknown West Coast acts playing small venues until they were walking down the aisle to pick up major music awards. Then he dropped the bomb:

"I never have told anybody this," he said. "But I used to have the most God awful crush on Loretta. I never said anything 'cause she had a husband and I had a wife."

The look of surprise on Loretta's face was priceless. Her eyes widened and her mouth dropped open, and she seemed to freeze. Buck continued his confession:

"I thought Loretta was the cutest little old thing I ever saw," he said. "When I first saw her, I went over and asked Mooney who he was. He said, 'I'm her husband!' "

Buck didn't tell Loretta about his crush for another thirty-five years, and though the watch she won on his show didn't work, she did have one lasting reward from her appearance on the talent show. The program was broadcast in Canada, where wealthy businessman Norm Burley heard her voice and was impressed enough to offer to pay for a recording session on a song Loretta had written called "Honky Tonk Girl." Burley not only paid for studio time in Los Angeles, he pressed up 3,500 singles on his newly formed Zero Records and mailed them to disc jockeys across the United States. When the song hit #14 on *Billboard*'s national charts, Norm Burley showed himself to be a class act. He paid for the Lynns' trip to Nashville, assuring Loretta that if she could find a major label who wanted to sign her, he would tear up her contract. It was a promise he kept when Teddy and Doyle Wilburn expressed a desire to handle the singer's career. Loretta again praised Norm Burley's generosity when I interviewed her for *On the Record,* and she explained how Doyle Wilburn got her a recording contract:

"I went in and cut a demo of nine songs," Loretta recalled. "I wrote some of them, and we got others from the Wilburns' publishing company. Every cut except one ended up being recorded by someone. When Doyle played the tape for Owen Bradley at Decca, Owen said he wanted to record 'Fool Number One' on Brenda Lee. 'I'm not pitchin' the songs,' Doyle said. 'I'm pitchin' the artist!' Owen said, 'I've got all kinds of artists, Doyle. I don't need a girl artist because I've got Kitty Wells and Brenda Lee.' But Doyle held out, and Owen finally said he'd take the song for Brenda Lee and also take the artist."

But according to Chet Atkins, Loretta had other options. Chet once told me that he wanted to sign Loretta to RCA the first time he heard her sing on the Grand Ole Opry. "I called Doyle Wilburn and asked him about her," Chet recalled. "And he said I was too late, that Owen Bradley was going to sign her."

The Owen/Loretta teaming proved magic from the beginning, and Loretta's first #1 single, "Success," was cut during her initial Decca sessions. Owen says finding the right songs wasn't easy at first. "I tried to encourage people to find the right songs—songs that would work for *them*," Owen reflected. "When we first started looking for Loretta, we were trying to do songs like Kitty Wells would sing and that didn't work because Loretta isn't Kitty. Loretta's type of song is more like 'If you don't straighten up, I'm gonna knock the hell out of you.' And it's sort of true. That's more Loretta's philosophy. 'You Ain't Woman Enough to Take My Man' and 'Fist City' tell it all about Loretta."

Once Loretta started writing most of her own material, she was on her way to becoming one of country music's most legendary singer/ songwriters. She opened doors for strong women performers and women writers who had something to say. But she did it in such a down-home way that no one ever felt threatened by her, even when some in Nashville were turned off by what they perceived as militant feminism. It's possible that only Loretta could have recorded a song like "The Pill" in 1975 and got away with it, and she almost didn't. As she told *Penthouse* in 1980, " 'The Pill' . . . was banned all over. I couldn't understand why anyone would even think about not playin' a record called 'The Pill' when women had been taking the pill for twenty years. What was the big deal? When 'The Pill' came out, southern preachers gave Sunday sermons about the record and how I was preaching having sex in a different way. The next day, half the congregation would go buy the record to see how bad it was. It wasn't bad at all. A lot of doctors told me they'd been trying to get birth control information to country women who were back in the woods and that my song had done more for them than all the literature they'd put out."

Loretta caught some backlash from her male fans about the song, too. "Our house was swamped with calls from men, and they weren't complimentary. Disc jockeys were a little bit hateful about playin' the record, and I remember one of 'em calling me up and saying, 'Good morning Loretta. Have you taken your pill today?'

And then I had all kinds of people asking me if I was a women's libber. I'm for women, but I'm not the kind that marches in the street and burns my bra and carries on. But I do think that if a woman does a man's job, then pay her equal."

"The Pill" was a top-5 country song, and one of only five of Loretta's single releases that made it into the pop charts. Her other "crossover" songs included 1970's "Coal Miner's Daughter," 1971's "I Want to Be Free," 1973's "Love Is the Foundation" and Loretta and Conway's 1971 debut as a duo, "After the Fire Is Gone."

One thing Loretta didn't do was sit down and think, "This is topical. Maybe it's a hit." She's too honest and quick to shoot from the hip. As I said, if Loretta thinks it, she says it. That's why her very personal songwriting became so important throughout her career. Owen Bradley placed equal importance on the singer and her songs, but says it is probably her persona that outshines it all. "There is no question that Loretta's honesty endeared her to her fans," he told me last year. "Early on, I went to Las Vegas to see Loretta perform. To be completely truthful, I was worried about the show and how she would relate to the Las Vegas audiences. Conway often played there, and of course, he carried it off easily. But Loretta was a different story. She stepped on the stage and started telling stories right away—stories you wouldn't believe. She'd talk about marriage and men, and the women in the audience would shout, 'Tell it like it is, Loretta!' Then she started off on this story about growing up in Butcher Holler, and how her daddy sent her to the store to pick up some Eskimo Pies for the family. She got some Baby Ruth candy bars, too, and couldn't eat them all on the way home, so she stuck one half-eaten one under a rock near their cabin. The next day she went out to get the Baby Ruth and found it covered with ants. 'I just knocked 'em off and ate it,' Loretta said. This was not a sophisticated tale you'd expect a Las Vegas audience to appreciate, but everybody just loved it."

LORETTA WILL SAY anything. Conway once told me that when he and Loretta were a duet team, rumors started flying that they were having an affair. Conway was horrified by the talk, but Loretta seemed to think it was humorous. It got so bad that fans would ask them straight out if they were sleeping together! Conway said that one night when they were signing autographs after a show, a woman blurted out the Big Question. "Loretta, are you and Conway . . . uh . . . you know . . . dating?"

"Nope," Loretta said, with a grin in Conway's direction. "We're just shackin' up."

Conway said he just threw his pen up in the air and headed back to his bus.

LORETTA HAS HAD a lot of losses in her life. Her beloved brother, Jay Lee Webb, died on July 1, 1996. The next month she lost her longtime love when Mooney died after a long bout with diabetes. Mooney's death hit her hard; she had, after all, grown up with him. She lost her son Jack some years earlier. And, of course, she was with Dee Jenkins at her dear friend Conway's side the night he died. Yet she continues on with her life and career, relying on that strong coal miner's daughter spirit she brought with her from the Kentucky hills.

"THEY FIRED HIM FROM THE OPRY"

IN HANK WILLIAMS Jr.'s 1983 tribute to his father, "The Conversation," Hank Jr. and Waylon Jennings sing: "They fired him from the Opry," referring of course to the widely believed story that the Opry folks got fed up with Hank Williams and Jim Denny canned him. I believed the story for years, only questioning it recently when Irving Waugh, who was in the Opry management at the time, told me, "We didn't fire Hank. We couldn't even find him!" Drifting Cowboy Don Helms told me it wasn't a firing, but a leave of absence:

"When Hank took his famous leave of absence from the Opry, none of the Drifting Cowboys chose to go with him," Don said. "He planned to go back to Shreveport and Montgomery and play some dates down there. All of us guys were playing spots with other artists—people like Ray Price—on the Opry, and didn't see any point to losing those jobs. Hank said he was coming back, and Mr. Denny said Hank was coming back.

"Hank's drinking sprees had become more frequent there toward the end. He'd missed some dates and showed up for some shows he should have missed. Mr. Denny was getting pressure from some of the other artists asking why they couldn't straighten Hank up. Finally Jim Denny came to Hank and said, 'Hank, I hate to do this, but you are going to have to go get your head on straight. Take a little leave of absence and find yourself, then come back.'

"I don't believe that Hank was ever fired. Mr. Denny was just trying to make him straighten up, because it was beginning to affect the image of the Opry. Hank wasn't mad about it. I went over to Hank's house on the afternoon that Johnny Wright was to drive Hank back to Montgomery. Hank had been drinking that day, and needed a driver, I guess. I went over to bring him a couple of things I'd borrowed; I had used one of his shotguns and the watch the city of Montgomery had once presented him. We were out on tour once and I needed a watch and Hank let me wear that one. He wasn't upset about the leave of absence. When they pulled out of the driveway he gave me the thumbs up, grinned and said, 'I'll see you soon Hoss.' "

I always regretted not meeting Hank, and am always on the lookout for Hank Williams stories. Here are a couple Chet Atkins told me:

"I first met Hank in 1949, after 'Lovesick Blues' had been on the charts quite a while," Chet recalled. "Hank walked into one of the dressing rooms at the Opry and introduced himself. He was very skinny, and looked like he was in bad health. In fact, as one guy around the Opry commented, Hank was so skinny his ass rattled like a box of carpenter's tools. I remember being amazed at the color of his eyes. They were almost black. But he was very open and friendly."

I once asked Chet to try and describe the magic that Hank Williams had onstage, and Chet says it was in large part the way Hank moved. "It was mesmerizing to watch his body language when he sang," Chet said. "It wasn't anything all that rhythmic, but more like the wind blowing a limb in rhythm with the music."

Chet moved to Nashville in 1950, and soon thereafter he ran into Hank Williams at the Opry again. Hank remembered him, and got right to the point.

"I hear you write songs," Hank said.

"Yeah," was the only word the startled Chet Atkins could say.

Hank nodded. "Then we'll get together sometime and try to knock one out."

Chet was floored. Hank Williams asking to cowrite with someone? But Chet gave him his phone number, and true to his word, Hank called him and set up an appointment.

"I went out to Hank's house and we tried, but I just couldn't write with him," Chet said. "I was so in awe of the man that I choked. I've still got fingerprints on my neck!"

Chet says Hank was always writing. He wasn't one of those guys who sets aside a time to be creative, writes his song and goes on about his day. Every time you'd see him, he'd just finished a tune.

"Hank would come up to you and say, 'I got a new one for you, Hoss,' " Chet says. "Then he'd get right up in your face and sing it, and usually the smell of bourbon would be pretty strong. Then he'd play something like 'Mansion on a Hill' or one of those unbelievably great songs. He'd say, 'How do you like it?' I'd say I liked it fine, but if somebody like Ernest Tubb or Hank Snow was standing around, they'd say, 'I'd like to record that, Hank!' Hank would narrow his eyes and say, 'No, it's too good for you. I'm gonna record it myself.' I think they were his test runs. If Ernest Tubb and Hank Snow wanted the song, Hank knew it was a hit."

4

ALAN JACKSON:

THE ART OF THE DEAL

If I've learned anything in my years in broadcasting, it's that new artists will always come along and replace established ones on the airwaves, and that no matter how diverse our music becomes, there will always be a place on the radio for traditional country music. There's room for many kinds of artists and songs under country's umbrella. There are times when pop-flavored music steps to the fore; at others, the edgy "outlaw" rock-tinged music seems the flavor-of-the-day. But there will always be a place for traditional artists like George Strait, Randy Travis and Alan Jackson.

Alan is such a big star now that it's hard to remember that he struggled five long years in Nashville before securing a recording contract. It's a well-known story, how Alan's wife, Piedmont flight attendant Denise Jackson, stopped Glen Campbell in an airport as he was traveling from a Boca Raton, Florida, show to a tour of the Eastern seaboard. Usually the story jumps from that chance meeting to Alan's first hit, 1990's "Here in the Real World." But here in the real world of country music, the road can take a lot of detours and turn downright bumpy. I thought it might be interesting to take a look at the road Alan took. If you're thinking about coming to Music City, keep in mind that the wheels sometimes turn mighty slow.

When Alan wrote those lines in "Chasin' That Neon Rainbow,"

"I moved on up to Music Row/Lordy don't the wheels turn slow," he wrote the story of his life during the latter part of the 1980s. "I got passed on by every record label in town, and some of 'em twice," Alan told me in 1990, when the stardom that had seemed so elusive finally happened. "I was like a lot of people who come here," he recalled. "I'd worked a lot of different jobs—sold cars and houses, drove a forklift—and played music on the weekends. It was almost like a hobby for a while. But around the time I turned twenty-five, I realized music was what I wanted to do with my life. I just didn't know how to get started."

HIS WIFE, DENISE, got the ball rolling when she approached Glen Campbell in the airport. After giving Denise some words of encouragement for her singer/songwriter husband, Glen suggested she have Alan call Marty Gamblin at Glen Campbell Enterprises in Nashville. Since people on the road often wanted to pitch songs to Glen, his road manager even had a few of Marty's business cards in his wallet. A few days later, Alan Jackson made the phone call from Newnan, Georgia.

"I knew Alan had a lot of drive from the first time we spoke," Marty recalls. "I asked him when he wanted to get together and Alan said, 'Well, I can't get off work today.' "

The two met a week and a half later, on August 15, 1985, at Glen Campbell Enterprises' office located in the basement of the Music Mill, where Alabama and many other major acts have recorded their hits. Marty remembers the tall, shy Georgia boy walking in wearing a baseball cap and tennis shoes, and armed with a homemade demo tape of his songs.

"I liked Alan right off," Marty says. "It's hard not to. And while I liked his song ideas, I felt they needed fine-tuning. Since his own songs were all just a guitar and vocal, I asked him if he had any tapes of his performances, and he did have a tape he'd made off the board at a honky-tonk he'd recently played. I listened to his versions of John Conlee's 'Rose-Colored Glasses,' Conway's 'I'd Love to Lay You Down' and George Strait's 'They Call Me the Fireman.' The next song was David Allan Coe's 'The Ride' and his interpretation and delivery on that one sold me." Marty Gamblin became a diehard Alan Jackson fan that day, but it would be several years before he could convert the powers that be on Music Row to his way of thinking.

Alan said the first thing he believed he should do was relocate to Nashville. Marty agreed, but cautioned him. "It's nice to hear the stories of how Willie Nelson or Roger Miller came here and starved at first," Marty told Alan. "But those things make better stories than they make experiences. They make it hard on a family, and there's no job in the world worth losing your family over."

Alan assured him that Denise could just as easily be based out of Nashville as out of Atlanta, and that he planned on working a day job, as well. "Then try to get a job somehow connected to the industry," Marty advised. "Networking is an overused word, but it's just what you'll need to be doing."

That conversation took place on August 15, and on September 12, Alan called to tell Marty that he and Denise had rented a basement apartment in Gallatin, Denise was now based out of Nashville, and he had a job in the mailroom at The Nashville Network.

"I'd worked for a marina back home in Georgia, so I had a kind of connection to a boat company here in Nashville," Alan said. "So before I moved to town I went out to the plant where they built the boats we'd used and talked to them about a job. It was late August, and the plant was hot and the fiberglass fumes were strong. I drove away thinking, 'Boy, I'd hate to go to work there.' Then as I was driving down Briley Parkway, I saw the sign for the Opryland Hotel and decided to stop by their personnel office. When I told them I was getting ready to move to Nashville, they said they didn't have any openings at the hotel, but TNN needed someone in the mailroom. I interviewed for that job and two weeks later I started work."

I asked Alan if he sorted all the mail at TNN back then, including mine. "You got a ton of it." Alan laughed. "And I sorted about a million of those 'Let Minnie Steal Your Joke' cards and letters."

"Let Minnie Steal Your Joke" was a great segment we used to do on *Nashville Now*. People sent in jokes—not all of them clean, I might add—and Minnie Pearl picked her favorites to read over the air. Roy Acuff was one of the segment's biggest fans, and he'd watch the show from his dressing room at the Opry every time we did it. If Minnie got a little too close to blue humor with one of them, Roy would scold her about it when she left the TNN studios and went to the Opry. And maybe one of the reasons Alan Jackson was having to sort through so many jokes was that people used to send in the previous week's winner, acting as if it were a brand new entry! I guess they figured if it was good enough to win once, it was good enough to win twice.

"ASIDE FROM HIS obvious talent, Alan's strongest asset is his enormous drive," Marty says. "He has that ambition and drive in everything he does. Back when he was living in Newnan, he bought and sold cars as an additional income. He'd take out a ninety-day loan to buy a Mercedes or some other car that needed repairing, drive it around town enough to get interest stirred up, then sell it and go buy another car. Alan once told me he guessed there were people in Newnan who thought he was a drug dealer because of all those cars he drove. He did the same thing with houses. He'd buy a house, fix it up and sell it."

His drive showed itself at his new Nashville job, too, as he quickly became a serious student of both songwriting technique and country music history. He spent lunch hours in the Opryland music library, listening to song after song, picking them apart to see what had made them hits.

On October 10, 1985, Alan made his first recordings in Nashville at the Studio on the Pond in Gallatin, with songwriters Jim Weatherly and Carl Jackson. "We were just trying to get him used to the recording studio," Marty recalls. "So we took the vocals off a song of Carl's called 'I Couldn't Care More' and had Alan sing. Now, since Carl sings in about the same key as Vince Gill, it didn't work well, but at least Alan was getting the feel of recording with headphones. The other song we did that day was one of Jim Weatherly's called 'Her Love's on Hold.' "

Two weeks later they headed to Muscle Shoals, where an acquaintance of Marty's, producer Stan Cornelius, was recording an act. Again, they took vocals off other projects, and let Alan sing to the track. Since they had to wait until Stan's act was finished, Alan didn't get to begin singing until midnight. They started for Nashville at 6:00 A.M., and Alan went home, showered and shaved and headed for his day job at the TNN mailroom.

Marty kept pushing for his act to make an appearance on my show, and I was happy to have him. I always tried to have a well-balanced lineup on each show: an established act, maybe an Opry star; a current radio favorite; and a newcomer. I believed then, as now, that we as an industry must treat our legends with the respect they deserve, and we must keep encouraging new blood because that is the lifeblood of the business. On April 21, 1986, Alan made his first appearance on *Nashville Now*.

Alan was a big, good-looking guy with good stage presence. But what was phenomenal was the audience reaction. They screamed and hooted and hollered for him. I asked him if he'd brought his fan club and he gave me a sheepish grin. It turned out that a bunch of his friends and coworkers at TNN had turned out to show their support. Alan kidded me about the amount of mail I got, and I told the audience that from that day on, if I missed reading their letter on the air, they should complain to a young man named Alan Jackson. As a singer, I felt Alan fit into the David Allan Coe mold. He didn't really sound like David, and he certainly wasn't copying him. But he approached a song the way David does, with soulful emotion. Later, when I learned that Marty was first interested in a Coe song on Alan's demo tape, it didn't surprise me. And it should be no surprise that Alan has that soul-drenched country vocal on "Midnight in Montgomery," as haunting as David's "The Ride."

This performance started the buzz in Nashville. Charlie Craig, with whom Alan later wrote "Wanted," saw the performance and started calling his friends: "Man, I saw a guy on *Nashville Now* tonight who is gonna be a star." Songwriter Jim McBride also saw Alan's performance and became an early believer. Suddenly, many established songwriters were interested in writing with the new kid in town.

On June 17, 1986, Alan recorded his first real session in Nashville, paid for by his sister and a private investor, who put up $6,000 apiece. At first it looked like getting a record deal was going to be a piece of cake. Marty and Stan Cornelius contacted Curb Records' Dick Whitehouse, who loved the project. Cornelius called Marty and said they had a deal.

"Alan and I were so excited that we took our wives out to the Cherokee Steak House and celebrated," Marty says ruefully. "It turned out that the deal wasn't solid, and we learned a very important lesson: don't celebrate anything until it's on paper.''

But word of Alan Jackson's talent was spreading around town. Steve Popovich was running PolyGram at the time and Stan Cornelius was producing Johnny Paycheck for the label. Stan played Alan's tape for Popovich, who offered him a spot on a compilation album the label was calling *Trade Secrets*. Popovich was serious about his offer. This time, Marty was sent a contract.

"I was nervous about the deal," Marty confesses. "I didn't see exactly how you were going to market that many unknown acts on one album. And since I've always been on the creative side of Glen Campbell Enterprises, I sent the contract out to Glen's business manager, Stan Schneider, in Los Angeles. Stan is the one who does contracts, and he took one look and said, 'No.' The deal would have tied Alan up for years. So we passed on the offer. It's always made me wonder how things might have turned out. Maybe Alan's one song would have made *Trade Secrets* big, I don't know. But more likely, it would have kept Alan from his Arista deal a few years later."

In November 1986, Alan recorded seven of Jim Weatherly's songs, which Jim took to Jerry Bradley at 16th Avenue Records, owned by Opryland. Jerry, Owen's son, and former head of RCA Records, turned it down. "It was a big disappointment," Marty says. "But I understood why Jerry made the decision. Sixteenth Avenue was trying to revive the careers of both John Conlee and Charley Pride, and those two were their priorities."

When Glen Campbell heard the Weatherly project, he phoned Bruce Hinton, head of MCA Records, and several other heavy hitters. Still, they had no takers. But on December 5, Marty played the session for Shelby Kennedy, another second-generation music guy, the son of legendary musician/producer and label head Jerry Kennedy. Shelby was knocked out by Alan's vocals, and several years down the line, he played an important role in the Alan Jackson success story.

During the early months of 1987, Alan needed a bio to use for pitches to labels, television shows and venues. Fortunately, since he didn't have the money to hire a writer, he met a publicist who offered to write a bio if Alan would paint a fence for her. Alan agreed, and added another component to his presentation kit, which up until then was comprised of the Weatherly tapes and a copy of his *Nashville Now* appearance.

In April of that year, Alan played his first big show, the Lively Arts Festival in Meridian, Mississippi. "I'm originally from Philadelphia, Mississippi, which is close to Meridian," Marty explains. "So I called a friend of mine who was involved with the festival and he offered Alan a spot on the show. Ronnie Milsap was the headliner. Rehearsals got fouled up because of first one thing and then another, so the band rehearsed for the first time on the bus we'd rented from Keith Steagall, driving to the show. Alan played two shows, and was paid one thousand dollars. The audience reaction to him was overwhelming. While we were there, we stopped by WOKK in Meridian, and the disc jockey played 'Gone to Pieces,' one of the Weatherly tunes."

Alan returned to Nashville and played a showcase at the renowned Bluebird Cafe that April. Still, there were no takers. On May 27, he made his second *Nashville Now* appearance, which led to a two-week gig in Las Vegas. *Nashville Now* was taping in Vegas at the Landmark between June 21 and July 8, and Alan was booked to play those two weeks at the Landmark. That was a smart move on the Campbell team's part. With *Nashville Now* taping at the hotel, interest in country music ran high. Alan had a chance to perform nightly in front of a friendly crowd, and sharpen his stage show for the all-important Nashville dates that would inevitably come.

Marty took Alan to Fan Fair that June, and country music fans converged on him, thinking he was already a star. "He has the persona of a star," Marty says. "So people kept coming up asking him for autographs. That experience convinced me that we needed to have him out and seen at as many industry events as possible. So he went to SRO, and my wife, Cherie, and I gave Alan and Denise our CMA tickets that year. I always believed his overall appearance and charisma would play an important part in his success, whether it be in getting the record deal, or making it in a very competitive business once he did get signed."

But by January 1988, Alan was still unsigned. There was plenty of interest. Doug Grau at Warner Bros. liked his work; Bobby Young and Harold Shedd at PolyGram were interested. Jerry Bradley, while he had initially turned down Alan's project, still professed an interest. Around this time, Marty began to think he needed to involve a full-time manager in Alan's career. "I was running the publishing company, and working with Alan on his songwriting, as well as with Glen's other writers," Marty says. "Alan and I had a handshake deal on both the manager and publishing roles. So I approached him about getting someone else involved."

Alan balked at first, feeling that somehow Marty and Glen Campbell Enterprises would be shortchanged by any such move. Marty assured him that with his song publishing remaining with Glen Campbell Enterprises, the company would have no problem with another person's involvement. Finally, Alan capitulated. Marty approached three Nashville managers: Ken Levitan, who managed Nanci Griffith and Steve Wariner, Larry McFadden, and Barry Coburn.

"Since Ken and Larry were out of town, I met first with Barry," Marty recalls. "He was the only one I didn't know, but his wife, Jewell, had pitched songs to Glen and I knew of Barry through her. I put together what I thought was a powerful package, including several *Nashville Now* tapes and Alan's demo tapes. Barry listened, and watched the shows, then said, 'I've got seventeen artist packages on my desk, and all of them are looking for managers. I'll have to get back to you, because I don't want to overextend myself.' " Marty gave him two weeks to mull over the opportunity, and in exactly two weeks, Coburn phoned back. He was in, if the offer still stood.

With an expanded team in place, more meetings were set. Alan met with Bob Montgomery at Sony, who played him a tape of one of Alan's musical heroes, Vern Gosdin, singing "Chiseled in Stone." Alan and Marty walked out of the meeting without a contract, but knowing they'd just heard a monster hit. Indeed, it became the CMA Song of the Year in 1988. More meetings took place over the next few months. They met with Renee Bell at MCA, with Doug Grau at Warner and with Al Cooley at Atlantic. It was always the same. The A&R executives felt Alan was close, but not there yet. On the plus side, the doors were always left open.

In December Alan met with James Stroud, who was working for Jimmy Bowen at Universal Records. Stroud knew he was hearing a star, and he knew some of Alan's songs were smash hits, especially "Chasin' That Neon Rainbow."

" 'Chasin' That Neon Rainbow' is definitely autobiographical,'' Alan told me. ''Jim McBride and I wrote that song. Jim's a good ol' boy from Alabama, and when we got together to write, we started talking about where we came from musically. My family really didn't own a radio until my daddy won one. And my mama and daddy hated seeing me out playing in bars. Then of course, I came to Nashville and kept trying to make contacts and get a record contract. None of it came easy. So Jim and I started the song with the line, 'Daddy won a radio.' ''

Not everyone heard a hit when Alan demoed the song. Even Marty Gamblin worried that it might be too much of an insider song, about the trials and tribulations of trying to get a music career going. And one label head went so far as to call it a ''piece of crap.'' But Stroud heard it, knew it was a hit and was determined to get Alan signed with Universal.

In February 1989, Glen Campbell, Marty Gamblin and Alan Jackson went to Jimmy Bowen's home to make their pitch. It would have seemed to be a shoe-in, because not only had Stroud been pushing Bowen, Glen was one of the label head's oldest and closest friends. Bowen told Alan to go back and make him a tape of ten songs, and to sequence them as he would in a live show. ''I want to see how one of your shows would flow,'' Bowen explained. A week later Alan was back with his tape. Bowen listened, then told him that he was a year and a half behind the established acts like George Strait.

Marty spoke up: ''Then he's right where he should be, because these tapes are a year and a half old.''

''Get me something new,'' Bowen retorted.

Glen agreed to pay for a new session, and off they went. This time, however, Jim Weatherly was in Los Angeles working on a film project and was unavailable. ''Keith Stegall had been a fan since he first heard Alan,'' Marty says. ''So when Jim couldn't do the session, I called Keith. Glen and I sat down and talked to Keith about what Bowen had liked and what he hadn't. Then Alan and Keith started work.''

Bowen liked what he heard, and said he wanted to hear Alan's live show. In the meantime, James Stroud, still determined to sign Alan, called Marty and suggested they do a preliminary showcase, where he could see Alan's show before Bowen. If Stroud saw any

problems, he could help work them out before his boss saw the
show. On March 29, 1989, Alan played a show at Nashville's Hall of
Fame Motor Inn lounge, and Stroud gave them the go-ahead. But
before he played for Bowen, Alan played one more showcase, at the
Cockeyed Camel, where keyboardist Dave Gann sat in with the
band. Alan was knocked out by his playing, and asked him to join
the band permanently. "I'd love to," Gann replied. "But I just
started playing with a new guy on Capitol, Garth Brooks." That
spring, Dave Gann had two options, and both of them came from
future superstars. Gann still plays for Garth.

On May 2, 1989, Alan Jackson played a show for Jimmy Bowen at
Douglas Corner in Nashville. Bowen had told Marty to schedule the
show at 6:00 P.M., so he could attend on a break from recording the
Oak Ridge Boys. Marty phoned all the Alan Jackson fans he knew,
hoping to pack the club, and no one disappointed him. Bowen seldom was seen at showcases, so Marty stopped by the studio at 4:00,
just to remind him of his promise. Stroud phoned Marty soon thereafter and promised to corral Bowen and make sure he got there.

Alan started playing to a packed club promptly at 6:00 P.M., and
halfway through the second song, Stroud and Bowen walked in. An
immediate buzz went through the room. Bowen did not like showcases, yet here he was to see Alan Jackson. Bowen listened, and
made his exit, his mind still not made up. But as it turned out, the
showcase for Bowen did get Alan a record deal. Shelby Kennedy was
one of the fans Marty called, and Shelby in turn called his friend
Tim DuBois. Tim was in the audience that night, and Tim was impressed. On May 8, Clive Davis came to Nashville and announced
that his company, Arista Records, would open its doors in Nashville,
and that Tim DuBois would run the label. They would be looking
for a flagship artist with which to launch the company. While he
was in town, Tim arranged a meeting between Clive Davis and Alan
Jackson, at which time Clive gave Alan a sales pitch as to why he
should sign with Arista instead of the other labels who wanted him.

"It was so ironic," Marty reflects. "After all those turndowns,
Clive was trying to sell Alan. Although the interest was strong, we
didn't have any other firm offers. But it showed me that Clive believed in him, and that Arista was where he should be. For their
part, Alan was the perfect flagship artist."

Alan's first release was a song titled "Blue Blooded Woman," and as Alan explained to me, it didn't exactly blaze up the charts. "It got to the forties, then died," Alan said. "But the next release, 'Here in the Real World,' went to number three. It's amazing. I never thought that three minutes of music could have such an impact."

"Here in the Real World" was a result of a songwriting session that Alan was less than enthusiastic about. "I wrote the song with Mark Irwin," Alan said. "I wasn't excited about writing with him and I don't think he was all that excited about writing with me, either. Mark's from New Jersey, and I'm from down in Georgia. We didn't know how we'd geehaw together. As it turned out, I came to the session with a couple of lines scribbled down in a notebook: 'cowboys don't cry, heroes don't die.' I didn't know exactly where I was going with it, other than the way the movies relate—or don't relate—to real life."

And as it turned out, Alan and Mark geehawed together pretty good, because as Alan said, ". . . the lines fell out in about an hour." Even so, Alan didn't think the song was for him, and instructed Glen Campbell Publishing to pitch it to other artists. One person Marty Gamblin pitched it to was Blake Mevis, who cut it on an artist he was working with at the time. "Blake first recorded it with the artist's road band," Marty says. "He didn't think it came off as well as it should have, so he petitioned the label about hiring session musicians and redoing it. They said no, that the song wasn't a hit."

"Here in the Real World" almost didn't make it on the debut album. It was the last song cut, and only got recorded because producer Scott Hendricks believed in the song. And once on the album, it was not the song most at Arista believed should be the follow-up single, a crucial release. Marty explains: "I spoke with Tim DuBois after 'Blue Blooded Woman' died in mid-chart, and he scared me when he said, 'If we don't have a top-five record with the next single we're all in a lot of trouble.' Anthony Von Dollen was in A&R at Arista then, and he pushed for 'Here in the Real World.' The song became a career-making one for Alan."

"I wasn't a known performer then," Alan explained. "And the song kind of loped along on its way up the charts. Then it wouldn't die. It stayed on the charts until finally radio stations had to take it off." In fact, "Here in the Real World" stayed on *Billboard*'s charts for twenty-six weeks, much longer than most hit songs today, which have very short chart lives. The song also garnered Country Music Association award nominations for Single, Song and Album of the Year.

When Arista had its Fifteenth Anniversary party that year, Alan was invited to perform, the only country singer in a sea of pop stars including Whitney Houston, Barry Manilow and Hall & Oates. That in itself was a heady experience, but according to Alan, buying a bus was the biggest thrill of the newly won success. "I'm such a car buff that having my own bus was almost as sacred as a number one record," he said, laughing. That vehicle probably ran a close second in Alan's list of favorite vehicles, the first being a 1955 T-Bird. "I started to work when I was twelve years old," he said. "And by the time I was fifteen I had saved up three thousand dollars toward a car. I went to Atlanta and bought a 1955 Thunderbird—that had been the first year Ford made them. Daddy and I took it apart and rebuilt it. I drove that car all through high school, and finally sold it when Denise and I got married. We used the money to make the downpayment on our first house."

Arista threw Alan his first gold record party in 1990, five years after he arrived in Nashville in search of his dream. Alan went right out and bought a new hat for the event, but that afternoon, as he got dressed for the first of what would be many such celebrations, he had second thoughts. "Not long after I got to Nashville, I bought a hundred-dollar Stetson," Alan told me. "I wore that hat out playing honky-tonks. I wore it the first time I was on *Nashville Now,* and I wore it when I played at Arista's anniversary party in New York. I looked at that hat sitting next to my new one and told Denise that I just couldn't bring myself to wear the new one. I told her, 'This old one's been through everything with me. I'd feel like I was cheatin' on it if I left it home now.' "

Spoken like an ace country songwriter.

FAREWELL TO THE FIRST LADY

IT WAS A heartbreaking headline in the Nashville *Tennessean* on April 7, 1998: QUEEN OF HEARTACHE DIES. Tammy Wynette, the First Lady of Country Music, had died a day earlier at age fifty-five. This chapter of *The View from Nashville* started out as a short, funny vignette about Tammy's defending "Stand by Your Man" during the 1992 Presidential campaign. I'm so sorry it had to turn into a sad good-bye.

It had happened suddenly. Tammy had been feeling sick the night before, but had improved by morning. She lay down on the couch in a room just off the kitchen, watching television and dozing most of the day. Around 5:30 P.M. the housekeeper told Tammy's husband/manager, George Richey, that he should try and get some sleep since he'd stayed up all night with her. He caught a catnap, awakening at around 6:00 to find a note from the housekeeper saying she'd run to the store and would be right back. He checked on Tammy, who was still on the couch.

She smiled and turned over on the couch to go back to sleep. Richey closed his eyes for about another twenty minutes. This time when he checked on Tammy, she felt cold and didn't appear to be breathing. Panic-stricken, he called her doctor, yelling into the phone hysterically: "I think Tammy's dead!" Just then the housekeeper returned, took the phone from Richey and he rushed back to his wife's side to wait for the ambulance. Death had come swiftly, when a blood clot hit her lung.

At 1:00 on April 9 a private funeral was held at the Judson Baptist Church on Franklin Road, near Tammy's home. A public memorial was held at the Ryman Auditorium at 4:30 that same day. Thousands of people came from all over the world to say good-bye to the First Lady.

You no doubt saw the worldwide coverage of the public service televised extensively on CNN and MSNBC, where stars including J. D. Sumner and the Stamps, Randy Travis, Naomi and Wynonna Judd, The Oak Ridge Boys, Rudy Gatlin, Dolly

Parton, Merle Haggard and Lorrie Morgan spoke and sang. Those artists (with the exception of Rudy and Merle) also spoke and sang at the private service on Franklin Road, and the Bill Gaither Vocal Band performed at the church, as well. Loretta Lynn attended but was too distraught to perform. One of the most moving performances was that of Gospel Music Hall of Fame member Jake Hess, who performed a song that Tammy loved: "Death Ain't No Big Deal."

As I left the first service Tammy's friend and former publicist, Evelyn Shriver, handed me a Tammy Wynette backstage pass. "You'll need this for the special seating at the public memorial," Evelyn said. I thought, "How ironic that my ticket to Tammy's memorial service is one of her backstage passes." It was a show business send-off for an entertainment legend.

As I walked through the crowds, members of the media stopped me time and again for comments about the First Lady. Several asked how I thought she'd have felt about the worldwide attention that surrounded her death. "I think Tammy would love this," I responded immediately. "After all, she was an entertainer."

Evelyn Shriver told me later that she had at first declined requests to televise the memorial service, thinking it might become a spectacle. "But then my friend John Seigenthaler from MSNBC called and asked me why, if the public was being allowed in, were we unwilling to include all the public. I agreed." Evelyn had recently been tapped to head Asylum Records here in Nashville, the first woman president of a major Music City label. The last letter Tammy would ever send Evelyn arrived in the afternoon mail a few days after the star's death, a congratulatory note about the new job.

"I love you and I'm proud of you," Tammy wrote.

Nancy (Mrs. George) Jones told me that Richey was so devastated he had to be sedated on the day of the two services. His close friends, including the Joneses, worried he might not be able to go from the funeral to the memorial. Richey made it through, but just barely.

There were so many powerful moments at the memorial: The Oaks gathering around George Richey for a private prayer just before the service started; Norro Wilson's poignant tribute; the Oaks' heartfelt performance; George Richey's tearful thanks to his late wife's friends and fans. There were also some lighter moments that Tammy, with her sharp wit, would have loved: Wynonna calling Tammy a "legend in her spare time"; Dolly making a joke about people thinking both she and Tammy had slept with Porter Wagoner.

"Half the people won't believe we did and the other half will just think we had bad taste," Dolly quipped. Tammy had shared that same joke with me three or four years earlier when she taped *On the Record*.

I tried hard to get through that horrible day without breaking down. I'd made it through the first service, but at the public memorial, when Dolly Parton began singing "I Will Always Love You," tears filled my eyes. And watching George Richey bravely attempt to speak to the crowd was absolutely heartbreaking.

Lorrie Morgan comforted George on the stage of the Ryman, then, at his request she performed "Stand by Your Man." Lorrie hadn't planned on singing it, feared she might break down, yet, professional that she is, she complied with Richey's wish to hear it and brought the entire crowd to tears with her performance. That was the second time I wept, and I was reminded of something Lorrie once told Tammy on my show: "Tammy, your music touched my soul." I believe it touched the world's soul, too.

Through no design of her own, Tammy and her signature song had been intensely visible throughout the first months of 1998. Television replays of Hillary Clinton's faux pas trashing of Tammy and her song seemed to drone on endlessly as speculations about the President's sex life took center stage.

Tammy Wynette would just as soon have forgotten all about what I call the "Stand by Your Song" confrontation that had transpired between the First Lady of Country Music and a First Lady–hopeful six years earlier. And while it's an oft-told tale,

Tammy shared some information with me about that incident and I'll pass it along.

Tammy told me she couldn't believe what she was hearing on *60 Minutes* that night in 1992. Hillary Clinton was on the program defending her husband, presidential candidate Bill Clinton, who was under fire for allegedly having a long-running extramarital affair with a young woman named Gennifer Flowers. In what turned out to be a serious tactical error, Mrs. Clinton reminded the viewing audience that she wasn't "some little woman" standing by her man like Tammy Wynette.

"Stand by Your Man" had drawn fire from feminists at the time, but Tammy thought it was a dead issue until she heard it being reborn on national television over two decades later.

"They'd been asking Hillary questions about her husband's so-called affair, and I thought she was simply up there defending him," Tammy told me. "I couldn't understand why she'd want to pull me in on it! It upset me and it upset Richey. I think I was madder about being called 'some little woman' than I was about her degrading 'Stand by Your Man'!"

Tammy was by no means "some little woman." And if anyone knew anything about her background, they would have known she faced many of the problems feminists addressed. And she often faced them alone. For starters, she raised four children virtually on her own until her marriage to George Richey. When she was starting out there was no money for baby-sitters. She took her three children to the studio, to interviews and to business meetings. If the weather was nice enough, they stayed in the car. If it was very cold, very hot or very late, she brought them inside. I remember when she came to do my television show for the first time in December 1966. I walked her out to the car and there sat the three little girls: Gwen, age five; Jackie, age three; and Tina, age fifteen months. Gwen was in charge, and while she seemed to be very much in control of things, the sight of those three babies sitting quietly in the car startled me.

"Tammy, why didn't you bring them in?" I asked.

"I was afraid to," she stammered. "I didn't know if the station would allow it."

"Your children are always welcome at my show, Tammy," I advised. "Don't ever forget that."

Being a single mother with a blossoming and time-consuming career but little money wasn't her only problem, either. Talent booker Hubert Long, for example, agreed to help her get show dates in the early years after she'd been turned down by several agencies simply because she was a female.

"One booker told me he didn't have any luck with 'girl singers' because they wouldn't 'patronize' the bar," Tammy explained to me. "I told him I thought I was being paid to sing, not to patronize the men at the bar!" And when one artist manager insultingly said, "We all know how you women make it in this business," Tammy didn't put up with it, and came back at him with both barrels. She was no shrinking violet then and she wasn't when Hillary Clinton insulted her. "Steel magnolia" is a much better description of Tammy Wynette.

Tammy let it be known that she didn't appreciate the slam, and by the following morning, Mrs. Clinton was on the phone to apologize. I'd heard about that part of the story. But what I didn't know was that Tammy wouldn't take the call until Burt Reynolds interceded. Burt, of course, was a former lover and longtime friend of Tammy's. If anyone outside of country music understood her strong personality, it was Burt. After all, when Mr. Reynolds once asked whether she'd consider marrying him, Tammy shot back: "Not a chance. I wouldn't want to share the mirror." Burt finally convinced Tammy to talk to Hillary, who explained that the questions had been coming very fast and she hadn't meant to be disparaging or harsh toward the legendary singer or her biggest hit song.

Here's what Tammy said to Hillary: "Well, isn't that exactly what you are doing? Standing by your man?"

"I guess it is," Mrs. Clinton answered.

It's funny. Tammy didn't even like "Stand by Your Man"

when she recorded it, and in fact, begged Billy Sherrill not to release the song as a single.

"I didn't relate to it," she told me. "It was so different from the songs I'd been singing, songs like 'D.I.V.O.R.C.E.' and 'I Don't Want to Play House.' And I didn't think much of the melody, either. I absolutely hated the high notes and thought I sounded like a pig squealing every time I listened to the playbacks!"

Additionally, the song hadn't started out to be an anthem for women standing by their husbands, so Tammy thought of it as a two-way-street message. Billy Sherrill told me he had been working on the song for over a year when he asked Tammy to help him finish it. Billy explained:

"The original title was 'I'll Stand by You, Please Stand by Me.' I would have preferred the title 'Stand by Me' but couldn't use it because Ben E. King already had a hit with that title. Tammy and I were in the studio and someone must have mentioned the line 'stand by your man' and I saw how we could write the song around that concept. Tammy and I went in the office and finished it in fifteen minutes. It became the third song on the session."

Tammy laughed when she heard Billy telling about finishing a song and recording it the same day. "That's how Billy worked," she explained. "We never had all our songs ready for a session. Billy would just say, 'Lightning will strike.'"

And right he was. Lightning struck swift and sure with "Stand by Your Man." Billy Sherrill thought it was funny that Tammy recorded the song while she was leaving her second husband, Don Chappel, getting ready to marry George Jones. All the while, standing in the wings was a good friend, the man who would stand by Tammy Wynette for the rest of her life: producer/publisher/songwriter George Richey. He once told me he thought he'd always loved her, even while she was married to his friend George Jones. But until her fourth divorce, he never had the nerve to tell her. (He had to get roaring drunk to tell her even then, according to Richey!)

Billy Sherrill related these things to me when I interviewed him for Tammy's *On the Record*. It's very hard to get an interview with the publicity-shy Sherrill, but I got around it by offering to send a crew to Florida where he was boating and promising to keep the interview brief. I got even more than I'd bargained for. Billy explained that he'd come up with the idea of renaming Virginia Wynette Pugh "Tammy Wynette" because of the incredible popularity of the film *Tammy and the Bachelor,* starring Debbie Reynolds. Many couples were naming their baby girls Tammy because of the film and its accompanying hit single. People often wonder how stars get a certain "title," such as the First Lady of Country Music. In Tammy's case, it was bestowed on her by Billy Sherrill. He said that with Roy Acuff being the King of Country Music, Kitty Wells being the Queen, and other titles like the King of the Cowboys being bandied about, he thought Tammy should have something more American. Hence, the First Lady of Country Music. Her term of office was all too short.

It's ironic that Tammy's health came to be such a problem. She was a physically strong, athletic young woman who'd picked cotton side-by-side with grown men and been a two-time All-State basketball player in high school.

The problems started with a simple appendectomy after Georgette, her daughter with George Jones, was born. Her internal scars began to form adhesions, and down the road there were more surgeries to remove them. And the scars from those surgeries formed more adhesions. She was in pain a good deal of the time, resorting to pills until she realized they had become a problem in her life. She checked into the Betty Ford clinic, then collapsed just after completing the rehabilitation and had to be rushed into surgery to remove still more adhesions. The more they were removed, the faster they grew back. It was a vicious cycle.

In 1992 I did a *Nashville Now* tribute to Tammy Wynette, and she told me that she'd been having problems with her blood clotting. She had frequent checkups for the condition, was required to take blood thinners and often had to have clots dissolved. She privately worried that in the end, a blood clot would kill her.

Near the end of 1993 Tammy almost died. She'd been in the studio recording with Aaron Neville for her wonderful duet album, *Without Walls,* which included sessions with Sting, Elton John and Wynonna, among others.

In the middle of the night she started having powerful stomach pains and when Richey got her to the hospital she was diagnosed with a badly infected bile duct in the liver, caused by adhesions.

Tammy told me the illness was more terrifying to her family than to her, and she explained why. It's a story I recalled during the funeral when Jake Hess was performing "Death Ain't No Big Deal."

"I hadn't been checked in the hospital long when my blood pressure began to drop drastically," she explained. "The doctors told Richey I had about a ten percent chance of making it and to call the children. I remember waking up at one point and all of our kids were gathered around the bed. I thought, 'Gosh, that makes a pretty picture. But why are they here?'

"Something happened in that hospital, Ralph. I don't know whether to call it an out-of-body or a near-death experience. I was aware of my condition even though I wasn't conscious. I felt like I was floating in a bright light. I felt no pain, no fear. I felt safe. After I passed the crisis, I thought a lot about what had happened. I thought about the lack of pain and fear and the feelings of safety and detachment I felt. Finally, I decided it was God saying, 'Wynette, death ain't no big deal.' "

On April 27, 1998, Sting dedicated the Rainforest benefit he held in New York to Tammy Wynette and Gianni Versace. At Sting's request, George Richey, the children and grandchildren were in attendance. At the show, Elton John sang "Stand by Your Man" in Tammy's memory, and I thought it was wonderful that the man who paid a final musical tribute to England's Princess Diana did the same for America's First Lady of Country Music.

CARL PERKINS:

"SINGING WAS A WAY

OF SURVIVING."

The year is 1937. Rows of black field hands toil in the cotton fields near Tiptonville, Tennessee. Around 3:00 P.M., when the blazing sun finally begins to hang a little lower in the sky, an old man called Uncle John Westbrook starts to hum a familiar tune, "Umm-ba-ba-bum." Seven or eight rows down, Sister Juanita begins to sing in a rich, throaty voice: "*Gonna lay down my burdens, down by the riverside. . . .*" Two rows over, one of two small white boys in the field chimes in: "*Down by the riv-er-side.*" It is five-year-old Carl Perkins, toting a heavy bag, his fingers bleeding from the thorny plants.

"My dad was in poor health for as long as I can remember so my brother Jay and I had to start picking cotton when we were very young," Carl once told me. "Every afternoon in the fields was the same. None of us had anything to look forward to; you picked cotton all week and pecans on the weekend. We knew we were never going to have anything, not the food that other people ate or the clothes they wore. I guess it was just natural that we sang, singing was a way of surviving. Of course, nobody had any instruments out there in the field, so we tapped on our legs or arms or on the cotton sacks. If we ran out of verses, my job was to make one up."

After some weeks, Uncle John Westbrook noticed scars forming on the youngster's hands and taught him how to pick cotton without getting cut by the plant's sharp shells. "Uncle John didn't pick fast, or fight it—as they called it," Carl recalled. "He said, 'Little Carlie, if you'll go to the bottom of the stalk you'll be able to see every bole between your hands and the top of that stalk. You can pick cleaner and your little hands might not get cut so bad.' Uncle John had the system and he taught it to me."

Uncle John then set the boy on a path that would take him out of the cotton-picking business forever; he taught Carl Perkins to pick guitar. "Uncle John would break the top off of a pop bottle and put it on his little finger. Now they call that a slide. He'd use that pop bottle slide to get those blues tones on his guitar."

The first guitar Carl had was one his father fashioned from a cigar box, a broken broom handle and some bailing wire. "Cigar boxes were rare in Lake County, Tennessee," Carl said. "It was on the counter at Coats' Grocery and I had to wait two weeks for all the cigars to sell." Once Carl began to show serious interest in music and in playing the guitar, Carl's father bought his son a used guitar for $3.50.

"I loved that guitar," Carl said. "But I kept painting it so it would look new. I'd paint it a different color every week. Finally it had so many coats of paint on it that the sound was terrible and it was too heavy for me to hold!" A cousin helped out, trading Carl a small Gene Autry model for the full-sized painted guitar, which he then stripped. Carl carried the Gene Autry instrument everywhere, even on his first day of school.

"Mama and Daddy had a big discussion about whether to let me carry that guitar on my first day of school," Carl said, laughing. "I wouldn't leave it at home, and they were afraid I'd ruin it." Finally it was decided that Carl could take his guitar, and if he ruined it or if other children made fun of him for bringing it, the experience might be a lesson to him. Ironically, no one made fun of his guitar, just his worn-out shoes and patched clothes.

"I STARTED SINGING at school, or anywhere somebody would listen," Carl said. "But I had terrible stage fright. Once when I was in the fourth grade I had to sing two songs at a school program: 'Home on the Range' and 'Where Have You Been, Billy Boy.' Well, I got up there and got scared and sang them both in the wrong key. One would have been too high for Bill Monroe and the other had notes so low Ernest Tubb couldn't have hit 'em.''

Carl was a bright and imaginative child who understood himself very well at a very young age. In his biography, *Go Cat Go,* there is a particularly telling essay he wrote as a ten-year-old schoolboy. When asked to write a description of himself in 1942, Carl handed his teacher the following essay:

> *Hello, my name is Carl Perkins.*
> *I am a sharecropper's son. I work very hard for what I have to eat and a place to stay warm in the winter. My favorite fruit is the orange, although I don't get very many oranges. I love my mama and my daddy, and my two brothers, Jay and Clayton. And I don't want to grow up and be a man like Hitler.*
> *Someday I want to be a big radio star.*
>
> > *Thank you.*
> > *Carl Perkins.*

Carl's first influences were the blues, sung to a rhythm beat out on cotton sacks, but he soon began to listen to the Grand Ole Opry on his father's radio. Roy Acuff was an early favorite, soon followed by Bill Monroe and later, Bob Wills. "I'd be sitting in bed at night, playing my guitar in Uncle John's blues fashion, but what I'd find myself singing was Ernest Tubb's 'Walkin' the Floor Over You.' A country song with a blues guitar.''

In 1946 Carl and his brothers, Jay and Clayton, started playing some shows around Tiptonville billed as the Perkins Brothers. Carl later said when he first heard Clayton playing bass he began to hear the sound for which he would ultimately be known, rockabilly. His musical direction was rounded out when he added "Fluke" Holland on drums. At the time, Carl wasn't thinking about rock 'n' roll. Because even though he knew his music wasn't mainstream country, he was still shooting for the Grand Ole Opry.

Throughout the early 1950s Carl sent tapes of the Perkins Brothers to New York record companies. The rejection letters usually praised his original sound, but admitted they had no idea how to market the music. Carl took pride in the fact that they liked it and held onto the hope that one day he'd find someone who did know what to do with the music he was making.

The Perkins Brothers had included Bill Monroe's "Blue Moon of Kentucky" in their repertoire since 1947. Then, in 1954 Carl heard the song performed on a local radio station radio by a Memphis boy named Elvis Presley, and was astonished to hear the same arrangement he used and the same pronunciation and phrasing. Still, he knew a record label somewhere out there "got it." Carl later told me that unbeknownst to him at the time, Elvis's first manager, Bob Neal, had heard him sing the song.

Carl and his brothers went to Memphis to see Sam Phillips, and after some hard convincing, Sam allowed them to come into the studio and present their material. Sam stopped them in the middle of the first song, one of Jay's country tunes. Jay was incensed and wanted to leave then and there. "No," Carl said. "I'm going to play him one of mine."

Sam later said he was sold the minute Carl started to play the guitar break. "It's still country," Sam mused. "But it's got something extra." What Carl called "music with a beat" was ultimately named rockabilly. Carl never liked labels of any kind, though, and resisted it when people told him he was strictly a rock 'n' roller.

"You can't tell me I ain't country," was the answer he often gave.

Sun recording artists Carl Perkins, Johnny Cash and Elvis Presley soon became friends and touring partners. Since they were playing a similar sound, and aiming for the same audience, Carl knew he was being compared to Elvis at each and every show. Instead of feeling resentment toward his contemporary, Carl used the friendly competition to fuel his stage show. "Compared to Elvis I looked like an old country mule," Carl laughed. "I had to shake the stage down to get any attention."

Carl and Johnny Cash became like brothers. "We had so much in common," Carl explained. "We grew up across the Mississippi River from each other, me in Tennessee and John in Arkansas. We both came from sharecropping families, close families who lived from Saturday to Saturday waiting for payday."

Jerry Lee Lewis, too, hung out at Sun, first as a piano player, then as an artist. Carl once told me how he'd been there the first time Sam Phillips heard Jerry Lee sing. "I was in the studio recording

'Matchbox Blues' and Jerry Lee was playing piano. During one of the breaks, he started playing the Ray Price hit, 'Crazy Arms.' Sam looked up suddenly and said, 'I didn't know you sang, Cat.' Jerry Lee nodded and said he sang some. After we finished 'Matchbox Blues' Jerry Lee recorded 'Crazy Arms.' "

Carl played a role in The Killer's trademark concert finale when, while on tour in Canada, he told Jerry Lee he should stand up to play the very end of his last song. "You just tear up that last part," Carl encouraged. Jerry Lee stood up, but as Carl explained, he accidentally knocked over the piano stool. "Well, that made him mad, and he kicked it," Carl laughed. "And when he swung around to finish the piece, part of his hair fell down in his face. The crowd went wild and gave him two encores. When Jerry Lee came offstage he slapped me on the shoulder and said, 'I'll go back after that stool tomorrow night, too!' "

JOHNNY CASH GAVE Carl the idea for "Blue Suede Shoes" but while Carl thought it was an interesting idea, he couldn't come up with a hook. "Johnny and Elvis and I were playing a show at a schoolhouse in Parkins, Arkansas, when John brought it up," Carl told me during one radio interview. "Bob Neal was managing Elvis at the time, and he stood at the door with his cigar box, taking a dollar apiece from the people coming in. If you were under twelve you got in free. We each made sixteen dollars, so it was a big night for us. After the show we went to a truck stop to eat and Bob put the cigar box on the table and gave us each a dollar for dinner."

There at the truck stop, Johnny told Carl a story about a friend from from his military days. V. C. White, a black airman from Virginia, stopped by to see Cash one night on his way to town on a three-day pass. "How do I look?" V. C. asked. Cash told him he looked sharp, and V. C. grinned and said, "Don't step on my blue suede shoes." Cash reminded V. C. that his shoes were black, and the airman grinned bigger and said, "Not tonight."

Then on the night of October 21, 1955, while Carl was playing a show at the Supper Club in Jackson, Tennessee, he overheard a young man say to his date, "Uh-uh, don't step on my blue suede shoes."

There was that line again. Carl thought it was almost funny, the guy cared more for those shoes than he did his date's feelings. This time the line crystallized the idea for the song, and that same night he wrote the song that made him famous. "My wife, Valda, and I were living in a government project house back then. I got home from the show around one o'clock A.M. and I couldn't get to sleep thinking about the song. Finally I got up and went downstairs and got my guitar out and started picking on it. An old children's verse came to my mind. Did you ever play hide and seek? Remember saying: *one for the money, two for the show, three to get ready* . . . ? I put some music to those lines first, and started singing. The babies had kept Valda up off and on that night, and she called from upstairs, 'Whose song is that, Carl?' I called back up, 'It's ours, honey, hush!' She called back, 'Well, it sure sounds like a good one.' "

It was a good one, too. Released on February 19, 1956, "Blue Suede Shoes" quickly went to number one on the country chart, and number two on the pop and R&B charts, hit the top-10 in the UK and established Carl Perkins as one of the architects of rock 'n' roll.

RCA's STEVE SHOLES, who had just bought Elvis Presley's contract from Sun, almost had a coronary when he heard the record on the radio. "I've signed the wrong act!" he said to Chet Atkins. Then Sholes called Sam Phillips and asked if Elvis could record the song. Sam explained that since the song was already out, he couldn't stop anyone from covering it, but he hoped that RCA would not release it as a single since Carl's version was soaring up three charts.

Carl's life was forever changed when, on March 22, 1956, with "Blue Suede Shoes" the hottest song in the nation, Carl and his brothers were involved in a car accident while on the way to New York to appear on the *Perry Como Show*. Carl suffered a broken shoulder, fractured skull and concussion. Carl had only just been released from the hospital when Steve Sholes released Elvis's version of "Blue Suede Shoes." Elvis's cut only hit the top-20, but it did take the edge off Carl's newfound stardom. Sam kept on releasing singles while Carl recovered, but he had nothing in the can that could follow "Blue Suede Shoes." He never had another pop hit.

"Boppin' the Blues" rose to #7 in country, but stayed in the charts only six weeks. "Dixie Fried" was a top-10 record that stayed in the country charts a short two weeks. And "Your True Love" went to #13, lasting eight weeks.

In 1958, when Johnny Cash signed with Columbia Records, he brought Carl Perkins with him. Again, he failed to find a hit song. Carl later said that Don Law's attempts to record him in a more traditional country style was at the crux of his Columbia problems. Carl wanted to sing country, but his kind of country, played with his trademark beat.

IN 1964, CARL went on tour in the UK with Chuck Berry and at one post-concert party he met four fans he'd been unaware he had: John, Paul, George and Ringo. George Harrison insisted that Carl show him how he played the intro on "Honey Don't," then invited him to come with them to Abbey Road, where the Beatles recorded three of his songs, "Honey Don't," "Matchbox" and "Everybody's Trying to Be My Baby." Into the wee hours they talked music, sang and picked guitars. George, especially, couldn't get enough of Carl's advice. It has to go down as one of the most historic behind-the-scenes events in music history.

Carl came back to the States energized and began to tour with country artists including Faron Young and Webb Pierce. Then tragedy struck again when, while playing a show in Dyersburg, Tennessee, he caught his hand in a rotary fan and had to be rushed to the hospital for stitches. The attending physician wanted Carl to go by ambulance to a hospital in Memphis, but Carl declined, insisting he could drive the sixty miles home to Jackson. It was a good thing that state troopers were accompanying him on that drive, because Carl lost consciousness and had to be rushed to the emergency room in Jackson. The doctor later said when he performed surgery on Carl's hand, he worked as carefully as if it were his own; after all, a surgeon makes his living with his hands, too.

A year later, in 1966, Carl suffered still another freak accident. While hunting with a friend, his shotgun accidentally discharged and hit him in the foot. Once more, Carl faced a tough recuperation, and once more, Johnny Cash was there as a friend and comrade. With Carl's career stalled again, Cash offered him a job: playing guitar in one of the hottest tours of the time, the Johnny Cash Show. Carl accepted his invitation, and what he thought would be a short-term detour turned out to be a ten-year road gig, one that became an inspiration for Carl and a musical bonanza for Cash.

"Can you imagine how I felt, sitting on that bus and having Mother Maybelle Carter actually pass me her guitar to pick out a song?" Carl asked me.

Carl wrote one of John's biggest hits while the two were on tour in 1967. " 'Daddy Sang Bass' came about in a dressing room in Omaha just before Christmas," Carl told me. "I get pretty sentimental around the holidays and start thinking about Christmas with my family when I was a little boy. I was sitting in my dressing room remembering the singing we'd done around the house, especially at Christmas, and started playing the guitar and singing, 'Daddy sang bass, Mama sang tenor. Me and little brother would join right in there.' Johnny knocked on the door and asked me if I was busy writing. I said, 'No, I'm just messing around with an idea. Come on in.' So he came in and I played him some of the lines I'd come up with. Right then and there he told me he'd record the song when I finished it. Ten minutes later I chased him down and said, 'Here's that song you bragged about.' "

"Daddy Sang Bass" was released in December the following year and stayed at the top of the country charts for a solid eight weeks. "All writers have certain songs that mean a lot to them," Carl told me back in 1974. " 'Daddy Sang Bass' is one of those for me. I revealed more about myself in that one than in any other. For me, the song is about the American way, the American spirit."

And it was Carl who Johnny turned to on the stage at San Quentin, whispering: "Get me the words to that 'Boy Named Sue' song." Johnny had never performed the Shel Silverstein song in public, but this live recording became the follow-up #1 to "Mama Sang Bass."

"John was running low on material," Carl remembered. "He'd done all the prison songs he could think of, and the show wasn't over. So during Bob Wooten's guitar break on one song, he asked me to get the words from his guitar case. John strummed a few chords and I picked up on it. The rest of the band just followed along."

* * *

THERE WAS A dark side to those years. Cash was popping pills and Carl was drinking heavily. "I'm not proud of this part of my life," Carl once explained to my radio audience. "But I'm not ashamed to tell you about it, especially if somebody out there has the same problem. I drank a lot of hard liquor all through my early career. It gave me courage, cured the stage fright. I got to leaning on liquor as a substitute for nerve."

Johnny and Carl talked about their problems often, in dressing rooms, on the bus, sitting in truck stops in the middle of the night after a show. They knew they would one day have to give up their chemical addictions if they were going to live. As Carl put it to me, "What we were doing was doing us in." Sometime around 1970, the two gave up their demons cold turkey.

"When we finally did it, we were in California on a long tour. We'd talked about it and prayed about it, then made a pact about it. Johnny and I went out to the beach and I threw my bottle of whiskey into the Pacific Ocean. There were many times I'd have gladly gone swimming in an undertow to find it again, too. But with Johnny's friendship and the Lord's nerve, I didn't."

Carl tried to help his friend Elvis Presley kick his addictions, but it was to no avail. After seeing photos of an overweight, bloated Presley, Carl drove to Memphis to ask the King of Rock 'n' Roll to go on a fishing trip, where he hoped to convince him to do as he and Cash had done: get rid of the chemical abuse. But Elvis's uncle, Vester, met Carl at the gate and told him Elvis was asleep. Carl finally gave up and drove back to Jackson. Elvis's mother, the woman Carl called "Mrs. Gladys," weighed heavily on him in the days that followed. Had she lived, she would have been such a source of strength to Elvis. After much thought, Carl sat down and wrote a song titled "Mama" for his old friend. Elvis was planning to record it just before he died.

IN 1975 CARL left the Johnny Cash show and started playing shows with his sons, Greg and Stan. In many ways, these were the most satisfying years of his career. His writing was never better and he started racking up cuts on country artists' albums; he continued to record solo projects as well as working with Paul McCartney on 1981's *Tug of War* and doing 1986's *Class of '55* with his Sun Records friends, Johnny Cash, Jerry Lee Lewis and Roy Orbison. In 1985 he was named a member the Nashville Songwriters Hall of Fame and the following year "Blue Suede Shoes" was inducted into the Grammy Hall of Fame. He was featured in a 1986 Cinemax production titled *A Rockabilly Session: Carl Perkins and Friends,* starring George Harrison, Ringo Starr, Dave Edmunds, Eric Clapton and Rosanne Cash, among others.

On January 21, 1987, Sam Phillips introduced Carl as one of the new inductees into Rock's Hall of Fame; Carl and Keith Richards closed the show playing "Blue Suede Shoes." His "Let Me Tell You About Love" became a #1 song for the Judds in 1989. Carl and the duo became fast friends, and when Carl was diagnosed with throat cancer several years later, Naomi sent inspirational books, Bible passages and guardian angels.

During his recovery period, Carl had three songs at once charting in *Billboard:* "Restless," recorded by the New Nashville Cats; "Silver and Gold," by Dolly Parton; and "When You're a Man on His Own," by George Strait. In 1996 he collaborated with David McGee on a biography, *Go Cat Go.* In the book, Carl looks at his existence with beautiful simplicity, saying, "It takes a lot of ups and downs to get a life completed."

IN NOVEMBER 1997, Carl Perkins suffered the first of a series of strokes that would take his life on January 19, 1998. Musical tributes came in from stars including Elton John, Eric Clapton, Paul McCartney and Bob Dylan. Many stars came to Jackson, Tennessee, for the funeral. George Harrison and Garth Brooks sang "Your True Love" and perhaps Wynonna Judd summed it up best when she said, "Carl Perkins was the coolest cat I know."

I loved talking with Carl because of his great heart, his clear, discerning commentary and his willingness to discuss those ups and downs he went through while completing his legendary life. Carl liked coming to my radio shows, too. One night, as he was leaving, this was his exit line: "Ralph, I wouldn't trade this talk for a gold monkey!"

I TALKED TO Carl back in April 1997 at *Prime Time Country* about "Mama," the song he wrote for Elvis. As it turned out, that conversation was the last I ever had with Carl, so I'd like to share it in its entirety.

RALPH: *Tell me the story about Elvis being on one of your record sessions.*

CARL: About six months before Presley passed away, I wrote a song especially for him. It was called "Mama." I really put the boy's vision and his mama's vision in my brain, and I wrote it line for line for Elvis. I came to Nashville and I sang the song live for Felton Jarvis, who of course had produced all of Elvis's material for fourteen years. Felton said, "Boy, he'll kill for that song, Perkins!"

So I went back and made a little demo of the song. Just me and my guitar and I got it to Jarvis. I didn't hear anything about the song for quite a while. I did keep hearing through the grapevine that Elvis wouldn't record, and that RCA even put a truck behind his house at Graceland and told Jarvis, "Man, if he is singing 'Jingle Bells'—anything—get him to turn the recorder on!" Felton was even following him around with a microphone.

At any rate the night that Presley was buried, my wife Valda was in the hospital in Jackson so I couldn't go down to the funeral. I watched it on television from the hospital room, and I remember pointing Felton Jarvis out to Val since she'd never met him. Then, the night after Presley was buried, the phone rang in Val's hospital room at around ten o'clock P.M. It was Felton Jarvis.

"I really hate to call you this late," Felton said. "But I just had to tell you that a few days ago I called Elvis into the kitchen at Graceland and played him your song. I hadn't seen a tear in his eye for a good while. But tears rolled down his cheeks and he said, 'And Carl Perkins wrote that for me? So where has this song been? How long ago did he write it?' "

Felton had been carrying the song around in his briefcase for six months. "Elvis, I've offered to play this for you two or three times," Felton said. "You said: 'I don't want to hear nothing. I'm not singing nothing.' " Then Felton said Elvis got very emotional. "You've been toting that song for me that long? The day the tour is over book Victor's studio in Nashville. I am going to record 'Mama.' "

But of course it never happened. Felton said he just called to let me know that Elvis heard it and was planning to record it. He just never got the chance. When I heard from Felton a couple weeks later I asked him what he was gonna do with Elvis gone. He said there was one guy he wanted to record, and I mentioned that the guy was a lucky fellow, because Felton was such a great producer. Felton said, "I'm talking to him, Carl. I want to produce you." I said, "Are you kidding me?" And Felton said he's always wanted to produce an album on me.

That was all he needed to say. I came to Nashville and we got some great players together for the sessions. Felton asked me to sing "Mama," the song I wrote for Elvis. I did, and of course it was nothing like Elvis would have done it. I'd written it as a country song and that's the way I approached it.

But after we got through recording it we listened to a playback. The first thing we heard was an open G chord on rhythm guitar. Felton said, "Wait. Run that back a minute."

Jerry Shook was playing rhythm guitar, and Felton asked him if he'd played that chord.

"No. That's an open G," Jerry said. "That's the kind Presley made."

Presley wasn't a great guitar player. He could play rhythm and that's about it. Shook made the bar G. But this was a G string, open strings down to a little E, a very distinctive Presley G chord. Felton looked at me and said, "Carl, you didn't make that did you?" 'Cause I was playing my electric guitar. I said, "No that wasn't me." It got real eerie. Chip Young said, "It wasn't me. I'm sitting back here." We couldn't find nobody that did it. We put up every track. To this day, we have never found that G chord that is on the front of that record.

RALPH: *As I remember, the first time you told me this, you said that you would eliminate tracks looking for that guitar, and it would not be there. Then you would bring it all together and it would be on the record.*

CARL: Yes, and I never released the song. Felton just held it, saying, "We are going to find that G chord and then I will erase it. I gotta know where it came from."

But the strange thing is, after we first ran through the song that day, the door to the studio closed. Nobody was even close to the door, and the wind wasn't blowing.

Felton said, "Well, I guess he decided to leave."

It was an experience. Felton and I talked about it several times during the years after that. We went ahead and made this whole album. We remained friends until he died which was several years after Presley died. We mentioned that session a lot. I'd say, "Well what do you think?" Felton would shake his head and say he didn't know. Then he'd say, "You're the guitar player, you tell me how a note that's not on any of the tracks is on the record." I once thought it might have been a chord left on a tape from an earlier session, but then Chip said it was a brand new tape. So we were back to square one. It may have been one of these things that can't be explained by anything we know about.

RALPH: *Do you think it was Elvis?*

CARL: When I was a kid I was always thinking I heard ghosts. But my dad could always track it down to be a loose piece of tin on that old shack, something scraping in the wind. He'd say, "Oh, go on to sleep boys. I'll nail her down tomorrow." We could never nail down where that chord came from. I'm afraid to say. I believe that there was something very mystical about that. Elvis's chord was meant to be there.

RALPH: *Was the sound unpleasant? Felton said he had to get rid of it.*

CARL: Well, it was there and then there was a little space before we started playing. He said if it is left on there, we'd have to splice the tape. If it had been just a second later it would have been perfect to start the song with. It was like Elvis said, "I'll start it, but then I am going to mess it up for you." It's weird. A very spooky thing.

RALPH: *Carl, were you and Elvis close?*

CARL: Yeah. In the very early years Elvis and I were real close. I was there once, when Elvis made a statement to Sam Phillips. Elvis often came to Sun when I was recording. He'd tell Sam to let him know when I was going in the studio, because he wanted to be there. And once when he was at one of my sessions, he said, "If Carl didn't write and sing, I'd hire him to play guitar for me. I really like the way Carl Perkins plays guitar."

Scotty Moore has told me since then that Elvis would sometimes say, "You are playing it like Scotty, now play that blues lick like Carl." And Scotty would just say, "Well, Elvis, you'll have to get Carl then. I can't play that way."

RALPH: *I've often wondered if Elvis went to school on you.*

CARL: Well. I don't know. There is a disc jockey by the name of Bob Neal. Bob was Presley's first manager. Bob was one of the first guys to hear "Blue Moon of Kentucky." He heard me sing it up at the clubs. I used to do a lot of Bill Monroe stuff. Bill played that up-tempo bluegrass and was very instrumental in the lives of Presley, me and a lot of the Rockabillies. It was the kind of country music that the boys that played what was later called rockabilly liked. In the beginning we called it "Feel Good Music."

I think that the name rockabilly came about when some of the Nashville boys said "some of the Memphis boys are rockin' our hillbilly music." Anyway, I think that Bob Neal told me, "I heard you do 'Blue Moon of Kentucky.' " He'd come up to the clubs around Jackson where I played before Elvis recorded it in '54. But the first record that Elvis recorded was "Blue Moon of Kentucky." Then he did "That's All Right, Mama." Those two came out as his first single.

The first time I saw him I said, "My goodness, he's good and he's pretty too!" I knew that nothing was gonna stop this kid. He had no blemishes. I'd get close. I'd say, "I'm gonna find a birthmark behind his ear. There is a wart somewhere and it's hid under his hair." But it wasn't there. He had perfect looks.

Elvis and I worked together at Sun, and then along came a tall, skinny boy out of Arkansas named Johnny Cash. Bob Neal booked the three of us on the same show, and charged people a dollar bill to get in. We didn't have tickets back then. Back in those days you didn't have big coliseums, so we played in a school auditorium. Bob just charged adults, and several midgets later told me they got in free 'cause they looked under twelve years old!

RALPH: *Is this* 1955?

CARL: This is 1954. Elvis started in March or April of '54. I was there two months later. Cash came in early 1955. Elvis and I worked the summer of '54 together. Then . . . John, his first record was "Hey, Porter" and "Cry! Cry! Cry!" Cash took off like crazy so Bob booked all three of us together.

RALPH: *Did all three of you work with the same band?*

CARL: No. Elvis had Scotty and Bill. Elvis never had a Sun record that had drums. I had the first set of drums that went into Sun Records. He did not. He had Bill Black doing that "bica bica bica." It sounded like a drum but wasn't. And Holland had a great big old marching drum for a bass drum. He said, "What are you all doing with that thing in here? We ain't got no drums in here." I said, "You have now. You listen." That was the first drum on a Carl Perkins record.

RALPH: *Was it Fluke playing?*

CARL: Fluke used to come to the clubs and he'd beat on the side of my brother Clayton's bass. I said, "Do it louder." He said, "I'm blistering my hands now!" It was about no more than a couple months before I went to Sun. I said, "Boy, get you a set of drums and you can start playing with us." One reason I wanted Fluke with us was the fact that he had a 1948 Cadillac and my old Plymouth wouldn't start half the time! He even stenciled "The Perkins Brothers" on the side of that Cadillac.

But the main reason we needed him was the fact that he played drums on the side of the bass. It just made the sound fuller in those clubs. I didn't really like it when he first started playing the drums. I said, "Get on those brushes. I want it to sound like that bass." The minute he started on the brushes, I said, "That's it."

Sam said, "It's got something, let's do it."

Back in those years two-thirds of the songs that came along were just ideas you started making up. There were at least four of my early Sun Records that I hadn't written the words down when we recorded. Here's what it was usually like:

I'd say, "Get in E," and we'd start. Sam would be back there listening. He'd let me go all the way through it and I'd just be making it up.

"Do that again," Sam would say. I wouldn't remember the words that I did the first time, and would sing something else.

"Boy, I wish you'd do it like you did it at first," Sam would tell me.

"I was making it up while I went," I'd answer.

"Well, the first time you did it was a hit," he'd say. "It's not as good as it was but it's a good song." And then I'd write it down and learn the song so I could sing it on stage.

RALPH: *Did "Honey Don't" start that way?*

CARL: "Honey Don't" started in a club a week before I was to record. I was just making it up. I turned to my brother Jay and said, "Let's start in E." Then I told him to go to C.

"You can't go from E to C," Jay said.

"Try it, it'll work," I said. Going from E to C was way different. In 1955 you didn't put C with E in those days. That was one of the things the Beatles said to me in 1964. George Harrison said, "You know what really knocked me out was you went from E down to C and came back up. That's what started us going into faraway places and putting chords together."

So see it was an accident but it gave them an idea to expand on. It was about the only time I really hooked chords like that together. But to me it sounded right. So we left it.

RALPH: *You mentioned Bob Neal. How did Tom Parker get Elvis away from Bob?*

CARL: Simply by walking up to Elvis at the *Louisiana Hayride* and asking Elvis if he wanted to be a big star.

"Yes sir," Elvis said.

"You signed with anybody?"

"I got about a year with Mr. Bob Neal," Elvis said.

The Colonel then asked Elvis who Bob was, and Elvis said he was a Memphis disc jockey. Then Tom asked if Elvis minded if he came to Memphis to meet with him. He already knew Elvis was an only child and all he had to do was go through Mr. and Mrs. Presley and this little disc jockey Bob Neal. That wasn't a mountain for the Colonel. He showed up the next week after one of Elvis's Saturday night appearances. Elvis recognized him. He said, "Mama here comes that fella I was telling you about, that Colonel Tom Parker. The man in the white cowboy hat."

The Colonel walked up to Mrs. Gladys and said, "I can make a star out of your son."

I think Mrs. Gladys had her opinion of him. She told Elvis, "Son, he's a little swift. He's saying he's gonna get you on the cover of movie magazines. Now, that don't sound right. You're a little bit too young to be doing this."

"Mama, I think he can," Elvis said.

Mrs. Gladys said, "We've gotta be fair with Bob Neal." So they called him at home and he came over there. I think it was Elvis's daddy who said, "Mr. Neal, you've been awful good to our boy and we ain't gonna sign with this fella if you got any reservations about it."

Bob told the Presleys that he thought the Colonel could make Elvis a big star quicker than he could. According to Elvis, Bob said: "I think I could do it but it would take me a lot longer. He's had Eddy Arnold and Hank Snow." Bob knew the Colonel but the Colonel didn't know Bob. That's how it happened. They shook hands as the story goes in Elvis's living room.

RALPH: *Did he give Bob Neal any money?*

CARL: I don't think so. No. Bob didn't ask for any. He said, "Son, it's your decision. I don't blame you." The Colonel told Elvis he could have him on the *Ed Sullivan Show* in two months, and he did. So it was a good move.

RALPH: *Did you like the Colonel?*

CARL: I was scared of him, but I liked him. I liked anybody that showed courage, wisdom and backbone. He felt totally convinced that nothing could stop this boy, and he was right.

RALPH: *I'm doing one chapter in this book on the Colonel. It's because I have an interview I did with the Colonel that I never released. I've had it for three years. Not many people have an interview with the Colonel. We've done some research on him, and all the naysayers say he took too much of Elvis's money but I've always heard from people that were around in those days that if it hadn't been for the Colonel there wouldn't have been an Elvis. What do you think?*

CARL: Nobody was responsible for Elvis but Elvis. That doesn't take away the fact that the Colonel was a strong manager and did Elvis a lot of good. But would Elvis have done it anyway? Yes. Money and publicity can't make a star like him. You could have borrowed money from every bank in West Tennessee and not made a star on the level of Elvis. Elvis would have happened without a dime and publicity. He made his own publicity when he walked on and off the stage.

I remember once when Johnny Cash and Elvis and I were on tour. I was standing at the side of the stage when Elvis walked out, and there was this huge roar from the audience. I went on back to the dressing room and Johnny asked me what in the world Elvis had done out there.

"He hasn't done anything, Johnny," I said. "He walked to the corner of the stage and pointed at them kids and they went crazy."

I've seen teenagers bite fingernails until blood run down their fingers while Elvis was on stage. And I'd bet they didn't even miss their fingernails till the next morning when they woke up with sore hands. He just "tranced" them.

I always said, God put Presley on this earth to do exactly what he did. He made him look like nobody else. He was perfect. The one thing they did was darken his hair. Got him a Tony Curtis haircut. He always liked Tony Curtis's hair. But boy he showed Tony what hair was about.

RALPH: *Do you think the Colonel deserved the fifty percent?*

CARL: I never heard Elvis complain.

We chatted a little more about our families, and signed off. There's one more thing, though, that I wish I'd said:

Carl, I wouldn't trade this talk for a gold monkey.

REBA'S RED DRESS:
CMA AWARDS, 1993

REBA MCENTIRE SAYS she got more press coverage out of her infamous red dress incident, when she appeared "uncovered" at the 1993 Country Music Association awards show, than she would have if she'd won Entertainer of the Year. Reba's form-fitting, bared-to-the-waist gown had this town buzzing for weeks, partly because Reba was such an unlikely woman to show up in scandalous attire. It started a week earlier, when her designer brought the gown to Reba's office for a fitting. "This sheer front will fill in nicely with sequins," the woman explained, when Reba's husband Narvel dropped his jaw at the sight of his wife's almost bare chest.

The gown was whisked back to the design table, and Reba didn't see the finished product until twenty minutes prior to showtime when she was hurrying to ready herself for the duet with Linda Davis, "Does He Love You?" The dressing room was packed with costumes, dressers, hair and makeup women, and the lighting wasn't the best. Reba threw on the gown and turned to Narvel. Once again his mouth dropped open. "I thought you were going to fill in that front part," he gasped to Sandy.

"I did—quite a bit," she answered.

"Well I don't think 'quite a bit' was enough," Narvel sputtered.

It was too late, though, because the show's producers were calling Reba's name. She glanced down, couldn't tell just how sheer the material was, or how low there in the cramped quarters, shrugged off Narvel's concerns and sped out into the hall.

"It covers everything," she called back to Narvel, as she hurried to get to the stage.

"As I rushed down the hall, I passed Kris Kristofferson," Reba recalls. "His eyes got as big as tractor tires. That was when I realized that Narvel had been right. 'Quite a bit' hadn't been enough. I walked onstage and heard an audible gasp from the audience. I didn't dare look down.''

After the show, Narvel whisked his wife back to their offices, where Reba's parents and her sister, Christian artist Suzy Luchsinger, and her family awaited them. I asked Reba what Narvel had to say when they got into the car, and she said she better not repeat it. But she did say this: ''Mother told me that when I walked out on the stage, Suzy leaned over and whispered, ''Ohhh, Mama!''

That's pretty much what the entire audience was saying, too. ''Ohhh, Mama!''

6

B R O O K S   &   D U N N :

T H E   N E X T   B I G   D E A L

In 1967 there were six bands calling themselves "The Originals" in Shreveport, Louisiana. One of them had a twelve-year-old guitar player named Kix Brooks. "We played a little bit of everything," Kix recalls. "We played Hank Williams and Rolling Stones and the Beatles. We even auditioned for the *Ted Mack Amateur Hour.* We thought we were the next big deal."

All those kids out there playing in those eclectic country rock bands owed a big debt—whether or not they fully understood it—to Carl Perkins.

TWENTY-FIVE YEARS LATER, Ronnie Dunn was in the studio taping my syndicated show and listening to his singing partner tell my listeners about his early aspirations. " 'The Next Big Deal.' " Ronnie laughed. "That sounds like a good name for a band."

In 1991 a record came along that made Brooks & Dunn country music's next big deal. It was *Brand New Man,* and it blew me away. It blew a lot of other people away, too, because the CD sold five million copies, more than any other country music duo's debut. Ronnie's wife, Janine, inspired the song that put her husband and Kix Brooks in the marketplace and on the map.

"She was giving me one of those married couple, 'you better turn it around, hoss, and get it right this time,' lectures," Ronnie says. "So I went downstairs and wrote 'I saw the light, I've been baptized.' " Ronnie's title was "I'm a Changed Man."

When Ronnie played several lines of "Changed Man" to Kix, he suggested "Brand New Man" would have a better meter. Then, as Kix explains, the two took the song to writer/producer Don Cook: "Ronnie had the first verse, and I suggested the title. But we had a space right before the hook, and couldn't find the line. Don listened and immediately said, 'I'm born to love again.' That's the value of fresh eyes and ears. We might have stared at that paper all day and come up dry."

Kix and Ronnie had no idea that "Brand New Man" would explode like it did. Even the executives at their own label, Arista Records, said they'd be lucky to sell gold, which is a half million, on the album. Ronnie figured they'd be lucky to get a top-10. But the woman who inspired the song never wavered in her belief. "Janine thinks she can predict the hits when we hear songs on the radio. So she bet me our single would go to number one," Ronnie laughs. "Okie that she is, she wanted a truck if she won the bet. We'd sold our car to get to Nashville."

Once a song gets into the top-10, the competition is stiff. It's like Pam Tillis once told me, "That's when you run into the Garth-wall." The single was at #6, and Kix and Ronnie were on a plane to Albuquerque, New Mexico, when the captain announced, "Mr. Ronnie Dunn, please report to the front of the plane." Kix said, "Oh, cripes, now what did we do?" After the two made their way up front, the stewardess said, "Mr. Dunn, your wife called and says you owe her a new truck." Kix looked at Ronnie and all he could say was, "No way!"

Since that time, Brooks & Dunn have sold over sixteen million albums, been named Entertainer of the Year by both the Country Music Association and the Academy of Country Music and hold the distinction of being the third-highest-selling music duo of all time, following Simon & Garfunkel and Hall & Oates. *Brand New Man* stayed on *Billboard*'s Top Country Albums chart for over five years, the biggest-selling album by a country duo. In 1997 Brooks & Dunn were named the CMA Duo of the Year for the sixth consecutive time since 1992. The award was so expected that Tanya Tucker announced them as the winners even before she opened the envelope.

Backstage at the awards show, when Kix was asked to name his favorite duos, he cited Hall & Oates, Simon & Garfunkel, the Louvin Brothers, Conway Twitty and Loretta Lynn, and George Jones and Tammy Wynette. When Ronnie reminded Kix that the Judds, who won the duo award from 1988 to 1991, were powerful, Kix looked shocked. "Who?" he asked. "Don't say that, 'cause they'll come back! Don't even use the 'J' word. They terrify us!"

Leon Eric "Kix" Brooks III was born in Shreveport, Louisiana, on May 12, 1955. He was such an active baby that his mother dubbed him "Kix" while he was still in the womb. "About a month before I was born I started trying to pound my way out," he laughs. "So she branded me with that name, spelling it with an 'x' for a little added flair."

The Brooks family lived on Shreveport's Horton Street, named after country legend Johnny Horton, whose hits included "The Battle of New Orleans" and "Sink the Bismarck." Although Kix never met Johnny Horton, he does remember the star's death. "I was around six when it happened," Kix says. "My dad pulled the car up in front of the Hortons' house and just sat there staring at the wreath on the door. I asked him what was going on and he said, 'Johnny Horton died.'"

Johnny's widow, Billie Jean, who had also been married to Hank Williams, continued to live there on Horton Street, and Kix grew up friends with the couple's daughter, Nina. When Kix put together The Originals, one of his first paying gigs was playing at Nina's birthday party. "Billie Jean paid us five bucks to play out in the garage. I popped those bills and thought, 'Man, five big ones,'" he says. "Being in the Hortons' home really made an impression on me. I'd walk around looking at Hank Williams's and Johnny's gold records and guitars, and I'd think, 'This is real. These aren't just people in movies.'"

Kix continued to play music through school in Shreveport and the four years he spent at Sewanee Military Academy. He got a degree in speech from Louisiana Tech. "I started out to get a music degree," Kix says. "But I learned I'd need twenty hours of ensemble music—chorus, orchestra or marching band—and that just wasn't gonna happen. I was out playing in bars, and I didn't know how to play an orchestra or marching band instrument." Kix wrote his first song while at Louisiana Tech. He titled it "Tucker's Got the Mange."

"A girl I was dating was down in the dumps because her black Labrador retriever had the mange. So to cheer her up, I did the manly thing and wrote a song about it," Kix laughs. "The hook line went, 'We quit singing 'Home on the Range' when Tucker's got the mange.' Kinda gives you goose bumps, doesn't it?"

After college Kix moved to New Orleans and started playing in local bars. His father, a pipeline contractor and engineer, encouraged his music, but not his career path. "Dad told me to come to a music center like Nashville or New York or Los Angeles and butt heads with the big boys," Kix says. "He said if I wanted to be a musician and a songwriter, I should really try and not just waste my time playing bars for fifty bucks a night. His motto was: 'Do whatever you want, but take it seriously.' That helped me understand that my ambitions were not frivolous."

Ronnie Dunn's memories are not so positive. Born June 1, 1953, in Coleman, Texas, Ronnie had lived in thirty-three different towns in Texas by the time he turned eighteen. As a boy he didn't know why the family moved so often, but in retrospect, he believes it was because his father was an alcoholic who couldn't hold a job. Ronnie's dad was a musician who often backed up Sonny James and loved die-hard West Texas country music. But when Ronnie left college and moved to Tulsa, the musicians he played with were guys who often worked with rockers such as Leon Russell and Eric Clapton. One night, after Ronnie played his dad some of his demo tapes, the two even came to blows. "That was really the culmination of twenty-five years of alcohol abuse that goes way beyond the music," Ronnie admits.

There were two distinct influences in Ronnie Dunn's early life. On his mother's side was an extended family of staunch Baptists. His father was an All-American Hell-Raiser. Ronnie was torn between the two and tried to compensate by entering the ministry. He attended Abilene Christian University for two years, but wound up getting kicked out. "I got called in to the Dean's office one day," Ronnie recalls. "He said, 'I hear you're out playing in bars and you know our policy on that. We can't have a student frequenting these places, so you're going to have to make a choice.' I said I guessed I'd leave and try the music for a while. I'd already figured out that being a preacher meant I'd have to stand up and talk in front of a group on a regular basis, and I couldn't do that.''

Ronnie arrived in Tulsa during the *Urban Cowboy* era in the early 1980s. His first job was as a salesclerk in a store that specialized in wild-looking clothing favored by local rock musicians, including Eric Clapton's band. Before long, he was playing a house gig at a dance club called Duke's Country, opening for major acts such as George Jones and Ricky Skaggs. He also played a stint at the historic Cain's Ballroom, famous for both its spring-loaded floor that moved when enough people were dancing and for an early house band: Bob Wills and the Texas Playboys.

One day in 1988, a friend of Ronnie's happened to see an announcement for the Marlboro Country Showdown talent contest in a Tulsa convenience store. He took a sign-up form to Ronnie. The prize offered was $30,000 and a chance to record with producer Barry Beckett and engineer Scott Hendricks. Together with his friends who now form the Tractors, Ronnie performed Dean Dillon's "Holed Up in Some Honky-Tonk," and won first place. They split the $30,000 six ways, and with his share, Ronnie Dunn headed to Nashville. "I finally figured out that the music business wasn't gonna come to me," he says. "So I come to it."

When Brooks and Dunn first got together, they were both shopping solo projects in Nashville. They'd both guested on *Nashville Now* and, I hate to say, neither one had made a lasting impression on me as a solo act. When you host a show, you don't always concentrate on the musical performances. You're so busy thinking ahead, to the next commercial break or segment of the interview or the next guest, that you don't listen attentively. I learned far more watching the playback. When I finally put it together that both Kix and Ronnie had been on the show, I was amazed at what a genius pairing it had been. Ronnie has one of the finest voices in country music. Combine those vocals with Kix Brooks's showmanship, and their songwriting, and you've got a powerhouse act.

One of the record executives who had their solo tapes was Arista's Tim DuBois. "Don Cook had given me a five-song demo of Kix, and

I'd been aware of Ronnie ever since he won the Marlboro talent contest," Tim says.

Tim and his friend Scott Hendricks were driving to Knoxville for a University of Tennessee football game, when Tim played Scott the Kix Brooks demo and mentioned that he was thinking of pairing him with another artist as a duo. Scott just happened to have Ronnie's demo tape in his briefcase. On that tape were the following songs: "Boot Scootin' Boogie," "Neon Moon," "She Used to Be Mine" and a new song he'd written titled "White Lightning" (not to be confused with the Big Bopper–penned song that George Jones had a chart-topping hit with in 1959). Tim flipped over Ronnie's songs, his vocals and the potential blend of the two songwriters' voices.

Tim played Ronnie's "Neon Moon" for Kix and Kix's "Lost and Found" for Ronnie, and suggested the three of them get together at a local Mexican restaurant. "People are always asking you to meet this person or that person and see if you can write together," Kix says. "And I looked at it as 'What have I got to lose?' You just might write a hit song. Plus, we wouldn't have turned down Tim DuBois's invitation, because both of us were trying to pacify him in the hope of getting a solo deal. So we met with him and said we'd give the Brooks and Dunn idea a shot."

"That lunch only cost me about eight or ten bucks," Tim says. "They're cheap dates."

Since Don Cook had been producing Kix, and Scott Hendricks had been working with Ronnie, Tim decided to pair the two on Brooks & Dunn's first sessions. Before the release of *Brand New Man* Tim sat the two down and told them he had some advice for them. There were three things he wanted them to do. The two looked at each other nervously, as their label head spoke: "Keep your boots on. Keep your jeans on. And keep it country."

"Whew!" Kix recalls saying. "We can do that!"

The success came at an opportune time for both of the struggling songwriters, especially Ronnie Dunn. "Janine and I had come a long way down since we moved to Nashville," he admits. "We were way past running out of money. As a matter of fact, we'd lost just about everything and we were desperate."

If it hadn't been for Johnny Cash and June Carter Cash, Ronnie and Janine might have been in the streets. Janine and June had been friends for years, and when June learned the Dunns were planning to move to Nashville, she phoned Janine. "Honey, I'm so worried about you moving here and living in an apartment downtown," June said. "Why don't ya'll take this little log house we own in Hendersonville and stay there until Ronnie gets dug in." The couple took June up on her offer, but while their rent was a nominal sum, digging in took a long time.

The two families remain close. The black suit Ronnie wore to the *Brand New Man* album photo shoot is one of John's. "I'd mentioned to Johnny that one day I'd love to have one of his suits," Ronnie recalls. "So the next day he comes up in this big Mercedes, driving like a maniac, as usual. He pulls in the drive and does this big rock and roll stop, gets out and says, 'Here's a suit. Don't tell June.' " The suit fit with some minor tucks. But there was one problem."

"Ronnie called me up and told me Johnny Cash had given him a suit," Kix laughs. "I said, 'You dog! I hate your guts!' Then he told me the pants were bell bottom, and I said, 'Well, Ronnie, that's why God made tailors.' "

Would they have given up looking for record contracts if the Brooks & Dunn concept hadn't come along? Kix doesn't think so. "You get real jaded and frustrated in this business," he says. "You lay awake at nights wondering if maybe you'll never get anywhere. Maybe you're getting too old. Maybe you don't really have what it takes after all. But thinking about giving up and doing it are poles apart. After all, what are you gonna do about that twenty-year hole in your résumé? No, I think you just say, 'Hey, bein' a songwriter ain't too bad.' "

Being named Entertainer of the Year isn't too bad, either. In the beginning, it was Kix who was the showman. During their first label showcase, Kix was all over the stage while Ronnie stayed in one spot, watching his partner's antics with a shocked look on his face. After a few concerts, Ronnie approached Kix and said, "Maybe it's just an Okie thing, but where I come from, you just get up and sing your song. Maybe you could try to settle down some." Kix just laughed and said, "You got to sing to the girl over there in the corner, not just the one in front of you. That microphone ain't an anchor, pal!" They compromised, with Kix settling down a little and Ronnie loos-

ening up. Ronnie remembers Kix handing him a cordless microphone and saying, " 'Now take this and go to the left side of the
stage and sing the first verse. Then go to the center and sing a
chorus, and then move right for the last verse.' And I said, 'Shoot,
I can do this!' "

It took time for the two to build up trust to the point where they
could say, "We are partners. We're a duo and we can go the dis-
tance." Kix explains: "When we first met, we were both solo artists
and used to running our own shows. So for a while we tiptoed
around trying to figure each other out. We were like, 'Well, you do
your deal and I'll do mine and we'll see how it goes.' Then after we
had a couple of hits and people started showing up at our concerts,
we said, 'Well, dadgum! This might work!' "

One of the reasons it does work is that they understand that they
both need personal and musical space. Most bands and duos need
to get away from one another every so often. Years ago I traveled
around the country by car with Homer and Jethro. When we'd get
to a new town, the two would sometimes check into separate hotels
and not see each other until showtime.

Part of Brooks & Dunn's on-the-job training came from a world-
class entertainer, Reba McEntire, who, as they put it, loaned the duo
her audience for awhile. "It was a proving ground," Kix says. "It
showed us we could handle big arena shows."

Opening for Reba had promotional benefits, too. The first time
I went skiing with Reba and her husband/manager, Narvel Black-
stock, she wore a Brooks & Dunn cap on the slopes every day. Kix
laughingly claims that was part of the deal, that they'd open for her
for nothing if she'd wear their cap out in public. Reba did more
than wear their tour merchandise. She noted on one awards show
that "Boot Scootin' Boogie" was her son Shelby's favorite song.

Six years and fourteen million records later, Reba and Brooks &
Dunn share the bill equally, and it's the best country music package
I've ever seen. One night Reba opens the show for Brooks & Dunn
and the next night Brooks & Dunn open for Reba. I first saw the
concert in the spring of 1997 in Lexington, Kentucky, where Joy
and I were visiting with our good friends Ralph and Marilyn Hacker.
Ralph is the radio voice of the Kentucky Wildcats. Two other cou-

ples went with us: Chuck and Janice Sutherland and Bryan and Nancy Potter.

Reba was opening. Now, if you're going to try to follow Reba McEntire and keep the audience, you better have your act together, because she just wears 'em out. So I was interested in how Ronnie and Kix would do it, especially after Reba entertained the twenty-thousand-plus people in Rupp Arena so royally.

As I sat there listening to Reba, I got to thinking about something Keith "Short Man" Fowler told me one year when I hosted Alabama's June Jam. Keith booked Alabama for years, and he called me aside before the show and said, "You're going to see Alabama put on the best performance of their career today." I asked why, speculating that it might be because they were on home ground there in Fort Payne, Alabama. "No," Short Man said. "It's because I put Charlie Daniels right in front of them, and that SOB will make you work!" Keith's right, Charlie's a hard act to follow.

The minute Reba finished her portion of the show and the applause died down, Brooks & Dunn hit center stage and there was no question of how they were going to follow Reba's royal performance. It was instant party time, with so much bottom (bass) in the music that Rupp Arena rattled. They even played their biggest hit to date, "Boot Scootin' Boogie," the third song into the set. The audience went crazy, then even more crazy when scenes from Lexington began appearing on several large screens in the arena. They'd obviously sent in an advance team who really did its homework.

The show's close was spectacular. As soon as Brooks & Dunn finished and left the stage, the lights went down. No more than a minute and a half later, Ronnie Dunn seems to magically appear under a spotlight, singing "You Don't Know Me," the great Cindy Walker song. Ronnie sings a verse and a chorus and the spotlight shines on Reba. It was one of the damnedest duets I've ever heard. The two voices transcended country and got into soul. All the time I'm wondering how they are going to bring Kix Brooks back into the picture. What in the world could they do to top that performance? When Ronnie and Reba finished, the stage lights popped on again, one by one in rapid sequence, and then it seemed like all the fireworks in the world went off. Up comes Kix Brooks, wearing a University of Kentucky jersey belonging to the school's All-American, Ron Mercer. Kix skipped up one side of the stage and down the other, and the three singers rolled into a rousing version of "Cotton Fields." I'd never seen anything like it, and I've been in the business forty years. One woman in our party, Janice Sutherland, is a very wealthy socialite, the kind of wealth that involves homes all over the country, private planes and yachts. And she was standing up clapping and screaming like a teenager from the time they started playing "Boot Scootin' Boogie." Janice added several Brooks & Dunn CDs to her collection after that show.

"Boot Scootin' Boogie" is the duo's biggest record to date. Ironically, although it had a huge impact on country dance clubs, neither Ronnie nor Kix is a line dancer. When I mentioned that there were people who'd seen their show who swore they could and did line dance, Kix said, "Oh, they've just seen us stumbling around on stage." Ronnie, who wrote the song, even bought a T-shirt that read: Real Men Don't Line Dance. His kids took one look at the shirt and advised him against appearing in public wearing it.

Before "Boot Scootin' Boogie," dance mixes were unheard of in Nashville. "About a year earlier, I'd been out on the road with Alan Jackson," Scott Hendricks said. "I noticed that after the live show finished in some of the big clubs, a deejay played a mix of country songs and rock and pop songs. The fans were line dancing to all of it. The common denominator was a groove on the bottom end of the music." Scott thought certain country songs could replace the rock ones currently being played, and he believed "Boot Scootin' Boogie" was the perfect tune to try a dance mix out on. He took the song and the idea to engineer Brian Tankersley, and Brian put together a twenty-second sample. Once Scott heard the music he went to Tim Dubois and got the financing to experiment with the new sound. "Dance music isn't happening," Arista's chief of sales said when he heard the mix. "Why would you do this?"

"Publicity, if nothing else," Scott said. Against the advice of Arista's sales chief, Tim Dubois took a chance, pressed ten thousand copies and shipped them to radio and retail. The label finally stopped pressing the dance mix single after sales had topped the 400,000 mark.

Ronnie got the idea for "Boot Scootin' Boogie" during the early 1970s while he was in college in Abilene, Texas. "One of my buddies happened to mention that his band was going to play a 'boot scoot' in Stanford, Texas. I said, 'A 'boot scoot'? Man, what a great term! That was the first time I ever heard that phrase." Ronnie carried the title around with him for several years. He finally wrote it during a stay in Grove, Oklahoma, where he spent a few months living by a lake and concentrating solely on his songwriting. It was a productive time, for Ronnie not only penned "Boot Scootin' Boogie," but "Neon Moon," "White Line Casanova" and "She Used to Be Mine."

He demoed the "Boot Scootin' Boogie" in Tulsa, and the guys who played on the original session later went on to become the Tractors, also on Arista Records. Asleep at the Wheel founder Ray Benson heard the tune and recorded it as a swing tune. But it didn't come into its own until Brooks and Dunn cut the raw, honky-tonk version that made them superstars.

But even superstars can be awed by their heroes. Garth Brooks once told me he'd been very reluctant to meet George Jones. When I interviewed Brooks & Dunn for *On the Record,* I learned that although Merle Haggard was a hero of Ronnie's, the two had never met. Merle and I are good friends and go way back, so I arranged for Merle to be on the show via satellite from California. I asked Ronnie on the air if he'd like to meet Merle, and he said, "No." He explained that he would be too nervous, and interestingly, Merle Haggard, talking to Ronnie from his California recording studio, understood completely.

"When I was sixteen years old somebody dragged me backstage to meet Lefty Frizzell," Merle said. "I wouldn't have gone except the guy doing the dragging was pretty big. But Lefty listened to me sing, then shoved me on stage with his own guitar. That inspired me for a long time, but I still couldn't believe I'd gone back to meet him. The problem is that you only have a few minutes and you don't get to know them as a human being, like you'd want to."

Kix Brooks did meet Merle. Brooks & Dunn played a festival with him, and Kix wanted to get his guitar signed by the legend. So he had his road manager take the guitar on the bus to get it signed. When the fellow came back he told Kix Merle wouldn't sign it. "Well, shoot," Kix recalls saying. Then he was informed that Merle had insisted he come on the bus and get it signed himself. He went back and asked Ronnie if he wanted to go with him. "No way," Ronnie said.

"Stepping on that bus felt like stepping into the corridor to Oz," Kix says. "But Merle couldn't have been more cordial. The bad thing was, he signed it right where my elbow rubbed against it, and I rubbed the signature off and had to do the whole thing all over again when we both played Vegas. I went over to his soundcheck and got him to sign it further down that time." You can see that signature in one of the duo's videos, "She's Not the Cheatin' Kind."

Being "the next big deal" has its price. The downside of superstardom is that you are away from your family for long periods of time. As Ronnie points out, "On the one hand is the dream you are fortunate enough to be living. On the other is your family, the thing that matters more than gold records and concert tickets." Kix Brooks concurs, but remembers that his father was also away working as a pipeline engineer for periods during his childhood, and the family remained happy, close-knit and well adjusted.

From the sound of it, Ronnie's and Kix's children are all well adjusted, too. Kix says only seldom do his son and daughter appear to have much interest in the fact that their father is a star. "I'll come home from an awards show and ask Molly and Eric if they saw Daddy on television, and they'll say, 'Nah, we were playing Nintendo,' " Kix laughs. One of my favorite stories involves young Molly Brooks. She was helping her dad wash the car one afternoon, and Kix noticed her staring off into space, in deep thought. When he asked her what she was pondering, she said, "I just can't believe I'm the daughter of Brooks and Dunn!" Eric sees the music business in economic terms.

"The family was in Panama City, Florida, for a vacation and Eric and I rented Sea-Doos," Kix says. "By the time we got back, Ronnie had bought a pair of them and they were out on his driveway. Well, this was the first time Eric understood that jet skis were something you could go to a store and buy. He thought they were just something you rented. So he started working on me to buy some. I told him we'd see. He hadn't mentioned them in a while, until we drove by Ronnie's house again and there the Sea-Doos set on the drive. Eric stared at those skis, deep in thought, and finally said, 'I'm gonna sing me a couple of songs and buy me a couple of Sea-Doos.' "

And who knows. Maybe he'll be the next big deal.

THE SLIPPERY MIND OF ROGER MILLER

THE ONE THING I miss around Nashville and the music business these days is great characters like Roger Miller. If you've been around this town at all, you've probably heard a story about Roger. One of my favorites is the time he stood on a balcony watching the sun come up over the City of Angels. Roger'd been up roaring for days. He turned to his companion and said, "Here comes God with his headlights on." Another time he was listening to a political conversation and quipped, "Well, it seems to me that selling arms to Iran is about like letting Charlie Manson loose with a map to the stars' homes."

Willie Nelson told me that a little boy had approached Roger in an airport and asked him if he was Roger Miller. Roger said, "Yes I am. How old are you, son?"

"Seven," the boy answered.

"When I was your age I was nine," Roger retorted.

Roger probably had the fastest wit of any star I've ever met, and I could always count on him to be interesting on my radio shows. Now the record labels send their artists to "media training" to make sure they don't embarrass themselves in public. I promise you, Roger was one of the biggest stars in country music history and he was no star school graduate.

Roger could flip from poignant to playful at the drop of a hat. One time when he visited my show he got to talking about his home near Santa Fe, New Mexico. "We have a place outside of town where the creek runs, the horses whinny, the dogs bark and the coyotes howl," Roger said in an almost reverent manner. "There's a quality of life there. From my house I can look down and see the Santa Fe Opera House, and sometimes on a summer night, if the wind is right I can hear the opera right along with the coyotes. In the afternoons you can watch skiers making their final run before the sun sets."

I asked Roger if he skied, since he lived right by a ski run. "No, but I'm slippery and I skid a lot," he said, eyes twinkling.

I knew Roger Miller ever since he first came to Nashville more than thirty-five years ago. I thought I'd heard all the Roger Miller stories, but in 1997 I heard one I'd missed. It was about pills, amphetamines—or as we used to say, Old Yellers. This is the story: When asked how he handled life on the road, Roger said, "You've got to be careful and remember which pocket you put your change in and which pocket you put your pills in. The other day I wasn't feeling too well and before I knew it I'd taken thirty-five cents."

Roger's sense of humor never left him, either. I'm told that just a few days before he died of cancer he turned to a friend and said, "Well, wouldn't you know it. Just when I need some spare parts California enacts a helmet law."

7

THE GOLFER FORMERLY

KNOWN AS VINCE

ountry Music Fan Fair, when over thirty thousand fans gather for a week every June in Nashville, is one of those events you have to see to believe. Hundreds of stars and would-be stars design costly booths where they hold court, signing autographs, posing for photos with fans and politicking in general.

A lot of today's stars got their first brush with fame when they attended this weeklong event as fans. Patty Loveless recalls standing in line to meet Vince Gill long before she added those heavenly harmonies on his breakthrough hit, "When I Call Your Name." A lot can happen between Fan Fairs; a hopeful who walked among the masses unnoticed one year can become an overnight sensation who gets mobbed by the crowds the next. The most visible difference is the number of security guards it takes to usher someone to his booth.

But there is a certain kind of star who, no matter what his stature, appears to be such a downright regular guy that he can combine superstardom and normalcy even at this event. Vince Gill is one of those guys. A couple of years ago one of the Fan Fair security guards told a story about Vince that pretty much sums up the star's character. It seems that too many artists were arriving at once and the security station was short of men. A brand new artist who had arrived in a stretch limousine with an entourage was standing there throwing a fit because he believed he needed a full escort instead of the one or two men available. Finally, they loaded this character onto the last vehicle and started through the crowd.

As they pulled out the guard noticed a car pull into the artist parking area. It was Vince Gill, the biggest star on-site that day, unescorted and seemingly unconcerned about it. Vince glanced around, didn't see a guard or a vehicle, and simply strolled into the crowd. When the security guard last saw Vince, the superstar was walking toward one of the buildings, accompanied by a dozen or so fans who thought they'd died and gone to heaven.

It was a very typical move on Vince's part. He once told me about going on tour in Europe, and being met by five security guards at a German airport. "What do you guys want?" Vince asked. "We're here to see you through the airport," one answered. "Oh, I won't have any problems going through this crowd," Vince responded. I asked him if it turned out that he needed them and Vince just laughed, "Nobody in that airport knew who the hell I was." Maybe not, but he was pleasantly surprised when the entire audience at one of his Dublin, Ireland, shows began singing along on "I Still Believe in You."

"It was amazing," Vince recalled. "You don't see as much of that with American audiences. But in Europe they seem to know the words to every song."

Vince is one of the most down-to-earth stars I've ever met. He really does want a normal life, where he can play golf in peace and make music he loves without worrying about charts, critics and comparisons. He can find humor in almost any situation, including a dangerous one. Take the time he was playing golf in the Bahamas and two masked armed robbers jumped out from behind some bushes on the third hole. One waved a sawed-off shotgun and the other carried a rifle and demanded the golfers' wallets. Vince told me it didn't hit him until he got home just how close he'd come to being killed. I asked him if he'd surrendered his wallet.

"Of course I did," he laughed. "I even offered them golf lessons!"

I THINK PART of the reason Vince takes his superstar status with a grain of salt is that it took him a long time to achieve it. Born in

Norman, Oklahoma, on April 12, 1957, Vince was an outgoing little kid who liked to introduce himself by either saying "They call me Vincy Grant Gill! Beep beep!" or "They call me Snorter Gill! Snort snort!" These days he sometimes refers to himself as The Golfer Formerly Known as Vince.

Vince's mother, Jerene Gill, once showed me what her son gave her for Christmas back when he was around seven years old. It was a bottle of Tarn-X silver polish. Vince laughs about it today, suggesting he was even then hoping to line her walls with platinum albums and he'd seen her clean her silver with toothpaste once too often. And he was always fast on the draw. When he signed up for a junior football league the coach tossed him a ball and asked him if he thought he could pass it. "Pass it? I don't think I can even swallow it," Vince quipped.

Vince started working with bluegrass bands early on and in high school he joined a band called Mountain Smoke. When he was seventeen he had his first brush with the big time. "One night around six o'clock P.M. we got a call from a promoter asking us if we could put a band together and get down to the Civic Center by eight o'clock," Vince says. "So we hurriedly got some guys together and rushed down there. The sign on the marquee said KISS. I assured everyone that KISS was probably playing the following night and we were there to play a Shriner's Convention who wanted a bluegrass band. It was KISS all right, and we walked out to open for them with banjos and fiddles."

I asked Vince if the KISS crowed booed them, and he said, "Oh, yeah. Big-time booing. We only lasted four or five songs. I'd never seen that many people that mad. When we left the stage I mooned the crowd and got a standing ovation from the police stationed around the stage."

"Mooned them? Did you drop your pants?" I asked.

"No, but they got the idea," Vince laughed. "I gave them the international signal that goes with it."

When he turned eighteen Vince moved to Louisville, Kentucky, to join the Bluegrass Alliance, which included the world-class mandolin player Sam Bush. He sharpened his already formidable skills as an acoustic guitar player for a year in Kentucky, then accepted an offer from Byron Berline (an alum of Bill Monroe's band) to join his band, Sundance, in Los Angeles. It was there that he met Rodney Crowell.

"The first time I heard Vince was in 1976 at the Troubador in LA," Rodney told me. "Vince was just a pup and so was I. He was playing with Byron Berline's band, and all of a sudden he started singing one of my songs, 'Till I Gain Control Again.' It was just stunning. I sat there thinking 'Who is this guy standing up there singing my song so much better than me? Stop it!' "

Vince and Rodney became close friends and stayed in touch over the next few years. Rodney was playing with Emmylou Harris's outstanding Hot Band and busy penning future hits like "Leaving Louisiana in the Broad Daylight," which the Oak Ridge Boys would take to the top of the charts in 1980. Vince joined Pure Prairie League as lead vocalist, even though Rodney offered him a gig playing with the Cherry Bombs, a band he'd formed in 1980.

"I can't believe I turned that down," Vince laments now. "I still think it's the best band I ever got to play with and probably ever will."

A few years later one of the former Cherry Bombs, a piano player named Tony Brown, got a job in A&R with RCA Records in Nashville. Tony was still a teenager when he went on the road with the Oak Ridge Boys, leaving them in 1975 to play piano for Elvis Presley. His love of eclectic music and unconventional artists would make him one of Nashville's foremost record men in the 1990s. Among the people he signed to recording contracts are Steve Earle, Patty Loveless, Trisha Yearwood, Lyle Lovett, Marty Stuart, Mark Chesnutt, The Mavericks and Nanci Griffith. He was still a pup himself, though, when in 1983 he signed Vince Gill to RCA and released a mini-album, *Turn Me Loose.*

Vince decided he needed to be in Nashville if he was going to make his career work. Some artists, George Strait most notably, are able to forge careers from somewhere other than Nashville. But being out of the loop makes everything just a little bit harder. You don't hear a hit that's just been demoed. You aren't around if someone cancels a television appearance and gives a newcomer a shot at national exposure. You don't have your ear to the street. "I thought

it showed my belief in myself and my recording career to relocate,"
Vince reflects. "Plus I had a lot of friends here, including Rodney
Crowell and Emmylou Harris."

Vince and his wife, Janis, moved to Nashville between Thanksgiving and Christmas of 1983. "We left sunny California like the Beverly Hillbillies," he laughs. "I didn't have any money so I had to
drive it myself. I rented a U-Haul or a Ryder or some kind of truck
and towed my car behind it. The whole experience was a nightmare—everything that could go wrong did go wrong. The car even
came off unhitched from the truck once. Then when we got here it
was seventeen degrees below zero. I thought my wife was going to
kill me for talking her out of California and bringing her into this
cold."

For almost a decade Vince would walk just a step shy of stardom.
The second single from *Turn Me Loose,* "Victim of Life's Circumstances," hit top-40 and Vince was named the Academy of Country
Music's Top New Male Vocalist. But the next three singles failed to
provide a breakthrough hit and Vince didn't see country music's
top-10 until he teamed with Rosanne Cash on 1985's "If It Weren't
for Him." Vince's singles on RCA didn't burn up the charts, but
Vince was firing up recording sessions all over Music Row during
those years. He became one of the most in-demand session players
and harmony singers in the business, and it began to cause him
some problems.

"I was just playing the cards I had," Vince said. "But everybody
started thinking, 'Well, he must like session work more than doing
a solo gig.' Hey, at every point of my life I've done whatever I could
do, whatever I was allowed to do. I still think session work is the most
challenging work I've ever done. The supporting roles on making a
record are every bit as important as who the star or the singer is. All
you have to do is listen to Patty on 'When I Call Your Name.'"

Vince's daughter Jenifer even got into the act, requesting her father accompany her on guitar when she performed a solo at a junior
high music festival. Vince told me it was a great experience, but
maybe not a great career move. "The Opry called and asked me to
make an appearance on that night," he recalls. "I said, 'Nope, I'm
already booked.'"

I asked Vince if he believed his years at RCA were productive, even though he didn't record any big hits. Sometimes seemingly unfruitful years spent at a label can be learning years, other times they're just wheel spinners. "I have no animosity toward RCA," he said. "The label did as good as they could with the music I gave them. The success or failure of my music will always be on my shoulders."

Ironically, while Vince languished at RCA, his wife's career took off over at CBS. Janis Gill and her sister, Kristine Arnold, billed themselves the Sweethearts of the Rodeo, named after the Byrds' country rock album. Janis met Vince when the Sweethearts played a show with Pure Prairie League, but by the time the couple married and moved to Nashville the sisters were no longer performing on a regular basis. Kristine moved to Nashville soon after Janis, and local interest in the act heightened. In 1985 they were offered a deal with Columbia Records. Between 1986 and 1988 the Sweethearts of the Rodeo had seven top-10 releases. I'm sure the tables turning like this surprised Vince, but I never heard him say a word about it other than to praise Janis's success.

Within a year of Vince's signing with RCA, Tony Brown had the opportunity to move to MCA Records and produce records. He asked Vince to join him at his new label in 1989. Vince's first MCA album contained "When I Call Your Name," and from then on "Snorter Gill" took a backseat to no one. Mama Gill probably goes through a lot of Tarn-X these days, because every one of her son's seven MCA albums has sold platinum or better. At last count he's won eight Grammy Awards, seventeen CMA awards including Entertainer of the Year in 1993 and 1994, nine TNN/*Music City News* fan-voted awards, nine *Music City News* songwriter awards, four ACM awards and thirteen BMI awards, including two Songwriter of the Year nods from the performing rights organization. That's nothing to snort at!

Vince told me he'd rather win Songwriter of the Year than Entertainer of the Year. "This community has existed on songs a lot longer than on entertainers and it always will," he explained. "That's what makes the town work. To be considered one of the greatest songwriters means longevity, since the songs last a lifetime. My popularity as a singer will not last a lifetime."

One of my favorite recordings made in the 1990s is a wonderful project on MCA called *Rhythm, Country & Blues,* and as a result of his duet with Gladys Knight on this CD, Vince became one of the few white men to ever grace the cover of *Jet* magazine. Together they performed the 1968 Marvin Gaye/Tammi Terrell top-10 R&B hit, "Ain't Nothing But the Real Thing."

I have always considered blues and country musical cousins, and the close ties are clearly reflected on this album. Vince told me that he thinks the only real difference in country and blues is the kick drum. "The kick drum is the thing that makes music feel like it's in your chest. On an R&B recording they funky it up a little more, while on country they usually play it a little more straightforward."

Since Vince and Gladys were the first two artists to agree to make *Rhythm, Country & Blues,* I asked Gladys if she had immediately liked the idea of mixing country and blues. "Without a doubt," she answered with no hesitation. "If you think about it, all my hits have been country songs, written by a country writer and producer, Jim Weatherly. Think about it—'Neither One of Us (Wants to Be the One to Say Goodbye),' 'Midnight Train to Georgia.' I've been waiting a long time for people to catch up with me. Let's just sing and make good music and stop categorizing everything."

"I think the music community is color-blind," Vince added. "I know it was some people's perception that the R&B audience and the country audience are at arm's length, but I think in the case of this record, people judged with their ears, and not their eyes. This wasn't about image, just music."

Image is a dirty word as far as Vince Gill is concerned. He has never had a particular image, except that of country music's guy next door. He dresses casually and has been known to cut his own hair. In fact, last year he went a little overboard and clipped his locks so close to his scalp that he finally gave up and shaved his head. Vince liked the idea of not having hair to worry about and kept the look for a while. You'd have thought he'd been arrested for armed robbery. The fans got up in arms, and Tony Brown had to talk him into growing it back out. Vince has hair again, but he never did understand what all the commotion was about.

And that's just part of his charm.

MEMORIES . . .

WHEN YOU'VE BEEN in show business for over forty years you tend to get a little jaded; nothing much gives me chills these days. But two incidents in the past decade stand out as goose-bump moments. The first one involved Minnie Pearl, one of the grandest ladies I've been privileged to meet in my life.

In 1990 TNN decided they wanted a presence at the ACE cable awards show produced by Dick Clark, and asked Minnie and me if we'd attend and present an award. Joy and I and Minnie and her husband, Henry Cannon, almost missed the plane because of Minnie's penchant for stopping to talk with any and all who waved her down in the airport. People recognized her everywhere, even when she was not in costume, without what Sarah Cannon called her "Minnie." She just loved people and always had time to chat. Henry was familiar with Minnie's little airport visits and reassured us she'd make it to the plane. "She's always like this," Henry said. She did make it, but barely.

We flew to Los Angeles and went to the green room at the Wilton Theater to wait to play our role in the awards show. Minnie was now in full "Minnie," in costume and ready to greet the audience with "Howdee!" For most of the first part of the evening, Minnie sat on a couch in a big conversation with Cicely Tyson, the actress. Then all of a sudden a group of boxers arrived, to participate in a James Earl Jones segment on boxing. Evander Holyfield walked in and several others. Then there was a magic moment when the legendary Muhammed Ali walked in, clearly held in the highest esteem among the boxers.

Then, for a brief moment in this crowded room, the waters parted, as it were. On one side of the room stood Muhammad Ali, and on the other side was Minnie Pearl. When Ali saw her his face lit up into a broad smile. He, of course, had Parkinson's disease and had some motor skills problems by then. But he lifted his arm just to waist height, and waved to her. I could tell by his face that he was delighted to see her. Minnie was equally delighted and waved back, thrilled that he waved at her. Then we went upstairs where we did our bit, presenting an award to Dick Cavett, who dropped his award on the way offstage. Minnie and I were going back to the green room, and up ran Whoopi Goldberg, who threw her arms around Minnie in a big hug. She, too, was obviously delighted to see Minnie Pearl.

On the flight home I was thinking about the beauty of a person like Minnie, so beloved by people of all races, from all walks of life. There at the awards, three of black America's legends singled her out as someone very special to them. Minnie grinned at the thought, and said, "You know, sometimes I think I get along better with black folks than I do with white folks."

A SECOND GREAT moment came about in November 1997 when former President Bush invited Joy and me to join him and about two thousand others at the opening ceremonies for the Bush Library at A&M University in College Station, Texas. It was a celebrity-studded affair with everyone from Kevin Costner and Arnold Schwarzenegger to heads of state. The Nashville contingent included the Oak Ridge Boys, who are such close friends of the Bush family, Loretta Lynn and Crystal Gayle.

Joy and I lucked out and got front row seats, so we had a close-up view of everything that happened. They started the ceremonies, and the six First Ladies walked out together, arm in arm: Barbara Bush, Lady Bird Johnson, Nancy Reagan, Rosalyn Carter, Hillary Clinton and Betty Ford. As they walked up the ramp together they literally took my breath away. They were followed by President Clinton, President Bush, President Ford and President Carter. The Presidents were impressive, but it was that line-up of First Ladies who gave me chills. I wasn't the only one who felt that way. I ran into the Governor of Tennessee, Don Sundquist, who felt that same "goosebump" moment at the sight of the six First Ladies.

"It made me proud to be an American," he said. And it did.

8

FARON YOUNG:

THE NEXT BIG DEAL—1953

Roger Miller once said that Faron Young had a heart as big as his mouth. Roger ought to know, because Faron gave him one of his first paying gigs here in Nashville. "Roger came up to me and said, 'I need a job,' " Faron recalled. "I asked him if he could play drums and Roger said, 'No, but I'll learn.' So I went down to the pawnshop and bought him a set of drums and gave him a job."

I asked Faron why in the world he'd hire a drummer who couldn't play drums. After all, on the road, it's important to have real musicians. Faron just laughed: "I wasn't much of a musician myself, and I figured his bad playing might distract the audience from mine!"

Faron soon learned that being on the road with Roger could strain your patience. "One night we were coming back from a show, and I'd had a touch of the grape that night and passed out on the bus. All of a sudden Roger started shaking me awake yelling, 'Sheriff, I've just written a smash hit song!' Then he sat down and started playing me a song that went, 'In the summertime when all the trees and leaves are green and the redbird sings I'll be blue 'cause you don't want my love.' There I was half drunk and half hungover and Roger is singing about trees and leaves being green! I said, 'Roger, if you wake me up again I'm gonna kill you and that's a promise.' Then about six months later here comes Roger on RCA singing

'You Don't Want My Love' and sure enough, he's got a smash hit song!''

Faron let some other songs slip by him, and one notable song-writer: Kris Kristofferson, who was doing a lot of odd jobs in town trying to get noticed as a writer. Kris was also a highly educated young man, a Rhodes Scholar, making him suspect to some. And he had a very unusual voice, that wasn't always appreciated, espe-cially by Faron Young. "I hired Kris to put paneling up in the *Music City News* building at $1.25 an hour," Faron once recalled. "Kris would go back there with a hammer and work for a while, then he'd come up to my office and sing me a song. I said, 'Son, that singing is horrible. And if you are going to learn how to write, you are going to have to live it. Go down to Tootsie's Orchid Lounge or Line-baugh's and hang out with the winos.'

"Kris would go back and hammer and saw and in about thirty minutes he'd come back with another song. Finally, I said, 'I am going to tell you what, son. All I want to hear singing is that hammer and saw which will tell me that you are back there working.' Foolish me. I could have had his publishing for fifty dollars a week! He came down and would hang around. Next thing you knew, 'Help Me Make It Through the Night' hit and he wasn't pounding nails for me or anybody else.''

JOHNNY CASH SAYS Faron was a "world-class cusser." He could be stubborn and obstinate, and he would cuss you out at the drop of a hat. As Faron once told me, "I'm a hard man to kiss." And it didn't matter who you were, Faron would show off what he called his "ratchet jaw" to the President just as easily as to a would-be songwriter. Once, when he was playing in a golf tournament, he was lagging behind when President Gerald Ford's foursome caught up with him. The Secret Service informed Faron he'd have to move out of the way, because President Ford, Jack Nicklaus, Bob Hope and Jackie Gleason were coming. Faron threw down his golf club and was still cussing hell out of the Secret Service guys when the Presi-dent's group came on the scene. Jackie Gleason, who was a big fan of "Four in the Morning," quickly said, "You just take your time, pal." And Faron did.

*   *   *

FARON WAS COLORFUL and he was always animated. One time he was standing at the back of the lot at a car auction, talking to a friend and all of a sudden the auctioneer shouted: "Sold to the man in the blue jacket." Faron didn't pay any attention, he just went right on talking and waving his arms for emphasis. All of a sudden the crowd parted, and when Faron looked up the auctioneer was pointing straight at him.

"You can pick up your Rolls-Royce around back, Mr. Young," the auctioneer said over the loudspeaker.

Faron started sputtering and his friend shouted up to the auctioneer: "Hell, Faron wasn't makin' no bid, he was just makin' a point!"

Because of Faron's tendency to run off at the mouth, some people thought that he might make some racist statement that would offend Charley Pride. In fact, when Charley first came to town, several people told him, "If you can just make it past Faron Young you'll be okay." But instead of having any problems about Charley's race, Faron became his champion. And you've never had a champion until you've had the Sheriff in your corner. Faron was still in his heyday in the early and mid-sixties with hits like "Hello Walls" when Charley Pride released his first single on RCA in 1965, "Snakes Crawl at Night." The song didn't chart in *Billboard*, but it did stir up some national interest in Charley.

Once, Faron was having lunch with a disc jockey who happened to mention that "Snakes Crawl at Night" was the #1 song at his station. Faron didn't realize that RCA had sent the record out without photos and a lot of disc jockeys didn't know Charley was black, so he nodded his head and said, "That's wonderful. I'm sure happy to see a Negro finally have a number-one country record."

The deejay dropped his mouth and asked, "What Negro?" Faron had no idea the guy didn't realize Charley was black and said, "Well, sure. Charley's a Negro." The guy jumped up and left the table. When he came back he thanked Faron for telling him about Charley and said he'd told the station manager to take the record off the air immediately. This time Faron jumped up.

"Do you have any Faron Young records at your station?" he asked.

"Well, sure. Lots of 'em," the guy said.

"Well, throw 'em out along with Charley Pride's, then," Faron shouted. " 'Cause if I ever hear of your station playing one of my songs again I'll come back and burn the damn place down!" Then Faron stormed out. It takes a Faron Young kind of nerve to insult radio like that, but the Sheriff never looked back.

I will bet that he tipped his waitress before he walked out that day, though. Faron had a thing about tipping, and he'd tip a bad waitress just as quickly as a good one. "I don't want people running around telling stories about that 'cheap SOB Faron Young,' " he told me with a grin.

On the other hand, he'd still run his mouth to Charley in jest. When he and Charley traveled together on tour in the sixties at the height of the civil rights movement, Faron would say, "Now Charley, you know you're supposed to sit in the back of this bus."

Charlie would grin and say, "Nope, you little banty rooster. I'm sitting right up here with you."

Faron loved that, just like he loved it when Ray Charles met Charley Pride and said: "You look just like your album cover!"

FARON ASSISTED ANOTHER legend in the making when he and Webb Pierce helped Johnny Cash get his first Grand Ole Opry booking in the mid-1950s. "I'd worked a few dates with Johnny and had seen the crowd's reaction to him. So Webb and I went to the Opry and suggested they book him on the show."

"But the guy can't sing!" was the Opry booker's response.

"I don't know if he can sing or not," Faron countered. "But I've been out there and seen him mesmerize people."

Against what they thought was their better judgment, the Opry people allowed Cash on the show. He got six encores, and Faron stood backstage and said, "You people didn't know if he could sing, and right now he owns the place."

As I said earlier, I've always regretted the fact that I didn't get to know Hank Williams. But Faron knew him well and had some great stories about him. The two met when Faron was still a teenager and hanging around the alley behind the *Louisiana Hayride* building. Hank stepped out back for a moment, and Faron shouted, "Hey, Hank!"

"Hey, boy! How're you doin'?" Hank called. Faron told me that Hank Williams never called anybody by their first name. It was always "boy."

"One of these days I'm going to be right up on that stage with you," Faron hollered.

"I hope you do, boy," Hank said. "Lots of luck."

Faron never forgot that moment, and when he finally made it to Nashville and joined the Opry, he reminded Hank that he'd been ". . . that smart alec teenager who'd hollered at him out behind the *Hayride*." Hank stood backstage and watched Faron's portion of the show, and when Faron came off stage, Hank stopped him.

"Hey, boy. You are going to do all right in this business," he said.

"That was like the Lord putting his hand on me and blessing me," Faron recalled. The two became fast friends after that, sharing bottles, cars and even girlfriends, as it turned out.

"Hank had broke up with Audrey and was dating some girl from Pennsylvania," Faron explained. "I was dating a girl named Billie Jean at the time, and we went over to a little house where Hank had moved. He'd been drinking and was already half shot by the time we arrived. Hank loved guns, so I wasn't all that surprised that he had a big suitcase full of pistols in the living room. I swear there must have been fifty pistols in that suitcase. What did surprise me was the sudden interest Billie Jean developed for weapons. She sat there on the floor beside the suitcase, smiling at Hank and asking him all kinds of questions about those guns."

"What is this, Hank?" Billie Jean asked.

"That is a forty-five automatic," Hank replied, clearly thrilled at her interest.

"What is this?"

"That's a thirty-eight Smith and Wesson."

It kept on going on, and finally Faron said, "What in the world is going on here anyway?"

Hank went in the other room and yelled to him, "Hey boy, come in here."

Faron told me he went in the other room and Hank stuck a .38 right in his stomach.

"I don't want no hard feelings but I'm in love with that girl," Hank said.

"Son, you got her," Faron said with no hesitation.

Hank did marry Billie Jean Jones Eshlimar, a few months before his death on December 31, 1952. Less than a year later, Billie Jean married Johnny Horton, who died in a car accident several years later. After Johnny died, Faron ran into Billie Jean, greeting her with the candor for which he was known:

"I'm damn glad I didn't marry you," Faron blurted out. "I'd probably be dead by now."

Hank never let Faron get too big for his britches, either. "I remember one time I was taking Hank to the Ernest Tubb Record Shop," Faron recalled. "I was driving this Cadillac convertible of his. Every time I would hit a bump it would squeak. I said, 'Hank this thing has a squeak in it.' He said, 'Yeah. You'd like to have one that squeaks like this wouldn't you?' "

A few years back, I asked Faron what he thought Hank Williams would be doing if he'd lived. Would he have continued to make hits, or would his career have faded? Could he have survived in mainstream country music into his sixties? Faron didn't hesitate.

"He'd be the main Hoss, to this day."

Faron's first career dream was to be a sportscaster. "I always wanted to be the guy who announced the ball games on the radio," Faron said. "Even when I was a kid, I'd take a tin can and go out behind the house and pretend it was a microphone and I was calling a game." That early dream was replaced by his high school years with the desire to become a pop star, and he began performing around his hometown of Shreveport, Louisiana. He entered as many talent shows as he could sign up for, citing Frank Sinatra as his idol. "I never listened to country music until around 1950 when I was in high school," he admitted.

Hank Williams changed all that. "I snuck into the *Louisiana Hayride* one night and saw Hank sing 'Lovesick Blues,' " Faron recalled. "That did me in. Besides Hank, another thing stuck with me about that night. I had to sneak in the show because I didn't have any money, and that show made me different somehow. So after I started playing a lot of shows, I'd tell my roadies not bother kids if they tried to sneak in. If they didn't have any money and wanted to hear me sing, let 'em come."

Faron's high school football coach had a country band that

played in the Shreveport area, and he asked Faron if he'd join them as the front man. Faron jumped at the chance, but he had a private agenda. "I blackmailed my way into football games," he explained. "I was only around five foot six—too little to be any good, but I love a good scrap, so I always wanted to play. If we'd get ahead a touchdown or two, I'd sidle over to the coach and tell him if he wanted a singer on Saturday night, he'd better make me a football player on Friday."

The band was soon performing country music at local VFWs, hoedowns, nursing homes and lodges. Faron quickly gained a reputation as an up-and-coming regional act, but it took another Louisiana natural resource, Webb Pierce, to help him break into national prominence.

Born in West Monroe, in 1921, Webb had his own radio show by the time he was sixteen, then, after a tour in the military, moved on to the *Louisiana Hayride* in Shreveport. His first recordings were on Pacemaker and 4 Star, and in late 1951 he signed with Decca to begin one of the most successful careers in Nashville's recording history.

Faron pitched some songs to Webb in 1951, but Pierce was more interested in Faron's voice than in his songs, and invited him to sing in his show at a local club. With Webb's blessing, Faron became a regular on the *Louisiana Hayride* that same year, playing alongside Pierce, Slim Whitman, Red Sovine and the Wilburn Brothers.

In addition to playing on the *Hayride,* Faron took his show on the road to small Louisiana clubs where, as he once put it, ". . . you had to have a switchblade to get in the door." These were places where not just your career but your health might depend on how the patrons accepted a song. "Down in Louisiana when people get a little kickapoo joy juice in 'em, they get to be music critics," Faron once told me. "One guy would come up and say, 'Sing "Walkin' the Floor Over You" or else,' and maybe flash a knife. I'd start to play and another guy would come up and flash his knife and say, 'Don't you *dare* sing "Walkin' the Floor Over You!" ' My answer was always, 'Go tell that guy with the knife. He's the one that wants to hear it!' "

Both Webb and Faron signed major record deals within months of each other, Faron with Capitol and Webb with Decca. Webb got a jump start on hit songs, though, when his debut on Decca, "Wondering," spent a month at #1 in 1952. Capitol released Faron's first chart single, the #2 hit "Goin' Steady," a year later.

Faron moved to Nashville, joined the Opry, and by 1952 was appearing regularly on WSM's morning show with Chet Atkins, The Carter Family and Carl Smith. Faron was on the early morning shift, and he didn't believe anybody was really listening to him. So one day he went on the show and said, "Anybody out there who wants a free picture of me, send a postcard to WSM." Well, about a week later he walked into the station and there were cardboard boxes stuffed full of postcards lined up against the wall. Faron asked the guard what kind of a contest they were running, and the guard said, "That's no contest. Those people want a free picture of Faron Young!" It cost Faron several thousand dollars in postage to make good his promise.

Faron was a great imitator of other singers, artists like Dean Martin, Eddy Arnold, Webb Pierce—and Hank Snow. Once when WSM was raising money for the March of Dimes, a caller offered to donate extra money if Faron would do an impression of Hank Snow. "I jumped right in and did it," Faron laughed. "And before I was finished, Hank Snow was on the phone wanting to talk to the guy who'd just tried to sing like him. He said, 'Young fellow, when you start to sell as many records as I do, then you'll have the right to try and sing like me.' So after I had some records out I ran into Hank and said, 'I guess it's time.' "

Hank and Faron had an ongoing feud after that, and Willie Nelson once told me about a funny incident that happened when the two men were part of a package show playing up in Canada. "Everybody was sitting around drinking in one of the motel rooms and as the night wore on, people started to leave," Willie said. "Finally nobody was left except Faron and Hank Snow. Faron said, 'Hank, here you are sittin' around swapping stories and telling jokes tonight. But tomorrow morning when you sober up, I'll bet you won't even speak to me.' Hank reared back and said, 'Oh yes I will, Faron. I'll say hello.' "

Faron used to tell another Hank Snow story. "Back in the old days everybody had one of those rube comedians that would black his teeth out and appear as a part of the show," Faron explained. "Hank Snow and I were playing a show in the Lyric Theater in Indianapolis. He had Sleepy McDaniels playing bass for him. Sleepy would play about three numbers and then lay his bass down and get this old wig and hobo clothes on, black his teeth out and come around to the front of the building. He'd start hollering, 'What is going on behind the stage.' Everybody looks and says, 'Nothing, why?' He'd say, 'Because there ain't nothing going on in front of it either.' That was his little comedy bit.

"One time Sleepy missed his cue. Snow had already sang 'Golden Rocket' and 'Moving On.' And no Sleepy. He ain't showed up yet. What had happened is that when he went out in front a guard thought he was one of the local winos and wouldn't let him back in the building. We was down in a seedy end of town. Snow kept on singing, and getting madder and looking for Sleepy. Finally Hubert Long went out front and found Sleepy arguing with the guard. Hubert assured the guard Sleepy was part of Hank's show and got him in the door. But Snow was mad as the devil by then. So Sleepy showed up and said his line, 'What is going on behind the stage?' Hank Snow said, 'Not a damn thing and you are fired!' "

FARON'S CAREER TOOK a detour right after he started recording for Capitol: the draft caught up with him. "I'd just started making money with the music when I got this telegram that said 'Greetings and Salutations from Uncle Sam,' " he explained. "I had a chance to make a hundred thousand dollars that year and I had to go in the military at $87.50 a month."

This could have spelled disaster for the emerging star, since his initial Capitol singles, including the self-penned "Tattle Tale Tears," hadn't charted. After he entered the army he recorded "Goin' Steady," but there was no obvious way for the soldier to go on the road to promote the record. Maybe his old high school talent show experience came into play here, because Faron entered and won an ABC-TV military talent search and replaced Eddie Fisher as the army's recruiting star. He had a freshman entertainer's dream job: fronting a band called the Circle A Wranglers on a military-

sponsored program that was heard on over two thousand radio stations. What a way to promote your new single! "Goin' Steady" hit
#2 in *Billboard*.

Of course, Faron may have been an idol to millions of women
right then, but he wasn't to some of his fellow military brothers. "I
had a Cadillac back then, and against regulations, I brought it to
the post," he laughed. "I was a cocky little guy and drove this big
blue Cadillac with a fifth wheel right up beside my company commander's Ford. That did it, brother. For fourteen days I was scrub-
bing commodes and cleaning garbage cans. The commander said
to me, 'Boy, you *will* get that car off this post, and you *will* make
that commode sparkle!' Up until then I'd thought I was a big shot."

Thus began a period of exceptionally high visibility for Faron,
and Capitol utilized the publicity to its best advantage. By the time
Faron was discharged in 1954, he was a national celebrity/hero with
four hit records. The day Faron was a free man, his biggest song to
date, "If You Ain't Lovin'," was headed straight to the top of the
charts, and a signature song was just around the corner. On April
4, 1955, Capitol released the honky-tonk classic "Live Fast, Love
Hard, Die Young" and the song spent three weeks at #1 in *Billboard*.

His appearance in televised advertisements for the Grand Ole
Opry attracted Hollywood producers, and Faron contracted for a
string of movies, including *Hidden Guns*; he played the local sheriff,
giving him the nickname The Sheriff, a name he liked so much he
even renamed his band The Country Deputies. Some of his films
included *Stampede, Daniel Boone, Country Music Holiday* and *Road to
Nashville*.

After releasing eight more top-10 hits in the fifties, Faron had
another trademark release in '58, "Alone with You," which stayed
at #1 for thirteen weeks. He had a #4 hit with 1960's "Riverboat,"
then went into a career slump. None of his next three singles even
made it out of the 20s on the country charts. By 1961, Faron badly
needed a hit.

He found it in "Hello Walls."

Willie Nelson told me about how he wrote the song. "Hank Cochran was almost a writer on 'Hello Walls,' " Willie said. "Hank and
me were trying to write in a little one-room house out in back of
Pamper Music. It didn't have a phone and it only had one window.

I'd just told him I wanted to write a song called 'Hello Walls' when someone came out and told Hank he had a phone call up at the office. I told him I'd start on the song while he was taking the call. He was gone about ten minutes, and when he came back I'd already finished it. It's your basic ten-minute song.''

Willie had been pitching the song at Tootsie's, and according to Porter Wagoner, it had become a joke around the bar. "Everybody was making fun of it," Porter recalled. "Other songwriters were going around saying, 'Hello glass. Hello table. Hello commode.' " But Faron recognized it as a hit, and Willie, who was broke at the time, offered to sell it to him for fifty dollars.

"I won't buy it," Faron said. "But I'll record it and loan you the fifty bucks."

He ended up loaning Willie five hundred dollars, and then went a step further in helping both his and Willie's fortunes by recording another Nelson composition, "Congratulations," during the same session.

The studio musicians who worked on the "Hello Walls" session were as unimpressed with the song as the Tootsie's crowd. "Everybody thought it was stupid," Faron later told me. "It was just like down at Tootsie's. They'd sit there tuning up and say, 'Hello guitar.' The musicians thought 'Congratulations' was the big hit, but I knew 'Hello Walls' was the one."

I knew it, too. Faron and I were on the road together in 1961, and he approached me backstage and said, "Ralph, let me play you a little song that's about to come out. I think it's going to be a hit." Boy was it ever. Faron was banking on a song that had become the butt of jokes all over town, and it became his biggest seller, staying at #1 in *Billboard's* country charts for nine weeks in 1961 and hitting #12 in the trade publication's pop charts. Faron was back with a vengeance, and Willie Nelson was no longer broke.

"I walked into Tootsie's one day and Willie waved a check for twenty thousand dollars in my face, bent me over and kissed me," Faron laughed.

Faron sure didn't give me a kiss that August, when I released the follow-up song to "Hello Walls," a great tune appropriately named "Hello Fool." It was a song Hank Cochran discovered one night when he was hanging out around back of the Opry. Jim Coleman came up and told Hank he'd written the answer to "Hello Walls," and showed Hank the lyrics written on a paper bag. Hank knew it was a hit, and got the fellow to put Willie's melody to it. I was signed to Liberty at the time, and the song went to #4 in *Billboard* and stayed on the charts for fifteen weeks. Faron dropped by WSM while I was enjoying my one hit as a solo artist, and jumped on me about it.

"What did you mean calling me a fool, Ralph?" Faron said with a big frown.

"It's only a song, Sheriff!" I protested.

He groused a little, but let it drop.

FARON ALWAYS BELIEVED that Willie would be a star, and over the years told him so time and again. "I kept telling him that and saying he was just a little bit ahead of his time," Faron later said. "When that time came, Willie Nelson became a giant."

The five-hundred-dollar loan? Willie used it to move to a small farm at Ridgetop, Tennessee, and he told Faron he was going to get a bull and after about six months, he'd slaughter it and give Faron the beef as payment. Willie ended up losing his house in a fire and moving back to Texas, and the mysterious bull got to be a joke between the two. "Willie got bigger and bigger, and I never did see any bull," Faron recalled. "One day he was in town and I said, 'Willie, how big is that bull these days?' Willie didn't miss a beat. 'He's about twelve thousand pounds now,' he said. 'You ought to see him.' "

A few weeks later Faron got a message saying to be sure and be at his office at 3:00 that afternoon. Faron wasn't even sure where the message came from, but he went down to the office and waited. Promptly at 3:00 P.M. a truck pulled in hauling a tractor-trailer carrying the biggest bull Faron had ever seen.

"What in the devil is this?" Faron said.

"It's the bull Willie Nelson's been raising for you," the driver said. "Sign here."

*   *   *

"I COULDN'T ALWAYS pick a Willie Nelson hit, though," Faron once said. "I turned down 'Funny How Time Slips Away,' and when Billy Walker had a hit with it, I went out and bought myself a machine that kicks your rear end."

Faron stayed with Capitol three more years, then left to record for Mercury, where his career nearly skidded to a halt. Between 1963 and 1969 Faron only had two top-5 singles and four top-10s out of twenty releases. In today's record market that would spell the end of a career. But in early 1969 Faron recorded a song he and his manager/business partner, Billy Deaton, had written. "Wine Me Up" hit the #2 spot on country's charts and the Sheriff's badge was shining once again. He remained a force on the charts throughout most of the '70s, making his mark on three decades of country music.

Faron once told me that he could never retire. "I get sick of people asking me if I'm ready to come in off the road and sit in the rocking chair," he told me. "Ralph, I think the only way show people can really retire is to die." I told him I thought he was a sure bet for the Country Music Hall of Fame, and even that notion unnerved him. "I don't want to go in anytime soon. Seems to me they put you there right before you die."

ALONGSIDE THE TALES of his larger-than-life personality, there's another thread that runs through Faron's story: alcoholism. And that is where the Faron Young saga ultimately turned dark; when his years of two-fisted drinking and his chain-smoking finally caught up with the Sheriff. In the last few years of his life he suffered from emphysema, and drinking left him depressed. Booking agent Jim Case saw Faron fairly frequently during the last two years.

"Faron didn't feel good a lot of the time, and he left his answering machine on all the time," Jim said. "The only way I could get him to pick it up was to threaten to come over and kick his door down if he refused to talk to me."

In 1995 Faron's son Robyn received a phone call from a coworker in the Nashville sheriff's office. "Your father was brought in last night on a DUI," his friend said. "We all knew who he was right away, but he specifically asked us not to call you."

"Is he all right?" Robyn asked.

"Oh, he's fine," the friend said. "In fact, we didn't even put him in a cell. He entertained us all night long. He's a very funny guy."

The friend didn't have to tell Robyn about Faron. He knew all sides of his father: county music superstar, practical joker, natural comedian, generous friend, loving husband and father. He also knew the Faron Young who, when drinking, could turn from funny to abusive in a split second, the Faron Young who once said, "The bottle cost me my wife, my grandchildren and a couple of million dollars."

I don't think there's any doubt that Faron loved his family deeply. When he visited me on the radio show he always talked about his wife, Hilda, and his four children. And he was candid about his drinking and his wild lifestyle, often telling the listening audience that Hilda put up with a lot from him. Finally, in 1986 Hilda could no longer put up with his hard drinking, and she filed for divorce, citing years of abuse. Robyn testified on her behalf, and Faron turned his back on his son. The sad fact is, that meant turning his back on grandchildren Faron would have loved and should have known.

Robyn Young says that although Faron was ill, none of his conditions were life-threatening. It was widely circulated that he had prostate cancer, but Robyn says it was simply an enlarged prostate. His emphysema caused him discomfort, but he wasn't in immediate danger because of it. The problem was that he faced life without many of his family members, and without his music.

In the end, the Hall of Fame became an issue for Faron. "Faron did want to be inducted into the Hall of Fame," Jim Case said. "I think the music business broke his heart. He'd say, 'Look at the way things go now, they pay these kids who've barely had one hit thousands of dollars to play a show and they want to pay me peanuts.' " The last time Jim spoke to Faron was during the Thanksgiving holidays in 1996. "He seemed in a pretty upbeat mood," Jim reflects. "He'd been off liquor a year and he sometimes went to AA."

But still another friend said that when he spoke to Faron during the second week of December 1996, Faron was despondent. "He said he was going to have to go on oxygen soon," the friend said. "Faron saw that as the beginning of the end."

On December 9, 1996, at age sixty-four, Faron Young lay down on his bed, put a pillow over his face and shot himself in the head; his hit song "Live Fast, Love Hard, Die Young" became his epitaph.

His estranged son, Robyn, along with the rest of his children, rushed to his hospital bedside. The neurosurgeon in attendance told Faron's children that he believed Faron could hear, and that he was capable of making "purposeful movement" on his right side. Robyn took his father's right hand. "I told him I'd never stopped loving him," Robyn explained. "He squeezed my hand and I knew we were at peace. In the end, we were reunited."

Faron's children and his former wife, Hilda, stayed with him throughout the night. Robyn, a fine singer himself, sang some of his father's glory-day hits, including "Hello Walls," and Faron seemed to respond.

When I think of Faron, I'll think of the days when he helped Charley Pride, Johnny Cash, Roger Miller, Willie Nelson and so many others. I'll remember the funny stories about this unbelievable talent. But I'll also remember him saying, "Ralph, the only way show people can really retire is to die."

Faron was cremated, his ashes strewn over Old Hickory Lake near Johnny Cash's house. I hope Faron will soon be inducted into the Country Music Hall of Fame; the plaque hanging in the museum will be his only headstone.

SOAP SISTER ON A SOAPBOX

I CALL NAOMI and Wynonna Judd the Soap Sisters. The two were always enterprising, and long before they had a record contract I started booking them on my early morning show on WSMV-TV in hopes some record executive might be up early and discover them over coffee and Cheerios. Naomi always had some little bit of homespun wisdom, or a recipe or mothering tip to add to the show. That portion of her persona is not something a publicist invented to add an extra dimension to the Judds. One morning Naomi brought in a recipe for home-made lye soap, and we started getting piles of requests for it. When they returned several months later I found my brain was still asleep and I couldn't remember their names.

"Ladies and gentlemen, please welcome the Soap Sisters," I said, looking for a quick fix of some kind. That started it, and Naomi still gets a kick out of me calling them by that nickname.

A lot has happened to Naomi and Wynonna since then. Their signing to RCA became a bit of country music legend when, in 1983, the two women sat down in label head Joe Galante's office and performed with only Wynonna's acoustic guitar as accompaniment. Joe listened to a couple of songs and signed them on the spot. They've had twenty-three hit singles, sold in excess of ten million albums and become one of the most awarded duos in country music history.

Life was just about perfect until Naomi was diagnosed with hepatitis C, no doubt infected when she was still working as a nurse in a Nashville hospital. "Hepatitis C is the one you don't want to have," she said. "That one's the booger." The doctors told her she'd probably had the disease for five or six years, and one suggested she had maybe six months to live.

"You don't know that," she said. "You're not God."

She began taking interferon to help shore up her immune system, and while it helped for a while, within six months she could tell the effectiveness was wearing off. Things started to unravel rapidly. "It was pretty stinkin' melodramatic," she told me. Wynonna was in a clinical depression, fearing that their final year's tour could kill her mother. Naomi was depressed, too. As she says, "Hepatitis makes you depressed, because you know that your body is poisoned."

When Naomi and Wynonna convened a press conference to announce that the mother half of the act would retire in 1991, they wanted to return to the RCA building where they'd first performed for Joe Galante. In the ensuing years, RCA had moved into a formidable-looking steel-and-glass office tower on the other side of Music Row, and Naomi wanted the old familiar—kinder and gentler, if you will—building they'd first called home.

Their staff made the arrangements, but unfortunately, Naomi hadn't a clue as to what was going on with their old home. Like many old homes, it had fallen into a state of disrepair and was being gutted for remodeling. On the morning of the press conference, Naomi was so sick she couldn't dress herself. When she and her daughter arrived, they found television cameras set up facing a threadbare couch in a room stripped down to ancient, rotting drywall. She made it through the announcement, but barely remembers anything except the empty, used-up room which seemed analogous to her life. Falling apart, stripped down and rotten.

Ultimately, she fought back with characteristic positive thinking and a strong faith in herself and her God. She went on to write a memoir, to work tirelessly for liver research and in 1997 she wrote a cookbook titled *Naomi's Home Companion,* filled with recipes, health hints and personal philosophy. Food for the stomach and the soul.

When she arrived at the studio to film *On the Record* with me in November 1997, I figured that her primary agenda was to promote the book. It wasn't, and I've seldom had as hard a time at keeping an interview on track. Naomi is a spokesperson for the American Liver Association, and she's worked hard in that role. She used the money raised in the *Judds' Farewell Tour*

Pay-Per-View event to finance the Naomi Judd Research Fund, which provides grants for research into liver disease. Naomi Judd was in her spokeswoman mode.

"I am in great shape," she said. "And it's because I took control over my body and my condition. That's the message I want to send to people who are suffering from hepatitis. Four million Americans have this disease, and many don't know they're suffering from it. When you're sick you feel like a veil is wrapped around you and you tend to turn inward. You have to come out and fight, be involved in your own healing.

"I knew from years of hospital work that the mind can control the body, so I went on what I call a voyage to self-discovery. There are eight things that exist in a person who survives catastrophic illness: One) faith; Two) a sense of humor; Three) a support system; Four) a connection to nature; Five) having a purpose and a goal; Six) good diet; Seven) exercise; and Eight) an open belief system, the willingness to experiment. I work hard at keeping these qualities in my life and my outlook.

"I believe in complementary medicine. Because I'm a nurse, I would never advise someone to replace recognized medical procedure, but to add to it. I am a believer in acupuncture, herbal therapy, aroma therapy—the help is out there. Complementary medicine comes naturally for me, I'm a harmony singer, after all. My job has always been to complement my daughter's voice."

Naomi kept going, a woman with a mission. She wanted people to know that individuals could take stock of themselves and their illnesses and fight back. She wanted people to know that you don't have to accept a terminal diagnosis and simply slink off home to curl up and die. I wasn't sure how to divert her back to her cookbook without appearing indifferent to hepatitis sufferers. I wanted to allow her to state her case, and offer advice and hope, but I knew I couldn't let the show turn into a medical program. Even after I eased Naomi back into a more diversified conversation, she often slipped back into acting as a spokeswoman for liver research.

I spent hours reviewing the rough footage, trying to balance the interview, and was reminded at every turn of Naomi's dogged determination in getting her message out to the public. Imagine my surprise to pick up the newspaper that same week and read that two hepatitis activists arrived at Naomi's book-signing to confront her on her lack of public support. It takes a lot to render Naomi Judd speechless, but from what I read the accusations just about did. So right now, I'd like to go *On the Record:* Naomi, I applaud your indefatigable efforts. You're one hell of a woman. And a tough edit!

THE FOUR HORSEMEN:

BRADLEY, ATKINS, LAW

AND NELSON

January 7, 1998, was a dismal, rainy day in Nashville. I'd just completed a lengthy phone interview with the founder of Capitol Records' country division, Ken Nelson. We'd spoken about his legendary career as one of the architects of the Nashville Sound, about mutual friends in the business and how Nashville had emerged as a major recording center.

A month or so earlier, Owen Bradley, another legend in the business, had told me that he felt Ken Nelson had never received due credit for his contributions to country music, and that it was a shame Ken was not yet in the Country Music Hall of Fame. Owen had been in the Hall for over twenty years, and I remember laughing when I heard what Chet Atkins said to him about the 1974 induction: "You've been sick, so I knew they'd put you in. They always put people in the Hall of Fame if they're sick."

Owen and his brother Harold had been on my mind that morning, because my book collaborator, Patsi Bale Cox, and I were double-checking some facts about the succession of recording facilities the Bradley brothers built in Nashville. Owen had been sick with the flu, so I put in a call to Harold at his office at the Musician's Union. As it turned out, Harold was at a friend's funeral, so I left word, then made a mental note to make sure the Country Music Hall of Fame had copies of the Ken Nelson interview. Patsi and I were just about to fire up the tape recorder again when my associate, B. J. Haas, came in the room, visibly shaken.

"There's a reporter on the phone who wants a statement from you," she said. "Owen Bradley just died."

A preacher once told me that there are no experts at a funeral, and that goes for giving statements to the press about a recently departed friend. I could barely hold my emotions in check while I spoke to the reporter just moments after hearing of Owen's death. I couldn't come up with any flowery words, just that everybody loved Owen and he loved everybody. He was one of the most genuinely kind individuals I'd met in this business, and without him I doubt that Nashville would have become the recording power it is today.

The Nashville Sound is sometimes equated with a dilution of pure country music when the industry emphasized the lush strings of a Chet Atkins production or Owen Bradley's trademark Anita Kerr harmonies. I think it's better described as the time when Nashville expanded its technology, production techniques and outlook to compete with rock 'n' roll. The Four Horsemen—Owen Bradley, Chet Atkins, Don Law and Ken Nelson—recognized a need for a more sophisticated sound and they developed it. Owen wryly explained the Nashville Sound as "Five or six German echo chambers turned wide open."

But not all records were lush productions. Owen could and did have it both ways: he stayed true to the more traditional music of artists like Bill Monroe and helped make Patsy Cline a crossover sensation. Chet Atkins produced the gamut, from the stone country music of Hank Snow to the pop-flavored Jim Reeves. Don Law's artists at Columbia ranged from Flatt & Scruggs to Johnny Cash to Marty Robbins. Ken Nelson encouraged the fiddles and steel guitars of Buck Owens yet developed the smooth sound of hitmaker Sonny James. Hardly a cloned roster.

As I reflect on Owen Bradley's life and his career, it tickles me to remember how he never flinched under any criticism the Nashville Sound received. Some people complained that the records of the era sounded "vanilla," or watered down. But if Owen's Patsy Cline records are homogenized, then the word must be synonymous with "timeless." Owen had a sense of humor and irony about it all. The last time I sat in his office, just a couple of months before he died,

I noticed a small sign on the wall: "Vanilla still outsells all the other flavors."

Some criticized the use of the A-Team, a group of session musicians who were hired on most Nashville recordings: Floyd Cramer on piano, Buddy Harmon on drums, Bob Moore on bass, Boots Randolph on saxophone and Grady Martin, Hank Garland, Harold Bradley and Ray Edenton on guitars. Others came and went, but these were the core team. But these musicians enjoyed far more musical freedom in Nashville than their contemporaries in Los Angeles or New York. The musicians were left to improvise, add personal touches and interpret their parts on individual projects, and Nashville did just the opposite of what critics were decrying. Instead of making all the music sound alike, Owen, Chet, Don and Ken paid attention to each artist and I believe that for the most part they stayed true to the individual styles.

A-Team drummer Buddy Harmon agrees. "Every session was different, whether it was because of the producer or the artist," he says. "Owen was probably the most involved from a production standpoint. He'd usually worked out an arrangement well ahead of time, but still leave the musicians room to improvise. Ken Nelson and Don Law were more prone to have the musicians work things out. Don was the only one who wasn't a musician, so he gave us a lot of leeway. Chet varied. Sometimes he was very involved, and of course, he'd play guitar a lot of times. But there were other times that he stayed in the control room."

OWEN BRADLEY WAS born on October 21, 1915, near Westmoreland, Tennessee, close to the Kentucky border. In 1922 the Bradley family moved to Nashville, and Owen's father bought him a gift that would change his life: a crystal radio. The young boy began to play along on a harmonica to songs he heard on stations playing orchestra music, later learning the guitar and Hawaiian guitar. When his father purchased a player piano, though, Owen found his instrument.

"When that upright was delivered to our home it was a defining moment in my life," Owen told me. "I never got over my love affair with the piano." Later, when Owen was playing piano in Nashville sessions, he could never quite outdo the legendary Moon Mullican.

Once, when Owen was playing on an Ernest Tubb record, Ernest said, "Well, Owen, you're about half as good as Moon." From then on, Ernest referred to Owen as Half-Moon Bradley.

The Bradleys lived near stringband leader Paul Warmack of the Gully Jumpers, a regular act featured on WSM once the station came on the air in 1925, and Warmack became a mentor to Owen. By 1930, he'd quit high school to concentrate on playing music with Farris Coursey's Blue Diamond Melody Boys. Owen loved many forms of music, from the jazz influences of Louis Armstrong to Count Basie swing, and when he began working with Beasley Smith on WSM's pop music show, *Sunday Down South*, in 1940, he had the opportunity to work with pop superstars including Bing Crosby and Dinah Shore.

But pop was by no means his only interest. Owen got his jazz musician brother, Harold, involved in country music when he urged him to join Ernest Tubb's band in 1943. While Harold spent time on the country circuit, Owen did time in the military. Bill Anderson recalled that while Owen was stationed in San Francisco, he could sometimes pick up WSM radio in the afternoons. It made Owen homesick and he started writing songs to pass the time; among them were Roy Acuff's hit "Night Train to Memphis." He joined the merchant marine, playing in a San Francisco–based band initially fronted by Ted Weems. When Weems left, Owen took over as bandleader and stayed with the gig until he was released from the military in 1945. Once back in Nashville, he started playing as many sessions as he could book.

Owen hated the control that engineers held over artists and musicians. It stifled creativity to consistently be told what notes to play and when to play them, according to the young piano player. But musicians seldom got to control the sessions. For Owen to put his ideas to work, he'd have to move into executive status, and that seemed a hopeless dream to Owen Bradley in 1946.

But the following year something happened to change Owen's destiny. The New York–based head of Decca records, Paul Cohen, began using him as a freelance talent agent. According to music historian Bill C. Malone, Cohen is the man who ushered in the modern era of Nashville recording when he recorded Red Foley in WSM's Studio B in 1945. Prior to that time almost all country artists

were recorded in the field, using portable equipment. The following year is a historic one for Owen and country music, as 1946
marks the year Owen produced his first country session in the WSM
studios, "Blue Mexico Skies" with Zeke Clements. He was also involved with Bullet Records, who released Nashville's first million-
selling single: "Near You" by the Francis Craig Orchestra.

Owen's break came when Paul found he couldn't leave New York
to come to Nashville for an Ernest Tubb session, and he asked Owen
to step in, which he ably did. According to Owen it was an easy gig,
since Ernest came to the session knowing exactly what he wanted to
do and how he wanted to do it. The professional relationship between Cohen and Bradley grew and Owen was soon either arrang-
ing, producing or playing piano for many of Decca's acts, as well as
working on projects for Fred Rose.

In 1952, Owen and his brother Harold opened a small studio on
the top floor of the Teamsters Union Building at 2nd and Lindsley.
They paid the rent a year in advance, and at the end of that year
the rent was tripled. Owen and Harold moved their operation to a
building in Hillsboro Village, where they recorded Kitty Wells and
the Denning Sisters, among others.

"I had that studio for two years," Owen said. "It wasn't much.
The ceiling was so low it made it hard to work. But we did get some
good records out of there." When he contracted with Al Gannaway
to produce kinescopes of Opry stars for syndication, Owen moved
his operation to the Vanderbilt Theater. "We put in a little booth
in the top of the place," he recalls. "I had a Telefunken [micro-
phone], tied from a rope that we could drop. The sound guy could
pick up anything in the theater with that. It was really sensational
in those days, unheard of in Nashville."

The more Paul Cohen was called back to New York, the faster
Owen's star rose as a producer. Even though Paul was technically
the producer for Kitty Wells, he was often absent from the studio,
leaving Owen in charge. "It was no problem to be suddenly left in
charge of a Kitty Wells session," Owen said. "I never saw her come
to the studio any less than completely prepared. She is a real professional." He was at the helm for Kitty Wells's blockbuster hit, "It
Wasn't God Who Made Honky Tonk Angels," in 1952, and when
last we spoke, Owen chuckled over the listening sessions during

those days. "We got two big songs in one day. First, we found Kitty's debut hit, which was written as an answer to Hank Thompson's 'The Wild Side of Life.' The next song we listened to was 'Back Street Affair,' which we cut on Webb Pierce. The funny thing is, Billy Wallace wrote the song and when his wife heard it she got it in her head that it meant he'd been cheating on her, and turned it into a song. It caused quite a stir in their household for a while."

IN 1954 THE Bradley brothers bought a building at 804 16th Avenue South, and began renovations, including building a Quonset hut where they planned to continue their filmmaking. Owen could rightfully be called the Father of Music Row, since this studio was the first music-related business to open its doors on 16th Avenue. They opened their doors in 1955, the same year that Castle Studios, where most of Decca's recordings were made, closed.

Castle was Nashville's first major recording facility, formed in the post–World War II years by three WSM engineers: Carl Jenkins, Aaron Shelton and George Reynolds. For a time they operated from the WSM studios, later moving into what had been the dining room at the Tulane Hotel on Church Street. Decca's Paul Cohen was one of the first record executives to use the studio, followed quickly by Art Satherley and Don Law from Columbia, Lee Gillette and Ken Nelson from Capitol and Murray Nash from Mercury. Until Fred Rose, who guided Hank Williams's career and cofounded the mighty Acuff-Rose publishing empire with Roy Acuff, built his own studio, he too used Castle.

Legend has it that Castle's owners were not willing to change with the times, refusing, for example, to buy an echo chamber when artists began wanting them in an effort to compete with pop music's new sound. But there was an additional problem. WSM was sick and tired of three of their engineers moonlighting as studio owners and issued the men an ultimatum: get rid of the studio or resign. Since their lease at the Tulane Hotel was coming up, the men decided to stay with WSM and closed up shop.

Paul Cohen considered moving his recording either to Dallas, Texas, or to Springfield, Missouri, where Red Foley was having success with his *Ozark Jubilee* show. With his money tied up in film and audio studios in Nashville, Owen didn't think he could afford to move, and if Paul wanted a better facility, Owen was prepared to build it. Ultimately, Paul Cohen guaranteed Owen a hundred sessions a year and Owen guaranteed Paul a top-notch recording facility. The Quonset Hut, which had excellent acoustics, became that studio, the first such facility in the area now known as Music Row. By this time Owen's credits as an arranger or producer included Hank Williams, Kitty Wells, Webb Pierce and Red Foley, whose "Chattanoogie Shoe Shine Boy" became Owen's first million-selling arrangement.

Chet Atkins says that it was the studios that built Nashville's recording industry and that two labels, RCA and Decca, played the most crucial roles in the process by moving most of their recording to Music City. Men like RCA Victor's Steve Sholes and Decca's Paul Cohen seemed to instinctively know that the country artists would be served well recording on their own turf. But Capitol's Ken Nelson and Columbia's Don Law also welcomed the chance to record in Nashville rather than on one of the coasts or in the field.

COUNTRY WASN'T THE only music coming from the Bradley brothers' Quonset Hut. Rock and pop artists also came there to record; the now infamous session on Buddy Holly comes to mind. It was not quite the event portrayed in the 1978 film starring Gary Busey. In the movie Owen's character—he was never mentioned by name—just didn't "get" Buddy's music and Buddy walked out in a huff. In the movie, Owen's character took on exaggerated "hillbilly" or "hick" characteristics.

"I didn't see the movie," Owen admitted. "The first I knew anything about it was when my nephew came running in one day and said, 'Uncle Owen, did you get into a fight with Buddy Holly?' I didn't have any idea what he was talking about. That was one of those deals where Paul Cohen called me up and said, 'I want you to record some things on this guy.' He didn't tell me anything about him, and I thought he was a country singer so I hired all these country pickers. Buddy came in and we worked on his songs, but it didn't take. I knew he was in the wrong place and so did he. There were no bad feelings on either part, as far as I knew. Paul moved him to the Coral label and the rest is history."

Although Buddy's sessions were not fruitful, the Bradley Studio recorded pop and rock records with great success, including Brenda Lee's great rock 'n' roll catalog. Additionally, Gene Vincent's "Be-Bop-a-Lula," produced by Capitol's Ken Nelson and recorded in 1956, was made at the Quonset Hut. That Ken Nelson brought his rock act to Nashville to record in a new facility says a lot about his confidence in Owen and Harold Bradley. The session had Ken nervous, because he'd only heard one tape of Gene Vincent and was concerned that he might be making a mistake. Rather, he recorded a rock 'n' roll classic in the country music capital.

"Gene had a drummer with him," Owen recalls. "He was a great big guy and he beat the hell out of his drums. We couldn't handle all that sound, and we didn't know what to do with it. The drums were overriding everything, and we couldn't figure out how to get rid of them. Harold and I had just gotten started, really, and we were walking around trying to act like businessmen. Finally somebody suggested we back up the drummer a bit, but since we didn't see how that would make much difference, we decided to move the singer back. So we put Gene Vincent out in the hall of the Quonset Hut. That's how we learned about isolating people, and we started building little huts for them."

In 1998 Gene Vincent was posthumously inducted into the Rock 'n' Roll Hall of Fame. His trademark song, "Be-Bop-a-Lula," was the first million-selling single recorded at the Quonset Hut.

One of the reasons Owen and Harold became successful in the studio business was that they were always looking for ways to upgrade their equipment. Ken Nelson told me his biggest complaint with Castle was that the owners wouldn't get a separate microphone for the bass.

When Paul Cohen left Decca for Coral Records in 1958 he asked Owen to step into his old job, and the first artist the new label head inherited was fourteen-year-old Brenda Lee. Owen and Brenda were magic together and she became one of the biggest-selling artists in history with over 100 million in sales. I asked Owen if he'd been reluctant to work with such a young child.

"I was glad to record anybody! I'd been with Decca on an unofficial basis, with nothing except a piece of paper saying I wouldn't work for anybody else," Owen recalls. "I didn't have any authority. Of course, back in those days, Nashville didn't really have much authority. We were just trying to please New York and keep our jobs."

Owen's work with Brenda is detailed in another chapter, but it should be mentioned here that his breaking her as a rock act from Nashville was critical to Nashville's development as a recording center. When Brenda was inducted into the Country Music Hall of Fame in 1997, Owen said that she'd done more than anyone he could think of to heighten interest in this town's recording potential.

Over the years Owen's roster at Decca included Bill Monroe, Ernest Tubb, Webb Pierce, Jimmy C. Newman, Kitty Wells, Bill Anderson, Brenda Lee, Jack Greene, Bobby Helms, The Wilburn Brothers, Del Reeves, Burl Ives, Charlie Walker, Ernie Ashworth and Red Sovine. He signed Patsy Cline in 1955.

Owen told me that he often thought back to the day he attended a meeting in New York just after Decca had moved from 57th Street to Park Avenue. "They told me to go back to Nashville and make records that would last ten years," he said with a grin. He went back and recorded Patsy Cline and Brenda Lee.

Decca desperately needed him to make those lasting hits, because the label suffered during the rock years. Decca's sister label, Coral, had Buddy Holly, but they never succeeded in rock the way others did at the time. There are those who believe Owen Bradley kept the entire company afloat, but unlike today's record producers, he got no royalties, just a flat production fee. "I don't make a dime off any of the sales," Owen said ruefully. "If I did my great-grandchildren would be very rich people. I think Patsy Cline's *Greatest Hits* package is at seven million and still selling." He produced a history-making single in 1957 with Bobby Helms's "Fraulein," which became the longest-lasting chart hit in country music.

By 1961, when Owen was named *Billboard*'s country Man of the Year, the Quonset Hut was home to an astonishing seven hundred sessions yearly. It was the same year he signed Loretta Lynn to Decca and started to build his soon-to-be-legendary Bradley Barn in Wilson County. Eighteen years and nearly fifty hits later, he and Loretta were still a team. In 1979 Owen produced the soundtrack for Loretta's autobiography, *Coal Miner's Daughter,* which garnered him an Academy Award nomination.

IN 1972 DECCA became MCA, and in 1974 Owen was inducted into the Country Music Hall of Fame. His health failed some in the early

1970s. He underwent eye surgery in 1971 and abdominal surgery in 1974. Two years later he retired from MCA to spend more time producing and developing his publishing company, Forest Hills Music. In the 1980s and '90s Owen took on Elder Statesman status in country music. But he never retired and he never lost his touch in the studio. In 1988 he produced k.d. lang's *Shadowland: The Owen Bradley Sessions,* and even costarred with lang in an hour-long radio special about the project.

In 1994 he was presented with the National Academy of Recording Arts & Sciences' (NARAS) Governor's Award; in 1997 he received the Heritage Award at the Nashville Music Awards; and in 1997 Nashville's Metro Parks Board renamed Music Square Park, located on Music Row, Owen Bradley Park. Less than two months before he died, Owen and his Nashville Sound contemporary Chet Atkins were presented with Joe Kraft Humanitarian Awards for community service by the Nashville Community Foundation.

When he died he was producing Mandy Barnett, the young lady who starred in the Ryman Auditorium's *Always, Patsy Cline.* Mandy's debut album on Asylum had been critically acclaimed and she'd recently signed a new contract with Sire Records. Mandy says that she had always believed that if she could just somehow hook up with Owen Bradley, her career would take off. Owen had heard her sing because she'd been hired several times to dress up in her Patsy Cline costume and perform at tribute dinners. But he saw her as a world-class vocalist in her own right, not a Cline clone. The last time I spoke with Owen he was very high on Mandy's project, and the word on the street was that the sessions were every bit as brilliant as you'd expect. The recording sessions were completed by Harold Bradley, Mandy Barnett and Bobby Bradley Jr., the son of Harold and Owen's brother Bobby.

I hear a foundation is being established to raise money to build a statue of Owen in what is now known as Owen Bradley Park. If I know Owen, he'd probably say that there should be three men standing by his side in that park.

CHET ATKINS WAS a contributory factor in the careers of Eddy Arnold, Bobby Bare, the Carter Sisters, Skeeter Davis, Jimmy Driftwood, Red Foley, Don Gibson, Waylon Jennings, Ronnie Milsap,

Dolly Parton, Elvis Presley, Charley Pride, Jerry Reed, Jim Reeves, Hank Snow, Ray Stevens, Dottie West, Hank Locklin and Floyd Cramer to name but a few. Together with a handful of men, he changed the face of Nashville as a commercial center and country music as an industry, yet he was a reluctant executive, embarrassed by corporate titles and unable to comprehend the awe in which many of his artists held him.

Chester Burton Atkins was born on June 20, 1924, near Luttrell, Tennessee, in the northeast portion of the state. He was a chubby little kid, shy and plagued by asthma. "There's a few people that still call me 'Fatty' around home," the lean and fit Chet laughed years later.

His father, James, was a music and vocal teacher who moon-lighted as a piano tuner when he could find the work. Chet's older half-brother, Jim, played with Les Paul's orchestra, and frequently sent home radio recordings he'd heard in New York, instilling in Chet a love of big bands and orchestras. Chet says he learned to play guitar listening to the radio and to those recordings.

Chet's first radio performance was on Knoxville's WNOX, and he went on to work at many radio stations early in his career. "I've been fired all over the country," he laughs, explaining that back-slapping and company politics were never his strong points. His first dealings with RCA came to pass soon after one such firing, from station KWTO, in Springfield, Missouri. Following that pink slip, Chet took a job with the Shorty Thompson Trio in Denver, and it was there that RCA's Steve Sholes tracked him down and asked him to come to Chicago and make a record for RCA Victor, hoping to compete with Capitol's Merle Travis.

"I was lucky that although I was a Merle Travis fan, I hadn't had the opportunity to listen to him enough to copy him," Chet ex-plains. "I play an alternate bass and he played a thump, almost like a four/four. I always played with my fingers. I'd take a toothbrush made of celluloid, heat it up and cut off a piece with a pocket knife. Then I'd put it in hot water and fit it around my thumb to make my own thumb pick. That way I could play the arpeggios with the thumb and finger rather than with a straight pick. I think that helped set me apart from some of the other pickers and it helped me get work."

The unusual picking style impressed Steve Sholes enough to offer to record the young musician. Chet agreed, but when Shorty Thompson learned of the contract he approached his employee. "You can't sing, Chet," he said. "You ought to put me on your record." When Chet declined the offer, Shorty fired him.

Chet's first RCA recordings didn't sell well, and since he didn't have the job in Denver to return to, he asked Steve Sholes for session work in New York. Sholes agreed, and Chet recorded with Rosalee Allen, Elton Britt and the Beaver Valley Sweethearts. When work ran out, he went back to Knoxville, dejected and feeling like a failure. But Steve Sholes wasn't finished with Chet. He tracked him down again, and asked him to bring some musicians to the Fox Theater in Atlanta and record some new sides. Chet was by then playing around Knoxville with Homer and Jethro, so he took them and a bass player and headed to Atlanta, where they recorded "Galloping on the Guitar" using portable equipment.

Little by little Steve Sholes began to ask Chet for help with his country sessions, and to rely on the guitarist's musicianship and instincts. "Steve paid me about seventy-five dollars a week to help him. He'd call me from New York and tell me to hire a certain number of musicians and background singers so he could record some artist. Eventually he began to call and ask me to take charge of the sessions when he didn't have time to come down here."

After Steve Sholes signed Elvis he was promoted at RCA, and his new job and superstar signing gave him the clout to name his successor in Nashville. Chet was named Nashville's Director of Operations for RCA in 1957, and several years later he got a promotion he didn't want, the vice presidency.

"I really didn't want that title," Chet says. "I was ashamed of it."

I asked him why he'd be ashamed of the title, and Chet said it was in part because he didn't like to be thought of as an executive. "I wanted to be known as a guitar player," he confessed. "And it also embarrassed me because I didn't even have a high school diploma."

Chet told me that there was a certain amount of fear involved with the first Presley sessions on January 10 and 11, 1956. "Elvis was a little scared when he came to RCA. We were all nervous that we might lose the magic that Sun Records had got on his records.

It could have easily happened, we could have lost some small ingredient that was key to the sound. Luckily, we didn't.''

BY 1957 RCA had built its famous Studio B on Music Row and Elvis came there to record. Chet worked on the records for a time, but the Presley crowd's love of all-night sessions soon stopped Chet's participation. "I had to work during the day," he explained. "When Elvis first signed with RCA he recorded in the afternoons, but when he got so big he started coming in during the night so fans wouldn't congregate outside the studio. I finally started going in around ten o'clock P.M. just to say hello, then leave. They'd record a while, then send out for about eighty Krystal burgers, then do karate for a while. Elvis was making so much money nobody ever complained about the wasted time and money.''

THE RELATIONSHIP BETWEEN Steve Sholes and Chet Atkins was much like the one between Paul Cohen and Owen Bradley. In both cases, a New York executive came to rely heavily on a Nashville musician to hire other musicians for session work, listen to local songwriters and make hit records. In return, both Chet and Owen liked and respected their New York bosses. There was a great amount of trust on both parts, which was good, because New York definitely had the power and held the purse strings.

"It's a business, you know," Chet said. "You try to make records that will sell. You try something a little different on one, and if it works, maybe you'll use a little more of it. But you always have to keep going in different directions, because the public demands things that are fresh and new.''

"Today the artist and the people who run Nashville labels tell New York what to do," Owen Bradley said. "But in those days it was exactly the opposite. New York spent the money and we would say, 'Yes sir! Whatever you want.' We were like little dogs doing back flips. And Chet and I did a lot of flipping in those days.''

On the other hand, neither Chet nor Owen wanted the total business responsibility; both preferred sitting behind the console to sitting behind a desk. In Chet's case, he never wanted to have to let any artists go, so he left the dropping of an artist to New York. "I loved to sign them," he says. "I just couldn't stand telling them to go." The times Chet and I have discussed the executive side of his career, he has been more reflective, more critical of himself than I'm used to hearing from record executives. Perhaps it's because he never wanted to be an executive in the first place.

Not breaking Roger Miller is one of his biggest regrets. Roger had three moderately successful singles on RCA: "You Don't Want My Love," "When Two Worlds Collide" and "Lock, Stock and Teardrops." But his career didn't take off until he moved from RCA to Smash and released "Dang Me." "Everything about Roger was perfect—the writing, the voice, the charisma, even the name," Chet said. "But we couldn't make it happen. Willie Nelson is another disappointment. We had him from 1965 to 1972, but his biggest success came later on Columbia. So much of what happens in the music business is a matter of timing. I have to take the blame, I believe, for Roy Orbison's lack of hits on RCA. Roy told me later that he was afraid of me in the studio, and when he moved over to Fred Foster at Monument, he felt more relaxed."

Chet is such a mild-mannered gentleman that it's hard to believe people were afraid of him. Yet even the head outlaw himself, Waylon Jennings, admits he was nervous around Chet Atkins. In his 1996 self-titled autobiography, Waylon writes: "When I was normal I guess I was a little bit worshipful of Chet." To take the edge off his discomfort, Waylon says he'd pop a pill before going to visit Chet in the office. Waylon also told about his need for approval in the studio, a need Chet sometimes didn't fill.

"For Chet, a smile meant 'that sounds pretty good.' A grin was wonderful out of him in the studio. If he said, 'Man, I liked that,' it was probably a number one record. I often fantasized about being out in the studio recording, and Chet getting up in the control room, standing on top of the console, jumping through the plate glass window, rising up, wiping the blood off and yelling 'Goddamn, that is a smash!' "

I told Chet that I believed his enormous talent was more intimidating to the artists and musicians than his well-known perfectionism. And even though Waylon's book was not yet out, Chet seemed to echo the artist's assessment. "I don't know," he said.

"But if I had it to do over, I think I could be a much better producer. I look back and think I should have smiled more, or danced
around the room like Paul Cohen did if he liked a record. Paul
would jump up and down and say, 'This is a hit!' That is one of the
best attributes a producer can have—the ability to enjoy the music
and make the artist enjoy the experience."

Chet believed that his reluctance to pronounce a record a hit had
to do with the business side of the industry. "I knew there were so
many ingredients that went into making a hit that it scared me to
get someone's hopes up," Chet said. "There were so many times
that I made what I thought was a great record, and then it was lost
because of sales and promotion."

One time Chet broke his own rule, and pronounced a song a hit
as soon as it was recorded, even though it was a long shot. The song
was an instrumental: Floyd Cramer's "Last Date." "I was sure about
it," Chet said. "I knew it was a hit sound and that it would change
the whole industry as far as piano playing went. It reminded me of
how Bob Wills played fiddle and the sound would just ring your
heart strings."

"Last Date" only went to #11 in the country charts, but it stayed
at #2 in pop charts for over a month in 1960. The only thing standing between Floyd and the top pop slot was Elvis Presley's "Are You
Lonesome Tonight," which also featured Floyd on piano. It made
Floyd famous for the "grace note" or "slip note," which is two
notes in one, a technique the pianist learned from listening to songwriter Don Robertson's demo of "Please Help Me I'm Falling."

Floyd explained the technique thus: "You hit a note and slide
almost simultaneously to another," he said. "It's sort of a near-miss
on the keyboard. You don't hit the note you intend to strike right
away, but you 'recover' instantly and then hit it. It is an intentional
error and actually involves two notes. Steel guitar players often hit
similar notes through the use of their foot pedals. The result is a
lonesome, cowboy sound."

There's a personal connection to "Last Date" for me. When I was
married to Skeeter Davis, she recorded a version of the song and it
made it to the top-5 in country in 1961. Boudleaux Bryant wrote
the lyrics for Skeeter's version, and Conway Twitty wrote a different
set of lyrics and put it in his rock show. Later, after he was making

country records, Conway did a country version and took it to the top of the country charts.

FLOYD IS ANOTHER legend the industry lost in 1997. He died at home, at age sixty-four, after a six-month-long bout with cancer. I was vacationing in Colorado when Floyd died, and saw only a small item in the papers about his passing. It saddened me to think that his passing was only a side item in the national press. His influence and popularity cannot be overstated; he sold millions of records and had legions of fans. In 1984 the Jackson family invited Floyd to play at a private party for their mother, Katherine Jackson, a big fan of Floyd's. Floyd accepted the invitation and played piano while Michael sang "For the Good Times" and Jermaine sang "Moon River." Floyd changed the way we look at instrumental music and influenced generations of keyboardists. He should have made headlines.

EVEN THOUGH CHET seems to remember his disappointments, the music world remembers his achievements. Don Gibson is one of those artists who kept the nation interested in country music during rock's heyday. Born in Shelby, North Carolina, Don had cut records for several labels, including RCA, when Chet stepped in. In 1949 Mercury's Murray Nash had recorded Don and the band he called the Sons of the Soil. The following year RCA's Steve Sholes worked with Don and a band he called The King Cotton Kinfolks. In 1951 Steve recorded Don again with Chet Atkins on guitar. Don's own songs were overlooked on these sessions, and Chet wondered why. When he heard Don sing his own compositions, he heard hit potential. In 1956 MGM released Don performing one of his own songs, "Sweet Dreams," and although the song went top-10 in *Billboard* there was no follow-up. Once again, Chet Atkins listened to a Don Gibson song and wondered why he wasn't being encouraged to record his own material.

After another failed try on Columbia Records, Don found himself broke and living in a trailer in east Tennessee. One afternoon in 1956, after his television and radio had been repossessed, Don sat down and wrote two songs: "I Can't Stop Loving You" and "Oh, Lonesome Me." By this time Chet Atkins was running RCA, and when Don sent him those two songs he signed him. The New York office questioned Chet's judgment since Don had already bombed several times, but Chet remained steadfast.

"Mr. Sholes kept saying, 'He's been everywhere!' But I kept reminding them that his writing was going to make him a star, and it did."

They released "Oh, Lonesome Me" on February 17, 1958, and it went straight up the charts to #1 and stayed there for two months. "I Can't Stop Loving You" went top-10 for Don and went on to be one of the most-recorded songs in country music history. It's been covered over seven hundred times and received over four million radio plays. Don went on to be a mainstay for RCA during the Nashville Sound years, and his song catalog made a couple of bucks for the mighty Acuff-Rose Publishing, too.

Like Owen Bradley, Chet Atkins received no royalties from the recordings made in the early years. But Steve Sholes, in an attempt to pay his label head fairly, cut a deal whereby Chet owned one-third of the RCA building built in 1963. "Mr. Sholes was trying to take care of me," Chet says fondly.

By 1980 Chet was tired of being a record mogul and wanted to be known simply as a guitar player. He retired from RCA in 1981, turning the helm over to Owen Bradley's son Jerry, and in 1982 he began recording for Columbia Records. His work runs the gamut from jazz to country to rock, and has brought him eleven Grammys and overwhelming critical acclaim. And while we always point to Chet as one of the major architects of the Nashville Sound, I sometimes think it was always secondary to his guitar playing. Chet was a picker who accidentally became a history-making record mogul.

ANOTHER TO ALTER the course of Nashville music was Columbia's Don Law. He developed the careers of Columbia artists, including Johnny Cash, Flatt & Scruggs, Marty Robbins, Carl Smith and Lefty Frizzell. Don was born in London, England, in 1902, moving to the United States in 1924. He was a trained vocalist, but made no initial efforts to support himself with music in the New World, instead trying his hand at sales, farming and bookkeeping. Don Law was fascinated with the American West, and in an effort to find what was left of the Cowboy Era, he moved to Texas. In Dallas he found bookkeeping work at Brunswick Records. In December 1931, Brunswick was purchased by the American Record Company and Don met Art Satherley, a fellow Englishman with a love for all things Western, including music. When American became Columbia, Art and Don built the country division.

Art Satherley understood and loved the country traditions, and he passed that love along to Don Law. Art immigrated to America from England in 1913, and started his career in the recording business as an assistant to Thomas Edison, and perhaps his English upbringing allowed him to better appreciate the Anglo-Celtic roots of Appalachian music. Satherley once recalled talking with East Coast distributors about "hillbilly" music and its sales potential. "They thought it was trash," Art said. "Prior to radio few people realized there was a rural America. People thought America was New York. But to me America was the dialects, the stories, the rural heritage. That is what makes country music possible."

In 1945 Art and Don split the country division, with Art taking all the music made west of El Paso, and Don concentrating on all the music made east of that city. When Owen Bradley opened his studio on Music Row, Don was quick to take advantage of the hometown recording opportunity. And when Owen wanted to build a new facility in Wilson County, Don convinced Columbia to purchase the site where the Quonset Hut was located to house the country division of the label. Don was one of the first executives to see Nashville's potential as a music center, and when he died in 1982, Owen Bradley lamented the fact that he was not in the Hall of Fame: "If anybody deserves to be in there, he does," Owen said. "His feeling for the music and his loyalty to me and my brother Harold when we were trying to establish our studio meant so much at the time."

KEN NELSON PRODUCED one of the first major crossover records when he cut "Gone" on Ferlin Husky using the Jordanaires and a heavy rhythm section. Ken Nelson ran the Capitol Records country division from 1950 to 1976, producing hits including Faron Young's "Goin'

Steady," Hank Thompson's "Wild Side of Life," Wanda Jackson's "Right or Wrong," Sonny James's "Young Love," Ferlin Husky's "Wings of a Dove" and Gene Vincent's "Be-Bop-a-Lula."

Ken was born on January 19, 1911, in Caledonia, Minnesota. He started singing while he was still a child, working for a music store that sold ukuleles and kazoos in a local amusement park. The store also sold sheet music and Ken developed an appreciation for the publishing side of music. In 1928, when he was just seventeen years old, he was offered a job working for a local publishing company. It was a short-lived position, since the stock market crashed the following year and the company went out of business.

He found employment at WAAF in Chicago, which catered to the immense agriculture business headquartered in the city. "WAAF was the first licensed radio station in Chicago, which had the world's biggest stockyards," Ken recalled. "Since their primary news centered around the reports on the cattle, hog and grain markets, they decided to add country music to the shows. That was my introduction."

Luckily, Ken had met a fellow music-lover, singer Lee Gillette. "I played tenor banjo and Lee played drums, so we got another fellow and put together the Campus Trio, performing over Chicago's KOYW. But the only way talent got paid in those days was if you had a sponsor, and we didn't have one. So I quit and unsuccessfully tried for a solo career while the other two continued as a duo. Well, they got very successful and found a sponsor soon after that!"

The duo, renamed the Campus Kids and sponsored by Seagram's liquors, got work with the *Fibber McGee and Molly* radio show and relocated in Hollywood. In California Lee met a man named Glenn Wallichs, who worked for the company that made acetates of the *Fibber McGee and Molly* shows. "Lee was the guy who went to the company to pick up the acetates, and Glenn was the man who was recording them off the air," Ken explained. "Lee ended up leaving *Fibber McGee and Molly* and going with the Buddy Rogers Orchestra for a short while. When he decided to leave that job, he came home to Chicago, where I helped him get a job as an announcer at WAAF."

Ken eventually went to work for station WJJD as music director. The station had a live country music show each night called *Suppertime Frolics,* and when management decided to replace the live shows with recorded music, it became Ken's responsibility to purchase the records. When he was drafted into the military, Lee came to WJJD agreeing to fill in for Ken until he was released. When Ken returned, Lee was prepared to hand him back his job.

"I didn't want it," Ken says. "I was a single guy with no responsibilities, and Lee was married and had kids. I told the station manager to leave Lee in the position and I'd go out to California and look for work."

" 'You can't do that, Ken,' the manager said. 'I need you here. We have this new thing called FM, and I want you to handle it.' At that time there were no commercials, just music. So Lee and I both stayed."

In the meantime, back in Hollywood, Glenn Wallichs and Johnny Mercer formed Capitol Records. Glenn talked to Lee and asked him what he was doing. When Lee told him he was the music director at a radio station, Glenn said: "You're just the guy I'm looking for to handle the transcription department for Capitol Records."

"The FM side didn't require much work back then, because nobody had radios to pick it up," Ken recalled. "We were putting it out on buses and at Marshall Field department store."

A threatened musicians' strike sent record companies scurrying to get in as many sessions as possible. So Lee came to Chicago to record Uncle Henry's Kentucky Mountaineers, one of the bands who'd performed on WJJD's *Suppertime Frolics.* He'd no sooner set up the session, when he got called to New York. So Lee turned to his friend Ken Nelson, and asked him to fill in.

"I said, 'Lee, what do I do?' I'd never recorded anybody." Ken laughs. "Lee gave me a short course and that became my first session. Since the record company was still frantic to get music recorded, I did a record on the Denning Sisters, and it turned out to be a hit: 'Buttons and Bows.' " Ken moved to California after being offered a job doing transcriptions for Capitol's country division.

In 1951 Lee was made the head of the label's pop division. "I think Lee Gillette was one of the greatest pop producers of all time," Ken reflects. "He did Nat King Cole, Kay Starr, Dean Martin and so many more." Ken was named the head of Capitol country, with a roster including Tex Ritter (the label's first country act), Hank Thompson, Merle Travis, Tex Williams, Tennessee Ernie Ford and Jimmy Wakely. It would prove to be a wise move, for Ken turned Capitol into one of the most powerful and respected country labels and helped make Nashville a major recording center.

As it turned out, Capitol put the transcription companies out of business when they became the first company to issue promotion records. Before that, the stations had to buy records, and in some cases they could not even do that. A number of labels even had records marked "not for broadcast."

THE FIRST HIT Ken produced was Hank Thompson's "The Wild Side of Life." Princeton-educated Hank is a good example of why one should never label country singers as backward hillbillies. Capitol's first country signee, Tex Ritter, was impressed with Hank's western swing and honky-tonk performances in Texas and Oklahoma clubs, and brought the Texas native to his label's attention in 1947. He recorded some hits between 1947 and 1952, most notably "Humpty Dumpty Heart," which peaked at #2 in the charts during mid-1948. When Ken began producing him they cut "The Wild Side of Life," which spent a whopping fifteen weeks at the top of the country charts during 1952. The song stayed on the charts the better part of a year and firmly launched the careers of both artist and producer.

Ken Nelson didn't learn to drive until he was fifty years old. When he went on scouting trips to find regional acts, he hired a driver or took buses and trains. By doing so, Ken believes he saw the country and its people a little better, spending time listening to folks talk in train stations, concentrating on local radio shows in the car rather than worrying about the road maps. Once, on a trip through the South recording some regional acts, Ken tuned in to a country music show coming from Shreveport, Louisiana. He heard a voice that knocked him out.

"I said, 'Gee, that guy's great. Who is he?' Then the announcer came on and said, 'You're listening to the Webb Pierce Program' and I thought, 'Well, forget it. Webb's signed to Decca.' Then this voice came on again and sang another song, and I realized that it wasn't Webb. I told the guy driving me to go on back to Shreveport. When we got there I went to the station and talked to the announcer. I didn't want to tip my hat, because I'd heard that the station manager was capable of hornswaggling artists if he thought they were about to be signed to a record label. I asked who was the kid singing with Webb, but I didn't say who I represented."

"It's a guy named Faron Young," the announcer said.

Ken went back to the car and drove to see a music manager he trusted, Hubert Long. Hubert was managing Johnnie and Jack at the time, and Ken asked him if he thought he could get Faron to sign a contract with Capitol Records. Hubert agreed to be the go-between, and then pitched Ken an act of his own, the wife of Johnny Wright, one half of the Johnnie and Jack team.

"Her name is Kitty Wells, and she's a hit act, Ken," Hubert said.

"Oh, sure, sure," Ken laughs. "I turned her down and told Hubert that girl singers didn't sell well, and of course, they didn't at the time."

The irony of it was that Kitty signed with Decca and her first hit was the answer to "Wild Side of Life."

But Ken did sign some great "girl singers." Jean Shepard was born in Pauls Valley, Oklahoma, but raised in Visalia, California. Ken said that Hank Thompson had always wanted to record in California, and while he was in the state he heard a group called the Melody Ranch Girls, featuring Jean Shepard. Hank loved Jean's pure country vocals, and asked Ken to go hear her sing. She signed with Capitol in 1953, and had back-to-back hits with duet partner Ferlin Husky; "A Dear John Letter" stayed at #1 in the country charts for six weeks and was a top-5 pop hit as well, and "Forgive Me John" hit top-5. Jean was an unlikely crossover artist. She steadfastly refused to make any attempt to add pop flavorings to her music and continued to cultivate her cowgirl image. But she became one of Capitol's most popular stars of the era and was named Top Female Singer in *Cash Box* magazine in 1959. Jean married Hawkshaw

Hawkins, who was killed with Patsy Cline and Cowboy Copas in the 1963 airplane crash. She remains a favorite at the Grand Ole Opry in the 1990s.

Ferlin was going under the name of Terry Preston when Ken met him. "Ferlin, Terry Preston is a sissy name," Ken said. "Why don't you use your real name?" One day Ferlin and his father were driving with Ken and Ken brought it up again. Ferlin's father turned to him and said, "Ferlin you're never going to be successful unless you use your right name." "He did, thank goodness," says Ken.

Ken also signed Wanda Jackson, who was at one time considered the female Elvis, dubbed the Queen of Rock 'n' Roll in the press. Wanda was a guitar virtuoso by the time she was ten, and by age twelve, she landed her own radio show on station KEPR in Oklahoma City. In 1954, after hearing her sing and play on the radio, Hank Thompson invited her to tour with his Brazos Valley Boys show and she signed a recording contract with Decca. Wanda cut fifteen sides with Decca, all of them country to the core. But with the exception of "You Can't Have My Love," the label couldn't chart her. Her music began to evolve when she started touring with Elvis Presley in 1955, with Elvis encouraging her to try her hand at rock 'n' roll. Hank Thompson helped her get a contract with Capitol and Ken produced her somewhere between country and rockabilly. Her first release on Capitol, "I Gotta Know," went straight to #1. Ken guided Wanda to international success, recording "Fujiyama Mama," which made her an instant superstar in Japan. The rock 'n' roll stardom came with "Let's Have a Party," which was recorded during the same sessions as "Fujiyama Mama." It became a top-40 hit and a million-seller for Wanda and Capitol.

Sometimes you have to go out and beat the bushes for a hit artist, and sometimes you get one dropped in your lap. One day Chet Atkins called Ken and said he had a singer who had recently returned to the States after serving in the Korean War. "I like this guy, but our roster is filled," Chet said. "Would you come over to my house and listen to him?" Ken went to Chet's, liked what he heard and signed Sonny James, who became one of the most successful charting artists in country music history with seventy-two country hits, twenty-three #1 records and eighteen pop hits.

Ken produced over 150 artists in his career, many of them making just one or two singles. Ken blames the label's home office for losing many artists who should have been stars. "Capitol called our music hillbilly music at that time," Ken explained. "There was a lot of competition at the label between the pop and country side. Every week we'd have a meeting between artists and repertoire and promotion, and everybody would play their records. These guys would listen all the way through to the new pop music and say, 'That's great.' Then at the end of the meeting they'd start to listen to my country records. They'd play about eight bars and say, 'Oops, that's enough. Next.' They had no feeling or idea of country music."

One of the things that irritated Ken the most about that attitude was an incident with Roy Acuff. "Wesley Rose had come to me about Roy after he left Columbia. I produced several singles and an album. The promotion department just held their nose at the music. I put out the album, but nobody would do anything for the record. Wesley came back to me and said, 'Ken, something's wrong. These people don't care about this album or Roy Acuff.' I felt I should free up Roy to go elsewhere." Then about six months later the company started to notice that the album had been selling like crazy, even with no promotion. The promotion guys came back to Ken and said, "We've sold over a hundred thousand units! Why'd you let him go?"

"Because you dumb asses wouldn't do anything with him," Ken shot back.

KEN NELSON ALSO turned the Bakersfield Sound from a regional favorite to an international success. He always believed in the big "Telecaster twang" that developed in Bakersfield and encouraged the musicians to never let it be dulled. (The Telecaster is a semihollow body electric guitar made by Fender.) It was in Bakersfield that he found Buck Owens, who was playing guitar with one of the Capitol artists, Tommy Collins. Ken was initially impressed by Buck's guitar playing, but Buck kept pestering him for a vocal audition. "Finally he wore me down and I said I'd listen. After about sixteen bars of the song I said, 'Okay, that's enough.' I heard it right away.

When Buck came out of the booth he thought I was getting ready to turn him down since I had stopped the session. I said, 'I don't have to hear any more, Buck. You've got a record contract.' "

He discovered Merle Haggard singing and playing in the backup band at a tribute for *Cousin Herb Henson's Trader's Post* show, at the Bakersfield Civic Auditorium. Ken came to town to produce a live album at the event. "Merle sang during the show, but since he was signed with Tally Records, I couldn't leave him in the album. After the show I went up to him and offered him a contract."

"No," Merle answered.

"Why not?" Ken was stunned.

"Lou Tally and Fuzzy Owens gave me my first break," Merle explained.

"I admire your loyalty," Ken said.

Over the next months Ken started noticing Tally Records on the *Billboard* charts. Merle had four charted songs with Tally, including the top-10 "(My Friends Are Gonna Be) Strangers." Finally Ken called Fuzzy Owens, who managed Merle. Ken knew that without the distribution power of a major label, Tally would probably not have sales to match the chart success. He asked Fuzzy to meet with him and discuss a buyout.

Ken bought the masters from Tally. Once Merle couldn't get scheduled with Ken to record, so he came to Nashville and cut "Tonight the Bottle Let Me Down" without him. Merle says it came off so badly, he brought the master to Hollywood and buried it, then recut with Ken at the helm.

Ken brought Glen Campbell to Capitol, getting more than he bargained for in the process. "I signed Glen to a country deal in 1962, and he started out making great country records. But when he got his television show in 1968, he started playing rock and roll. I couldn't sell any country records if he wasn't giving them the exposure, and I got a little peeved at him. Al Delorey, another producer at Capitol, came to me and asked if he could produce Glen. I said, 'Be my guest.' It turned out to be the best thing for Glen, because Al knew better than I what to do with Glen. He put an orchestra behind him, and found the right songs."

Ken spent about six months a year in Nashville, and eventually he became so busy that Capitol opened an office, hiring Marvin

Hughes to produce some of the load. In 1976, after establishing Capitol as a major player in Nashville, Ken retired. He still lives in California, and is still an active man, spending his time traveling, playing golf and playing the piano.

Ken Nelson says he never considered himself a great producer, but if you look at his body of work you'd have to disagree. He was known for allowing artists to retain their personal style, for encouraging experimentation and standing solidly behind an act in whom he believed. And maybe his legacy is similar to that of Owen Bradley, Chet Atkins and Don Law: they were all men who first proved to the record industry that Nashville didn't have to take a backseat to anybody when it came to making hit records.

BATTLE OF NEW ORLEANS:
THE REMATCH

''THE BATTLE OF New Orleans'' was Johnny Horton's biggest song, staying at #1 in country for a whopping ten weeks and #1 in pop for six weeks. The story of how the song got recorded is interesting; the story of what happened next is bizarre.

After Arkansas history teacher and folksinger Jimmie Driftwood first recorded the song for use as a teaching aid in his classroom, publisher Don Warden signed him to a publishing deal. Don knew that Johnny Horton was looking for a follow-up to "When It's Springtime in Alaska," and sent him a copy of Driftwood's version. Johnny and his manager, Tillman Franks, weren't sure about the song.

I was one of the few deejays in the country who was playing the very lengthy Jimmy Driftwood version, and that's how I came into the story. I think my audience was primarily male, because most of the people who called in were men and they seemed to love the fact that Jimmy swore in "The Battle of New Orleans." Here's how his lyrics went: "Old Hickory [Jackson] said he didn't give a damn, he'd whip the britches off of Colonel Packingham. . . . We fired our guns and we really gave 'em hell." It's a good thing mine was the all-night show; I doubt that WSM would have allowed me to play this in the daytime. Remember, in those days the use of "hell" or "damn" was considered radical.

One night Tillman heard the song on WSM just as he was falling asleep. He awoke the next morning convinced it was a hit for Johnny Horton. (I was always afraid my show would put someone to sleep, but in this case we influenced one of the biggest songs of 1959 so I don't feel too bad about it.) It hadn't hurt that I mentioned the fact that the song was in my top-10, one of the most popular and and most requested on my show.

Both Johnny and Tillman knew they'd have to get Jimmy Driftwood to shorten the song to a more radio-friendly version, and to that end they invited the songwriter to Shreveport where he could play the *Louisiana Hayride* and rewrite. In addition to shortening the song, Johnny had Jimmy remove the swear words. That's why in the version most of you have heard, the line goes, ". . . we really gave 'em, *well*." By the time the song was finally released, Johnny Horton had decided it was not just a monster country hit, but a pop hit as well. I'm not so sure that it was a shrewd musical instinct that led him to that conclusion. When he recorded the song Johnny called a friend, Bernard Ricks, to his house for a listen, and Ricks claimed to have seen a dollar sign inside a bluish haze appear above the record player! Considering Johnny Horton's belief in the supernatural, it's no wonder he was convinced of the song's potential.

But that's not the bizarre part. That part of the story began when the song lived up to its potential and became one of the year's hottest releases in any genre.

Columbia Records saw the writing on the wall—or in the haze, as it were—and started releasing patriotic history lessons as fast as it could: Hawkshaw Hawkins ("Soldier's Joy"), Carl Smith ("Ten Thousand Drums") and Lefty Frizzell ("Ballad of the Blue and Grey"). Then the label went one step further and decided to release a version of "The Battle of New Orleans" to Canada and England.

Huh? The line goes: "In 1814 we took a little trip along with Colonel Jackson down the mighty Mississip'/We took a little bacon and we took a little beans and we caught the bloody British in the town of New Orleans." Easy enough for an enterprising record label to fix. Since the "bloody British" line probably wasn't going to play at the Paladium, Columbia rewrote the song without telling either Don Warden or Jimmy Driftwood. Now the lines went like this: "In 1814 we took a little trip along with Colonel Packingham up the mighty Mississip'/We took a little bacon and we took a little beans and we met the blooming rebels in the town of New Orleans."

It got even more bizarre. Both versions said, "We fired our

guns and the [British or rebels, take your pick] kept coming/ But there wasn't nigh as many as there was a while ago." Since the rebels were defending against the advancing British, that line got dicey.

The whole thing got even more dicey when Don Warden learned that Columbia and Wesley Rose had not only rewritten the lines, but had put Don's name on the tune as a new writer! By the time he found out what had happened and told Jimmy Driftwood, it was a done deal: the records were in Canada and England. I talked to Don about this fiasco not long ago, and asked him if he'd made any money on it. He said he doubted if he made anything, since the record mercifully stiffed in England. "If I found out I had," he said. "I'd donate the money to the Hermitage."

The Hermitage, of course, is General Andrew Jackson's historic home, where he is buried. "When I showed Jimmy Driftwood the new lyrics to his song he almost had a stroke," Don said. "He went right out to the Hermitage and got down on his knees beside Old Hickory's grave and asked his forgiveness."

10

TRAVIS TRITT:

A NEW GENERATION

OF OUTLAWS

Like the Nashville Sound, the Outlaw movement in its narrowest definition stands for the way in which records were made. In the mid-1970s, several artists, most notably Waylon Jennings, Willie Nelson and Tompall Glaser, fought to record with an edgier, rawer and rougher manner than was the prevailing fashion. Waylon, for one, wanted to use his own band in the studio; Tompall wanted to control his own publishing and booking, as well as his music.

Willie just wanted to be Willie. Back in 1975, I asked him what the term "outlaw" meant to him and he quipped, "Just that they're writing about me." Then he went on to explain how he saw the movement. "The word 'progressive' has been used a lot in relation to our music. But I really think it's the listener who is progressive. If someone can listen to a guy with long hair and a bandana sing country songs and not criticize him for the way he looks, that's progressive."

I asked him if he thought he could have gotten away with his style of dress back in the early '60s when he first came to town. "I might not have gotten away scot-free," he laughed. "But I think I could have gotten away without getting killed."

Waylon is probably most identified with the Outlaws, since he was one of the most outspoken artists. But if Waylon was the mouthpiece

of the Outlaw movement and Willie was its heart, Tompall Glaser
was the businessman. Back in 1962, he and his brothers, Jim and
Chuck, opened their own recording studio, publishing arm, production company and booking agency and began to assert control over
their music.

Once they met, Waylon and Tompall hashed out their common
gripes with record labels, record executives and what they considered watered-down music, then teamed up to take on Nashville's
music establishment. Waylon stopped using RCA's Studio B and
moved his recording to Glaser Studios, and used his own band instead of Nashville's A-Team pickers.

The Outlaw movement was given its name by Hazel Smith, a
music columnist who worked in Tompall's Music Row office. Hazel
was helping Tompall and Waylon with some promotional ideas
when an Ashboro, North Carolina, deejay called Tompall's office to
talk about an upcoming show that featured recordings by Tompall,
Waylon, Willie Nelson and Kris Kristofferson. Hazel threw him a
title right off the top of her head: "Call it Outlaw Music," she
quipped. The tag stuck.

Waylon's gamble paid off, and in 1974 he had back-to-back #1
records with "This Time" and "I'm a Ramblin' Man." It was the
first time in his ten-year stay with RCA that he'd had a chart-topper.
Two years later RCA decided to come to the party and released a
compilation of songs by Waylon, Tompall, Willie Nelson and Waylon's wife, Jessi Colter: *Wanted: The Outlaws*. It became the first
Nashville-produced million-selling album in country history. Ironically, the rock-tinged Outlaws movement had started as a reaction
to the slick Nashville Sound, and both eras had expanded country
music's audience in leaps and bounds.

The term Outlaw soon came to stand for people who broke tradi-
tion or balked at prettifying themselves or their music. The heir
apparent to Waylon and the Outlaws is Marietta, Georgia, native
Travis Tritt. He didn't start out in the Badlands, though, but in
church.

"WE ATTENDED THE Assembly of God Church, and after Sunday
school, they had adult church and 'children's church,' where we

did everything from sing to color and listen to Bible stories. One of the teachers taught us Ray Stevens's 'Everything Is Beautiful,' and I got to do the solo parts. We rehearsed for weeks and weeks before going upstairs to sing it for the big folks. I remember feeling so small and being really overwhelmed when I got a standing ovation. See, it wasn't considered appropriate to applaud a solo in our church. I heard the applause and I was hooked.''

He taught himself to play guitar when he was eight, and by the time he turned fourteen he'd written his first song, a love song he hoped would impress a potential girlfriend. ''I was fourteen years old and dating a girl who was eighteen,'' Travis says. ''Man, I thought I was hot. This girl and I even went to the Gulf Shores for spring break. I told my mother that I was going somewhere else, of course. Well, the very first day we were on the beach, the girl dumped me for one of the lifeguards. I remember sitting on a life-guard stand at four in the morning, waiting for him to come by just so I could hit him on the head with my guitar. He never came by, so I wrote this song I called 'Spend a Little Time with Me, Baby.' I didn't have any idea what I was doing, but I just poured my heart out.''

I'm sorry he lost the girl, but glad that the experience helped lay the foundation for one of the top success stories of country music in the nineties. ''I wanted to be an entertainer from the time I was a little boy,'' Travis says. ''But it was a hidden aspiration. My dad and grandfather were farmers, people who worked hard their whole lives. Most of the guys Dad knew who'd tried to be musicians were, in his opinion, just 'too sorry to work.' He reminded me of that all the time, usually adding that the pickers he knew were drunks or drug addicts who hung out in honky-tonks and bars. He'd say, 'That is exactly how you'll turn out if you do this, too!'

''So I tried to keep my dreams hidden. I'd go in my bedroom and lock the door and pretend a pencil was a microphone, singing songs along with the record player. My dad would scream, 'You need to get out of the house more! All you do is stay in the house and listen to records.' But I was enthralled with music.''

But after much soul-searching, Dad did relent and buy his son a twelve-string guitar when Travis was fourteen. Travis had been lis-tening to James Taylor and John Denver records, and since they both included twelve-string guitars, he wanted one, too. At first his father balked, saying it would make too much "racket." Travis knew his father wanted him to cultivate hobbies more along the lines of hunting and fishing, anything having to do with the great out-of-doors, so he decided to compromise.

"Dad loved being outside, especially watching the seasons change. Every fall we took a trip to North Carolina to watch the leaves change color. That was back before the park service closed off all the trash cans, so we'd see bears at the road stops. We would stop in Cherokee, North Carolina, to watch the Indian dances and that sort of thing."

With full understanding of his father's feelings, Travis gave his parents an option about Christmas, saying, "Well, if I can't have the guitar, can I have a twenty-two rifle?"

About a week before Christmas, Travis's dad and mother were having breakfast, and he suggested they go to the local music store when they finished. "Whatever for?" Mrs. Tritt asked her husband. "We're going to have to get Travis that guitar," he replied. "I know he's not going to be happy with anything else." Travis says it was the most surprised he's ever been on a Christmas morning, and he played that cherished twelve-string for the next six years.

"That guitar opened up a whole new world for me," he confesses. "Because I was able to learn to play better. I still don't consider myself to be a fabulous player, but the extra six strings on that guitar gave me a louder sound, and I was better able to accompany myself on solo performances."

Travis worked a variety of jobs through his teenage years. He worked for his uncles in their construction company, starting out as a gofer and working his way up to framing and trim work. He worked as a house painter, a bag boy at a local grocery store and even mowed lawns for extra money. After leaving high school, Travis went to work for a heating and air conditioning company, first as a truck driver, and later as a manager who distinguished himself by going up against company owners on behalf of his men.

"We were required to do inventory every April," Travis says. "It was an elaborate process, because there are so many small items in that business. For example, there was one bin with just screws— thousands of them that nobody wanted to count, but we did because we got an incentive bonus for each inventory. I was very responsible about doing those inventories, and I think that helped me get promoted into management. One day I came to work and was told that all our bonuses were being cut by seventy-five percent. I asked, 'Why?' They gave me a runaround about having to buy new trucks and new phones, and I said, 'Well, you should have told us before we did all this bean counting!'

"I went to my employees and told them I thought we should all hand in our resignations, and the next morning the vice president of the company had them all stacked on his desk. Every single person in the company went along with us, and my resignation was right on top. I was the leader of the pack. We ended up getting our bonuses and keeping our jobs."

When I asked Travis if he became a hero at the company, he just grinned. "Well, I did a lot of things that made people mad over the years," he said. "But it wasn't a question of being a hero, it was a question of doing the right thing."

Travis quit his job at the trucking company to pursue music full time, working in area clubs headlining everything from country and rock shows to sitting in with house bands at after-hours blues bars. His first band was named Southern Bred, after one of his favorite songs, "My Home's in Alabama," by Alabama. It was during this time that Travis came up with what he calls an Immutable Law of Honky-Tonk.

"If a fight ever breaks out when you're playing a honky-tonk, the first thing you should do is launch into a version of 'Silent Night.' I've seen big old two-hundred-fifty-pound men stop fighting and break down and cry at that song. It's amazing."

I knew of a few entertainers who would sing "The Star-Spangled Banner" to stop a fight, but I told Travis I'd never heard of anyone singing "Silent Night." "Well, I had always heard you should do a ballad," he explained. "And one night a fight broke out, and for the life of me I couldn't think of any slow song except 'Silent Night,' so I sung that!"

He eventually came to the attention of Warner Bros. Nashville-based pop promo executive Danny Davenport, who became a fan and worked two years to help Travis obtain a contract with the Warner's country division. Once signed, Travis remained fearless in his quest to be his own man. One of the first things the label told him was to change his name. "We started recording in 1987, and didn't release our first single until 1989," Travis says. "At that time, of course, Randy Travis was on the label and was hot as a pistol. The first thing I heard was, 'Everybody is going to confuse you with Randy Travis.' They were scared of it and started a contest within the label. They sent everyone a picture and said, 'You name this artist.' A lot of times they tried to incorporate my first name, James. There was James Hunter and a ton of different names that came down the pike. Finally, thank goodness, one of the vice presidents walked in and we were sitting around debating the issue and he said, 'Why don't we just let him keep his name? It sounds like a stage name. It sounds like a name that a performer would have. His music is so different from Randy Travis that nobody is going to get the two confused. Just let it go.' He was really the first real advocate for me keeping my own name."

The concern proved based in reality on at least one occasion, though. When I interviewed Travis for *On the Record,* he told me about playing a Las Vegas concert with Barbara Mandrell early in his career. The names Barbara Mandrell and Travis Tritt were twenty-five feet high out on the marquee, and Travis was impressed, thinking he'd hit the big time. That was before he had to walk past the crowd waiting for tickets.

"I had to walk past the line of people who were lined up outside waiting to get in the building and there was no other way to get to the elevators," Travis recalled. "I must have walked by six hundred people on the way to the elevators, and not one person recognized me. That deflated the old ego a little bit. I got up to my room and came back down and was standing in the elevator waiting to go back down to go onstage. There were two old ladies standing there talking and one said to her friend, 'I'm really looking forward to the show tonight.' The friend replied, 'Yes. I am too. What time does that nice young Randy Travis start playing anyway?'

"I thought, 'Ladies, we are all in trouble.' "

Travis is not a hat act, possibly due in part to the fact that wearing cowboy hats used to get him in trouble. "That was during the Urban Cowboy craze," Travis reflects with a laugh. "There were a few guys in my school who wore cowboy hats and boots, and we really stuck out. In one way, I think it was a way to get through an identity crisis by grabbing attention. More than one teacher told me to take off the hat or get out when I walked into the classroom. Being the outlaw I was, I usually got out. Luckily, I baby-sat the assistant principal's dogs, and he'd usually let me off easy."

There was initial concern about his music, with Warner fearing his raw sound would turn off country traditionalists. Still, Travis stood his ground. "I think if you are in country music these days and you want to do something different, and have a definite idea of what your records should sound like, how you want your career to progress, you should go with your instincts. It's a constant battle, though, because the professionals will always have different ideas. I've tried to follow the example of people like Waylon Jennings who maintained one thing throughout his career and that is his music. That's what I've tried to do. I write it. I sing it. I play it. Nobody knows it better than I do and that's why I do it my own way."

Waylon couldn't have said it any better.

It's easy to understand why Travis Tritt's music is diverse when you look at his influences, which range from Ray Charles and Muddy Waters to Willie Nelson and George Jones to Aerosmith and ZZ Top. That he loved the music of Elvis Presley is evident, and Travis says what impressed him the most about the King of Rock 'n' Roll was his obvious love of country and gospel music. Travis's diverse influences are evident in his live show, which includes everything from his rendition of The Eagles' "Take It Easy" to Steve Earle's "Copperhead Road" to Johnny Cash's "I Walk the Line" and Merle Haggard's "Mama Tried."

Another artist Travis loved from an early age was Roger Miller. "I've thought about it a lot over the years, and I think it was Roger's comedy that drew me to him. Songs like 'Do-Wacka-Do' and 'Burma Shave' caught my ear as a little kid. One of my first records was Roger Miller singing 'King of the Road.' You didn't have to twist my arm to sing it for other people, either. I could snap my fingers, and I'd break into 'King of the Road' at a moment's notice. It didn't matter if it was in the middle of a shopping center or a grocery store or in church on Sunday!"

Travis loves Southern rock, the musical form that he calls rock that's not afraid to show its country roots. "I wish I had a dollar for every time I camped outside a record store or a mall waiting for Hank Williams Jr. tickets to go on sale," Travis says. "Hank would always come in February, which meant the tickets would go on sale in January. But despite the cold weather, I'd get off work on Friday night and sleep in my pickup that night to be ready for the ticket office to open on Saturday morning. Hank Jr., Charlie Daniels, Waylon Jennings—those were my heroes."

One edge Travis believed rock acts had over most country performers was a high-energy stage show. Hank Jr. showed him that country could compete when it came to high energy. "A lot of the country performers just walked out on stage and sang," Travis says. "If you went to a rock 'n' roll show, you saw smoke and lights and people running around on stage having a good time. It appealed to me a lot more. Hank Jr. was the first person I saw in country who did that. He incorporated all the elements of a rock 'n' roll show, but put them in a country format. But he is also one of the first I ever saw who would walk out with just an acoustic guitar, and play five or six, maybe ten, songs with just his guitar accompanying him. It's one thing to perform for ten thousand people with a six-piece band backing you up. It's another to be stripped down to you and a guitar in front of a crowd. That's where the real entertainer comes in."

I found it puzzling that with all the edge artists Travis listed as heroes, he listed John Denver as a favorite. John was pretty mellow when compared to Hank Jr., the Allman Brothers, ZZ Top, Charlie Daniels *and* Travis Tritt. Travis explained that his affection for John's music was a result of his early upbringing.

"That is a side of me that came from when I was a kid doing gospel music. Waylon and Charlie Daniels might not go over too big with the church crowd, but they could dig John Denver. I was a huge John Denver fan—never missed a show when he played Atlanta. I watched all his specials, and at one point I even thought about being a forest ranger because of John's work on behalf of the environment."

Fortunately for his legions of fans, Travis chose music. He did have to make a few early concessions, such as cutting his hair, which he kept long because women loved it that way. He capitulated after getting a call from the label, who said they were afraid they'd run up against some radio programmer who'd been wanting his heavy metal–listening teenage son to cut his long hair. The programmer might be telling his son to get a trim, and hear the son say, "But Dad, you play Travis Tritt's records and he's got hair as long as mine." Travis cut his hair, and regretted it immediately.

"It is a mistake I made simply because I was young, inexperienced and hungry for a deal," Travis says. "All I wanted was to make music and records and I didn't know then a lot of the things I know now. I went with what the 'professionals' told me. I felt like I had sold myself out for what somebody else wanted and not done what I really wanted to do."

But Travis Tritt's career took off, and it didn't seem to matter whether his hair was long or short, his music edgy and his name similar to one of country's biggest stars. His first single, "Country Club," was released in September 1989, and it shot to top-10 in *Billboard.* The wait from 1982, when Warner executive Danny Davenport first heard him sing, until Travis's 1989 sessions must have seemed like an eternity, but it did serve a purpose. It gave Travis a chance to observe the industry as an insider, before his own career was on the line.

"I probably had a better idea than most performers coming in, because I was unofficially tied in with Warner Bros. for seven years before I had a release. I got to go backstage at a lot of shows, and it was like being a fly on the wall. I started to learn what to expect. But even with the advance knowledge, I wasn't completely prepared for it. Once it took off, it was like a hurricane. I've wished a million times that I'd taken the time each night to write in a journal or a diary. So many things were passing through my life in a short space of time. My advice to everyone—whether you are a performer or not—is this: Sit down every night and write down what happened to you that day. Sooner or later you'll forget it, and trust me, it's important stuff. It's your life."

Travis's life changed drastically with the success of "Country Club." The song broke debut single sales records, quickly selling over 220,000 copies. His second single, "Help Me Hold On," released in 1990, was his first #1. He followed that success with "I'm Gonna Be Somebody," which hit #2, and "Put Some Drive in Your Country," which only charted in the 20s, but defined the man and his music, becoming a concert staple. By 1991 he was back in the top-5 with "Drift Off to Dream" and "Here's a Quarter (Call Someone Who Cares)," which he'd penned when his second wife left him, then suggested a reconciliation on the very day he was served with divorce papers. It turned out to be one of his career records, and he soon learned a big lesson about song lyrics and overly enthusiastic audiences.

"I had to threaten to stop performing 'Here's a Quarter,' " Travis says. "People started throwing them on the stage and the band and I were getting hit. When you play a little club it doesn't matter, and in fact, the guys and I loved it because we'd scoop up the money and buy VCR tapes for the bus. But in an arena the throwing of coins can get dangerous. Lynyrd Skynyrd had the same problem when they released 'Give Me Back My Bullets.' People started throwing live ammunition at them! Once I explained to the audience that it's dangerous to throw a metal object at people on a stage, it slowed down. People do it once in a while, but not often. I hated to have to resort to the threat of walking offstage, because the fans are who got you there. But my fans seemed to understand."

His fans included those in the industry, and while Travis has not been the darling of the awards shows, he's won some coveted prizes, including the 1991 Country Music Association's Horizon Award. When he took the stage to accept the award, he cracked:

"Wow! Well, maybe now people will stop calling me Randy!"

The award brought immediate career results, upping both his album sales and concert price. "Awards haven't been a necessity for sustaining my career," Travis reflects. "There was a period of time when I was nominated for practically everything but Homecoming Queen. But I've learned that the most important award you can get is when they tell you you've sold a million, or two million albums. That means that the fans who work hard for their dollars have gone to the store and chosen to spend their money on your record. There's no politics involved in that. There's nothing but allegiance, the fans saying they love what you do."

In that case, Travis has at least fourteen million "awards," having sold in excess of that number of albums. Travis considers his first platinum album a career milestone, as was becoming a member of the Grand Ole Opry. Another personal and career highlight was his friendship and collaborative efforts with another country favorite, Marty Stuart, which resulted in winning a 1993 Grammy for their duet "This One's Gonna Hurt You (For a Long, Long Time)." What was it that brought the two stars together as friends and partners?

"I have Marty Stuart hair envy," Travis deadpans. "Seriously, Marty and I met as a result of one of Marty's songs, 'The Whiskey Ain't Workin'.' I'd met him at the 1990 CMA awards. I was walking down the hall, half shell-shocked. There's all these stars back there. You'll pass by Loretta Lynn and Johnny Cash and Garth Brooks and Randy Travis. You just can't take it all in. I was thrilled to be there, and couldn't quite believe I was a part of it all. So in the middle of everything I see this guy with really tall hair, and it's Marty. We simultaneously pointed at each other and said, 'I like what you do.' Then we kept on walking.

"A few weeks later Marty sent me 'The Whiskey Ain't Workin',' and we decided to do it as a duet. We really got to know each other when we shot the video for the song, and spent our time between takes sitting on Marty's bus. We talked about our backgrounds, and how we grew up. Both of us are sons of the South. We found we had a lot in common, and in the years since then, we've just grown better friends. He's the closest thing to a brother I ever had."

The success of "Whiskey" and the Grammy-winning "This One's Gonna Hurt You" resulted in two highly successful tours: No Hats, in 1992, and Double Trouble in 1997. The two continue to record and tour together from time to time, but don't compare them to another top team, Waylon and Willie. "I don't like that comparison, because I don't think there will ever be anyone as good as Waylon and Willie," Travis says. Travis invited Marty to be the best man at his 1997 wedding to Theresa Nelson, although, according to the groom, there was always the chance that pal Marty would find a job he preferred to Best Man duties:

"He could have decided to park cars." Travis laughs. "Because he's got some really nice valet jackets. I told him I'd prefer he didn't wear rhinestones because there is an airport close to my house and I was afraid planes would start crashing thinking there was some kind of a sequin beacon down on my lawn."

And while Travis and Marty dubbed the '97 tour "Double Trouble," Travis's life had settled down considerably since this last trip to the altar. Success and his second divorce had arrived close to the same time and ushered in a period of frantic partying for the young singer. The newly single new star found girls waiting at every stage door. And like the outlaws of old, he found them hard to turn down.

"You have to understand my background to grasp my frame of mind at the time," Travis explains. "I was never Mister Don Juan when it came to women. People laugh when I say that, but it's true. I was real shy while I was growing up. My guitar introduced me to every girl I ever met. As far as walking up and introducing myself to a girl, or asking her to go out to a club or to a dance—I was never good at any of that. I always thought of myself as semi-ugly. Then all of a sudden I didn't have to go looking for girls, because they were looking for me. I don't say that arrogantly or egotistically. It's just a fact of life when you're in the spotlight."

Travis says the groupie situation on the road was worse than drugs or alcohol. And even more dangerous. "AIDS can literally take your life, and until I thought that through, I was taking a lot of chances. I was playing Russian roulette out there on the road."

I asked Travis how he made the decision to stop, whether he read a newspaper article or watched a news broadcast. Travis attributed his lifestyle change to his mother and his grandfather, an Assembly of God minister. "I had a good upbringing," he says. "I've always been able to identify things that would get me in the long run. I smoked cigarettes from the time I was seventeen until I turned twenty-six. One day I quit, and it was because I knew they'd kill me someday. I drank enough liquor to float a battleship. I took pills, uppers. Like my song says, it made me feel like I was 'ten feet tall and bulletproof.' I talked to so many of my heroes about it—Johnny Cash, Waylon, Charlie Daniels. They all said, 'If you go out there and take a bunch of pills and drink, you'll feel good for a little while, but in the long run it will get you.' And I figured out the Big Lie about drugs and alcohol: when you are younger you think they are great, that you can run around and do drugs and drink and it doesn't faze you. But it's catching up with you every day. That understanding started a period of great change for me. Now I am straighter, cleaner and happier than I've ever been in my life."

On February 18, 1998, Travis and Theresa Tritt welcomed the birth of their first child, Tyler Reese.

WHATEVER IT TAKES

THE PETITE BLOND teenager strolled through the lobby of a downtown Nashville hotel with the self-confidence of a young lady meeting her parents for dinner and a show. But she didn't stop at the restaurant, taking the elevator to the upper floors instead. She alighted on the fourth floor, but when a group of partying tourists spilled out of a room, she returned to the elevator. On another floor she glanced up and down the hall, saw nothing and no one. She quickly hopped back on the elevator.

The third time was the charm. No one was in the hall, just a large, covered room service tray left for the housekeeping staff to pick up. She lifted the lid from the tray and hastily stuffed a partially eaten steak, an almost untouched baked potato and two rolls in her bag. Then she hurried back to the elevator and made her getaway. It was Dolly Parton's first meal that day, and she was glad to have it.

But at least she didn't feel guilty, as she so often did at the supermarket. "I went hungry a lot when I first came to town," Dolly recalls. "When I really got desperate I would go to Kroger's or Hill's and push a cart around like I was shopping. I'd stop at the deli and pick up a sandwich, unwrap it and eat it, then leave the cart and go home! I'm not proud of that, but once I made it I bought enough food there to pay them back."

That single-minded will to survive on the road to success is shared with many superstars, although I don't know if they've all been quite as inventive as Dolly.

11

RAY CHARLES:

COUNTRY'S IMPROBABLE

HERO

I first met Ray Charles when I was recording for ABC Paramount in 1965. My A&R guy was Fred Carter Jr., who, in addition to heading up ABC's Nashville office, was one of the greatest session guitarists in the business. Of course, these days he's probably best known as the father of one of this year's new stars, Deana Carter. Fred called me one day and asked me to accompany him to some ABC meetings in Hollywood, Florida. All the label's big brass and distributors and artists were going to be there.

I went to some of the business meetings with him and listened to all the speeches. We went to some label breakfasts, lunches and that sort of thing. One night there was a big "meet and greet" in one of the hotel ballrooms, where everybody got together for the first time. People were hovering all over somebody by the back wall, and when they thinned out a little, I could see that it was Ray Charles.

Ray Charles is an improbable hero in country history. Perhaps more than any singer from another genre, he brought a new fan base to country music. His *Modern Sounds in Country & Western Music* was #1 for fourteen weeks on the pop charts. The single, "I Can't Stop Loving You," was #1 for five weeks. The album's very title implies something different from normal country fare at the time: *Modern Sounds.* Ray recorded the album away from Nashville, utilizing pop-flavored arrangements. The result was that thousands of

Ray's fans—blacks, college students and pop music fans—heard country songs for the first time. And they realized how powerful these simple lyrics could be.

ABC hadn't wanted Ray to make the record, fearing he'd lose his fan base. But Ray thought otherwise. "I think I'll gain some new fans," he told ABC president Sam Clark. Country radio didn't play *Modern Sounds in Country & Western Music,* but I was very familiar with the album and appreciated what Ray had done for our music. Not long before ABC's convention in 1965, Ray had played a show in Nashville, and some very big stars had come out to hear him. I was hoping to have the opportunity to tell him about that, so when the crowd finally dispersed, I went over and introduced myself.

"Mr. Charles, are you aware that when you played Nashville a while back, both Chet Atkins and Jerry Reed were in the audience?"

He said he hadn't known it, but he certainly loved country music.

"Who's your favorite country singer?" I asked.

"George Jones," he answered without a moment's hesitation.

"What's your favorite country song?"

Again, there was no hesitation. "A Girl I Used to Know," which was a Jack Clement song that George Jones had a big hit with in 1962. We spoke for a while and I was impressed by Ray's knowledge of country music, but I didn't learn that he actually started out in country music until 1983, when he visited my syndicated radio show, which we taped at the audio facility at Channel 4 in Nashville.

I had Rick Blackburn to thank for having Ray come on the show. Rick was heading up CBS Records in Nashville, and in what Rick called "an irregular signing" had offered Ray a record contract. The two had been in contract negotiations for months. The irregular part came when Ray wouldn't let Rick bring the corporate lawyers! "Ray's a damn good street attorney," Rick told *Variety Weekly* in 1982. "I wasn't allowed to bring an attorney. That's the height of intimidation." But with or without lawyers on the front end, the two struck a deal. "There's a real fine line between black music and country music," Rick went on to say. "Both have a lot of feeling in what they do."

Ray Charles doesn't consider himself any specific "kind" of singer. He says he's not a blues singer or an R&B singer or a country singer. He's a singer who loves blues, jazz, country, pop—many

forms of music. Mainly, he likes songs that tell a story. He doesn't
believe in trends, which has certainly played a role in his longevity.
He was reared in the South and listened to everything from blues
to boogie to the big band sounds of Count Basie and Tommy Dor-
sey. He also listened to and loved the Grand Ole Opry. And he
started his musical journey in country music. By the time we did the
interview on WSM, I'd learned that the first steady gig Ray Charles
ever played was with Tampa's Florida Playboys.

"The Florida Playboys was a hillbilly group—or a country
group—I get confused to know how to describe it," he recalled. "It
was back in 1947 or '48, and I was around sixteen years old. What
happened was that one of the musicians worked at a record store
that I would frequent. I couldn't buy anything because I didn't have
any money, but I'd go there and listen and look at the pianos and
touch them and nobody would throw me out. Since I could play the
piano the guy took a liking to me. One day he said, 'You know, R.C.,'
that's what they called me in those days, 'our pianist is ill and since
you can play, how would you like to come out and make the gig?'
Well, naturally, if you're hungry you want to do it, so it's like, 'Boom,
let's go!'

"We went out the first night and I enjoyed myself, so when the
band asked me to come out on a regular basis, I said yes. I still
feel embarrassed talking about taking a guy's job who's sick. But he
couldn't continue, and I ended up getting a job with the Florida
Playboys. The good thing about them is that they worked all the
time. They played every night. We played a lot of small clubs, but it
was work. You'd make ten or fifteen dollars a night, which was pretty
good in those days."

Not only did Ray play the piano with the Playboys, he took the
lead vocals at times. One of his specialties was Eddy Arnold's "Anytime." That song includes a yodel, and to prove just how serious he
was about his country roots, Ray Charles yodeled on the airwaves
during our interview! "I think I'm a pretty good yodeler," he said.
"You know how they do in the Swiss Alps? I can do that kind of
yodeling, but I learned it from these guys."

I don't know if there is another major R&B artist who can yodel.
But I doubt it. Of course, there are few who have mastered as many
kinds of music as Ray Charles. His stylistic range is phenomenal:

blues, country, jazz, symphony pops, boogie. The thread that holds it all together is his unique approach to a song, and his love of solid material.

"I'm one of those kind of people who is very emotional," Ray explained during our talk. "I don't know if that's good or bad, but it's the truth. And songs do things to me. Music does things to me. When I told ABC Records that I was going to do a country record in 1962, the label discussed it and decided, 'If it don't kill your career, go ahead.' I asked them for songs so they talked to various publishing companies. I started listening and went through maybe 200 or 250 songs. I found this song of Don Gibson's, 'I Can't Stop Loving You.' What attracted me to the song were the two lines: 'I can't stop loving you. I've made up my mind.' *That's it!* Not that the rest is less, but the hook line was the thing that *snatched* me. There's a lotta people feel like that, people who think this way: 'You done did everything that you could possibly do to me, but *I can't stop loving you.*' That's what attracted me to it."

Willie Nelson went so far as to say that Ray's recording of "I Can't Stop Loving You" did more for country music than any other single release by an artist ever had. I told Ray that a lot of people, both country fans and non-country fans, had been affected by the record. I'd recently had the Oak Ridge Boys on the show. I knew Ray was making another country album and I asked them if they thought country fans would like Ray Charles.

"I think most of them already do," Duane Allen said. "Because Ray Charles has had a love for country music as long as I can remember. I remember that album with 'I Can't Stop Loving You' on it and a lot of other standards. The way Ray Charles sang them, they were brand new again." Joe Bonsall agreed. "Some of the ways I heard country music was listening to Ray Charles sing the songs back in Philadelphia. That's the way a lot of people heard country music for the first time."

When I shared that story with Ray, he was genuinely touched. He stammered at the praise, and admitted he didn't know how to respond to it. In fact, I was impressed at the man's honesty and lack of any pretense during the time we talked. His love of country music was obvious, and he knew a great deal about it.

One of the songs he cut on the session came about because of a

tip from a stockbroker. Ray was on an airplane coming back to the
United States from Europe, and he struck up a conversation with
the man seated next to him. It turned out the man was a stockbroker, a Texan and a great fan of both George Jones and Ray Charles.
The fellow told Ray that George Jones had recorded a Red Lane
song titled "Ain't Your Memory Got No Pride," and that he believed it would be perfect for Ray. "I'll have to be honest," Ray told
me. "I wouldn't normally pay much attention to a person giving me
recording ideas on an airplane. But the reason I listened to this guy
was because I couldn't imagine a stockbroker, dealing in gold, living
in Texas and liking George Jones and Ray Charles! Usually stockbro-
kers can't tap time to nothing. That's not where their minds are. So
when I got home I had someone find the record, and the song was
perfect for me. It spoke to me, and that's what I have to have in a
lyric. So I didn't get any market tips, just a good song tip."

Like Conway Twitty, Ray Charles is a friend to songs. He listens
carefully because he wants the song to say something, as well as be
right for him as an individual and an artist. "I always like to think
that songs have to fit the artist. I have to find good songs, but they
also have to be ones that I can fit. I don't want to say the song has
to fit me. I need to find ones I can fit. If not, I can't get into it. I'm
very much into lyrics that tell a story. It's very much like an actor or
actress who gets a script. You read the script and think to yourself,
'Can I put me in this script, can I become what this script says?' I
look for songs that tell me what I want to hear."

Ray Charles has been making music in that honest way since his
1957 chart debut on Atlantic Records with "Swanee River Rock
(Talkin' 'Bout the River)." In 1959 he made his move into the top-
10 pop charts with "What'd I Say (Part 1)," and 1960's "Georgia
on My Mind" established him as a star. He was born Ray Charles
Robinson on September 23, 1930, in Albany, Georgia. While he was
still an infant, his family moved to Greenville, Florida, where Ray
grew up. The family was very poor, and lived in what Ray calls a
"shotgun shack." When he was around four years old he was taken
under the creative wing of a saloon boogie-woogie piano player
named Wylie Pittman, who instilled in the boy a love for boogie and
blues. At age six he started going blind. Ray doesn't know what illness caused his blindness. He says it could have been something as

simple as childhood measles. Ray credits his mother with his independent streak. She taught him that his lack of sight didn't mean his mind or talent was lacking, and that being blind shouldn't stop him from making his own place in the world. That place was not on the street begging, either. Ray's mother was determined that her son be self-sufficient. He attended the State School for the Deaf and the Blind in St. Augustine, Florida, where he began studying piano, organ, clarinet and trumpet. Like the rest of the country, the school for the deaf and blind was segregated. "We stayed on one side and the whites stayed on the other," Ray says.

That experience and other hurts affected Ray, but not by making him bitter. On the contrary, if anything, it turned him more philosophical. "When I look at my life overall, I have to say that I've had just enough hurt to teach me. When my feelings were hurt, it inspired me in the end. Life will always provide two things: happiness and sadness. You have to understand that. If you can, you learn how to deal with the pain that comes from personal problems or race discrimination or whatever, and gain from it."

Ray Charles didn't come across as a civil rights activist. He has strong beliefs, but to draw them out in a radio interview proved tough. Just as he was an improbable country music hero, he is somewhat of a reluctant political activist. He'd much rather talk about music than discrimination. I told him I could recall the early '50s, when Nat King Cole came south with his shows. It was a time when this nation was in turmoil, and Nat had problems appearing in the South. I wondered what Ray's experience was.

"No, it never happened to me," Ray said. "Nat was in a different type of market. He was involved in the pop field, and had a lot of white clientele. A lot of his audience was white. I became an artist— a star if you want to call it that—in the black community, and the places I played were black clubs. The only problems I had were the normal ones, like when you gotta go to the bathroom, you can't. You want to eat, you can't. But nobody wanted to do something to me because maybe somebody wanted to hug my neck. That could have happened to Nat in the clubs he played. But not in the clubs I played. I stayed in rooming hotels that allowed blacks. I wouldn't be going to the Hilton or the Sheraton. I think it started to make some difference where you could notice it around the early sixties.

But I don't think it started to get to the point that you wouldn't be afraid. I would say it didn't change to where you could really go anyplace you wanted or walk into a restaurant without fear until 1964 or '65. Of course, we're still arguing about what we're going to do about the schools and this is 1983. Now you know why we better talk about music."

After establishing himself as a top sideman on the Florida music scene, Ray headed West in 1947 with $900 he'd saved. He ended up in Seattle, Washington, and soon formed a group called the Maxim Trio. The trio was a big success in Seattle's speakeasies, and the men were offered a local television show. Ray says he was still trying to emulate Nat King Cole and Charles Brown back in those days, but even though he had not yet developed his inimitable style, Down Beat Records signed him to a deal in 1948. Ironically, around the same time Down Beat changed its name to Swing Time, Ray Charles Robinson dropped his last name to avoid confusion with fighter Sugar Ray Robinson. In 1952, Ray's Swing Time contract was purchased by Atlantic Records and it was Atlantic chief Ahmet Ertegun who encouraged Ray to drop the Charles Brown imitation and be himself. What a difference it made, because Ray Charles's musical self is second to none.

When Ray came to visit me at WSM in February of 1983, over twenty years after his *Modern Sounds* album, he was promoting his upcoming CBS project, *Wish You Were Here Tonight,* set for release in July of '84. His approach was going to be different this time out. "Back in '62, I took country songs that I loved and did them in a contemporary pop manner. I might have had twenty-four strings in the chorus. But this time, we're really getting down to the nitty-gritty, using the flavor and seasoning of country music. It is a first for me in that way. I'm really getting into the music with the country musicians themselves. We've got that integrated thing where it flows."

I asked Ray if any country pickers had played on that first record, and he admitted he didn't have any idea. "I've found out one thing about musicians. You never can tell about them. I ran into a fiddle player today and he shocked me by playing jazz! He's playing country music here in Nashville and he starts playing me something by Miles Davis. So we mighta had some hillbilly cats on the first album,

The wonderful Loretta Lynn in a publicity shot with me just prior to telling her life story in the television series *On the Record*. When I rolled a clip of Loretta and Conway Twitty on the show, she said, "I can't look at that." *(Photograph by Jim Hagans)*

As a reward for a lifetime of devotion to her craft, Brenda Lee goes into the Country Music Hall of Fame, September 1997. Here a happy Brenda holds the plaque given to her by the Country Music Association.

(Photograph by Lee Cahn, courtesy of CMA)

What can I say, I love to hang with beautiful women. Like Faith Hill, Barbara Mandrell and Reba McEntire, in Aspen, Colorado, Christmas '95. The other beautiful woman in my life, Joy, took the picture.

A very pensive Faron Young alongside Kathy Mattea at a rehearsal for a tribute show. It turned out to be a nice surprise for me.

March 1991. My wife, Joy, threw a surprise birthday party for me and invited some of my closest friends. A few didn't make it but these did *(from left to right):* Tom T. Hall (what a smile); my family attorney, Tom Binkley, and his wife, Joyce; Leona Atkins (Mrs. Chet); Henry Cannon (Mr. Minnie); the birthday boy; Minnie Pearl (the last picture I had taken with her before her stroke the following June); the Godfather of the Guitar, Mr. Chet Atkins; Dixie (Mrs. Tom T.) Hall, a lady who loves dogs or couldn't you tell? It was a nice day.

Fred Foster pictured here, July 26, 1981, with June Carter Cash and Kris Kristofferson. In the book you will find the story of Fred giving this very talented man his biggest break. *(Photograph courtesy of Fred Foster)*

I was host in 1980 to a Nashville-based television show that never went into production. My guest was Ray Stevens. I was unexpectedly joined on the set by a "gorilla." When the creature pulled off its head, I discovered my wife, Joy, was inside the costume. *(Photograph by Don Putnam)*

Johnny Cash, Christmas special: "This Train Is Bound for Glory." Late '70s, taped at the Grand Ole Opry. *From left to right:* Carl Perkins, Roy Orbison, Johnny Cash, Jerry Lee Lewis. *(Photograph courtesy of Broadcast Music Inc.)*

This is just what it seems to be, an autographed picture Colonel Tom Parker sent to me after the rare telephone interview I did with him. On the back it has a poem written by the Colonel that was a tribute to Elvis.

THE
COLONEL
Longtime Friend &
Manager of ELVIS

THE COLONEL SAYS:
VISIT
Graceland
Memphis, TN

Ray Charles tells us in the pages of this book how his career started in country music. This is Ray as he appeared on the Johnny Cash television show about 1970. *(Photograph courtesy of Broadcast Music Inc.)*

Ronnie Dunn and Kix Brooks, country's hottest duo, who enriched the country dance scene in 1992 with their mega hit, "Boot Scootin' Boogie." They are great showmen. *(Photograph by Jim Hagans)*

I love this job. I get to meet the most interesting people. In this scene, I am sharing a laugh with country rocker Travis Tritt. I found him to be intelligent, with a drive to succeed. He doesn't avoid the hardball questions. *(Photograph by Jim Hagans)*

Two of the most berserk stories involved legendary country music singer Johnny Horton, who is pictured in 1959 with his producer, Don Law of Columbia Records. This was about the time of Johnny's multimillion-seller, "The Battle of New Orleans." *(Photograph by C. Escott)*

Picture of Hank Williams taken in his prime, probably about 1950.

Dolly Parton and some of her old friends gathered at Tootsie's Orchid Lounge to tape a segment for her television show. We told old show business stories for over two hours, and I think they used only three or four minutes of that. *From left to right:* Uncle Bill Owens, me, Faron Young, Porter Wagoner, Fred Foster, Curley Putman, Johnny Russell, Bill Carlisle, Bill Phillips (in the hat), who recorded Dolly's first writing success, "Put It Off Until Tomorrow," Buck Trent, and Jimmy C. Newman, who gave up a spot on the Grand Ole Opry so that Dolly could make her debut. Of course, the lovely lady in the center is Dolly Parton.

Eddy Arnold and me in Nashville at the opening of the second RCA studio in 1965. We televised the event.

Olivia Newton-John is a remarkable woman who beat breast cancer. Her attitude toward life is very upbeat. I am applauding her here at the conclusion of our interview in front of a live audience. *(Photograph by Jim Hagans)*

"A Tough Act to Follow": Reba hosted *Nashville Now* one night and brought in some of the hottest names in the business. *From left to right:* Vince Gill, K. T. Oslin, Alan Jackson, Reba, and Garth Brooks. *(Photograph by Jim Hagans)*

For a brief time in the latter part of 1996, I did a live morning TV show for TNN from the Opryland Hotel. This was opening day with Ronnie McDowell, Porter Wagoner and Lorrie Morgan.

I first saw this picture at the Bradley Barn the day I interviewed Owen Bradley. I said, "We've got to have it for the book." *From left to right:* Loretta Lynn, Kitty Wells, Owen Bradley, k. d. lang and Brenda Lee. A moment of fun after cutting a record and video session for k. d. lang. *(Photograph courtesy of Brenda Lee)*

I have titled this picture, "The Punch Line." It is obviously a reaction by the legendary Roy Acuff and Minnie Pearl to someone's very funny joke. They were like big brother and little sister who loved working together.

Minnie Pearl, *right*, shares a laugh with Barbara Mandrell and me during a 1989 break from *Nashville Now*. This is one of my favorite pictures.

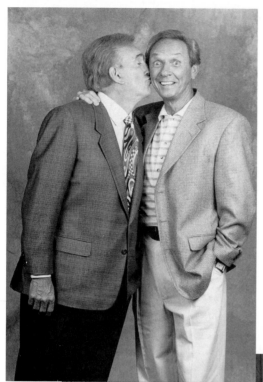

I love Mel Tillis.
Isn't it obvious?
*(Photograph by
Jim Hagans)*

A good picture of a very intense Patsy Cline. She is rehearsing for a show on Nashville's Channel 4 in the early 1960s. The guitarist on the left is the late Ernest Tubb. The mandolin player on the right is Rollin Sullivan, one half of the comedy team of Lonzo and Oscar.

(Photograph courtesy of the Country Music Foundation, Nashville, Tennessee)

April 1988. My dear friend Conway Twitty dressed in the style he found most comfortable. We had taken *Nashville Now* to the Grand Cayman Island.

(Photograph by Jim Hagans)

I call this my Simon & Garfunkel picture. It was the last week of *Nashville Now* and President George Bush honored us by coming to San Antonio for one of the final shows. We presented him with this special guitar and you will notice that he is a southpaw. Mr. President, if you're reading this, let's try "Mrs. Robinson" sometime.

(Photograph by Jim Hagans)

Roger Miller during one of his last visits with me. He died on October 25, 1992. *(Photograph by Jim Hagans)*

Chet Atkins was our special guest at *On the Record* with Vince Gill. He presented him with a guitar and played a duet with him. Chet told him if he didn't need another guitar, he could always use it as a boat paddle. *(Photograph by Jim Hagans)*

The first time I'd ever signed autographs in a bookstore. It was Dallas, Texas, December 1991, and this little girl's father asked if I would mind having my picture taken with her. She was eight years old at the time. Little did I know that I was meeting a future star—for this was the first time I ever laid eyes on LeAnn Rimes.

At the opening of the George Bush Presidential Library in College Station, Texas, when I saw the First Ladies come out of the front door, arm in arm, it took my breath away. This was November 6, 1997. *From left to right:* Lady Bird Johnson, Barbara Bush, Hillary Rodham Clinton, Betty Ford, Nancy Reagan and Rosalynn Carter. *(Photograph by Mark Sykes)*

Dolly tells a joke, to the absolute delight of Chet, myself, the live audience *and* Dolly. *(Photograph by Jim Hagans)*

This photo was given to all the artists attending the private funeral service for Tammy Wynette, to enable them to get into the public service at the Ryman. I think there is a lot of irony in the fact that a Tammy Wynette Backstage Pass was given out at her funeral. *(Photograph courtesy of Evelyn Shrider)*

I just don't know. But the concept was not to do the style of music, but to do the songs. I wanted to take Don Gibson or Hank Williams songs and do them with pop or contemporary arrangements. This time, what I really love is that we are really into the true flavor of the music itself. So I used some Nashville cats.''

Ray didn't know it until that day, but the Nashville cats who gave him the sound he wanted for *Wish You Were Here Tonight* were primarily guys from my *Nashville Alive* band. *Nashville Alive* was a weekend television show that I did for two seasons on WTBS, just prior to the arrival of The Nashville Network. He'd used Hoot Hester, Terry McMillian, Phil Baugh and Buddy Emmons, among others. He couldn't have found any better musicians anywhere, either.

Wish You Were Here Tonight didn't meet CBS Records's sales or chart expectations, and I think it was the material. Ray had great songs on there, but they were all unfamiliar songs. I think if they'd put four or five country standards on the album it would have been far more successful. The label followed it up with *Do I Ever Cross Your Mind* in 1984. But it was the next release that grabbed the interest of country fans and country radio: *Friendship,* Ray's collection of duets with country legends. "I started getting phone calls the minute word hit the street about Ray's initial signing,'' Rick Blackburn said. "Willie called. Merle called. Ricky Skaggs called. They all wanted to sing with Ray Charles.''

Friendship included duets with all three of the callers as well as with Johnny Cash and with Ray's favorite country singer, George Jones. CBS released five singles from *Friendship*. The first, "We Didn't See a Thing,'' went to #6 and featured Ray with George Jones, and Chet Atkins on guitar. "Rock and Roll Shoes,'' with B. J. Thomas, went to #14. The next release was the blockbuster. "Seven Spanish Angels,'' with Willie Nelson, was a #1 song and is still considered a classic of the genre. Although two more top-20 duets were released, "It Ain't Gonna Worry My Mind,'' with Mickey Gilley, and "Two Old Cats Like Us,'' with Hank Williams Jr., nothing came close to the Ray and Willie show.

"Country music is a lot like blues,'' Ray says. "It's simple, honest, and you don't have to be a genius to get it. If I was to direct someone to real country music, I'd send them looking for George Jones. I've been a fan of his since the early sixties. George has that real earthy sound of what I feel, like Hank Williams or Hank Snow. I'm not against modernization and I don't want to be misunderstood. But I love that real country sound in itself, the pureness of it without a room full of musicians. We should never let this sound—the sounds of the hills and mountains—slip away, no more than I think we should allow the genuine old-fashioned-type Muddy Waters blues slip away. Why? We Americans don't have nothing else, musically speaking. We don't have Bach and Beethoven or Tchaikovsky or Sibelius. They're other countries' music.

"But Muddy Waters, George Jones—we *own* that music! We can go to the bank with *that*."

A QUESTION OF GEOGRAPHY

I WAS HOSTING a morning television show on Channel 4 when, in 1965, Tom Jones burst onto the world's airwaves with back-to-back hits: "It's Not Unusual" and "What's New Pussycat?" Surprisingly, this international star was being managed in the United States not out of New York or Los Angeles, but by the Acuff-Rose organization in Nashville. My friend Joe Lucus at Acuff-Rose, who frequently called me to get their acts booked on the television show, let me know that Tom was in town. "Sure, bring him down," I said. "I'm a big fan."

Tom couldn't make it to the early morning live show—it was from 6:00 A.M. to 7:00 A.M.—so we taped him right after the noon show. He was a charming guy, and I believe, the first man I ever saw in person who had the long hair that became so popular during the '60s. And I think most of the people down at Channel 4 were in the same boat as me, since they kept stopping by the glass partition to stare at him. I know part of the attraction was that he was a big pop star, but we were still in the crew cut years here in Nashville and Tom certainly didn't have a crew cut.

Tom didn't yet understand the geography of the United States, just how vast this country really is. We were sitting in the studio talking about music and American artists he liked, when he suddenly said, "Do you have any idea where Jerry Lee Lewis is?" I told him I didn't, but that I'd call Jerry Lee's record label, Mercury, and find out. As it turned out, Jerry Lee was playing in Indianapolis, Indiana.

Tom turned to his manager and Joe Lucus and innocently said, "Could we run over to his show for a little while tonight?"

I said, "Tom, that's about a six-hour drive."

Tom must have thought it was like running down to the 7-Eleven.

Ten years later country radio "discovered" Tom Jones, and made his "Say You'll Stay Until Tomorrow" the #1 song in the nation.

12

PATSY CLINE:

IN SEARCH OF A SONG

Patsy Cline and Owen Bradley sat in his office one afternoon in 1958 listening to songs. They had stacks of them to go through, all sent by Four Star, the record company that had Patsy under contract. The songs were terrible, and Owen said so.

"I know," Patsy replied, close to tears. "Owen, they've got me cornered."

Owen told me his heart broke for Patsy that day, but he knew she was right. They had her cornered, and would continue to have her cornered for another three years. If there was ever an example of the importance of sacrificing the right songs for the wrong contract, it is the case of Patsy Cline.

Patsy's first big break came in 1948 when gospel singer Wally Fowler played a show in Winchester, Virginia, near Patsy's hometown of Gore. After Patsy maneuvered an audition, Wally invited her to Nashville, where he introduced her to the Opry's Jim Denny. Unfortunately, while Denny professed to love her singing, he wouldn't make the decision alone and asked for a second audition the following night. Patsy's mother didn't have enough money to stay at a motel, and they returned to Virginia. She continued to perform at local clubs and events, finally returning to Nashville in

1953. This time Ernest Tubb heard her and gave her a spot on his *Midnight Jamboree.*

In a classic case of two steps forward and five steps back, Patsy soon got involved with booker Connie B. Gay, and with Four Star Music's Bill McCall. Gay put her to work on his radio show at $50 per appearance, a definite step forward. But on September 30, 1954, she signed a recording contract with Bill McCall and Four Star, a California-based company she'd come in contact with though a songwriter friend in Washington, D.C. McCall knew that the real money in the music business was in song publishing, and he did get his hands on a few formidable copyrights, including "Walking After Midnight" and "Lonely Street." But in order to make sure the copyrights were profitable, he put clauses in his artist contracts that gave him control over what they recorded. The contract Patsy signed virtually shut the door on songs coming from outside McCall's publishing interests. Her contract was for two years and sixteen sides, with an option to renew. Rumor had it that whenever Patsy needed money, she went to McCall and he gave her a few hundred dollars and added an extra year onto his deal with her.

McCall did as he had done with several of his artists and approached Paul Cohen at Decca with a leasing agreement which turned over everything from production to distribution of Patsy Cline records to Decca. McCall's responsibilities seemed to be twofold: approving the song selections and sending out promo copies of the singles to deejays.

Paul Cohen sent Patsy to Owen Bradley on June 1, 1955, warning him that "this girl singer has a temper and could talk a tough game." As it turned out, the two became fast friends and a legendary team. "I never really saw that tough side people talk about," Owen said. "We'd sometimes fuss at each other but it was more like an old married couple than anything else." Owen said his immediate worry was that Patsy saw herself as a stone country singer, a kind of yodeling cowgirl. Paul Cohen did not care for yodeling cowgirls, and as Owen often said, he aimed to please New York and Paul Cohen. Moreover, Owen already had a great "stone country" star in Kitty Wells, and he believed he had to find a different approach if he was to make a success of Patsy Cline.

Patsy's first release, "A Church, a Courtroom and Then Good-bye," was written by Four Star's Eddie Miller, who'd penned "Release Me," a hit for both Ray Price and Kitty Wells in 1954. It stiffed and for the next two years Patsy and Owen worked to come up with a winning song. Finally it looked like they'd found it when Four Star sent "Walking After Midnight," which blazed up both the country and pop charts in 1957. On January 21, 1957, Patsy sang "Walking After Midnight" on *Arthur Godfrey's Talent Scouts,* and the audience responded with a standing ovation that froze the applause meter. It appeared that there was no stopping Patsy with a crossover hit and a newly won national visibility. But a star without a song doesn't usually go anywhere. She followed "Walking After Midnight" with "A Poor Man's Roses (Or a Rich Man's Gold)," which barely made it to #14 in country and failed to crack the pop charts.

For the most past, the contract she'd signed kept Patsy broke, off the charts and depressed. My then-wife, Skeeter Davis, and I went to a filming at the Methodist Film Commission one night in 1960. We were doing some Army recruiting shows with Faron Young and Ferlin Husky headlining, and Skeeter, Roy Drusky and Patsy Cline as opening acts. Patsy was really down, and it was easy to see why. Her career was going nowhere.

Owen agreed. "Patsy went through some very bad times. She was competing against her own labelmate, Kitty Wells. It looked like Kitty could never be dethroned as the top female artist in country music. And while Patsy didn't suffer from outright jealousy, it left her feeling down a great deal of the time."

I suggested that her financial status must have played into that, too. "Yes," Owen said. "That and those songs that Four Star was sending her. She was tied to that contract until around the time we got 'I Fall to Pieces.' She'd had 'Walkin' After Midnight' in 1957 and didn't have a hit again until 1961! It was a long four years." After such a strong start, with so much promise, her career had nose-dived. All because she couldn't dip into the rich well of songs Nashville had to offer. Owen even tried to get around the contract by recording some hymns, which were public domain. By the time she was released from the contract, Owen feared she was fed up with Decca.

"I was surprised Patsy stayed with us, to tell you the truth, because nothing was happening," Owen said. "We hadn't been able to break her at radio, and I really was afraid she'd sign with Columbia or someone else. But I got word that she wanted to stay with us, and all she wanted was a little advance when she signed the recording contract. That Four Star deal had kept her so broke."

Owen got Patsy the advance and he found the song to bring her back to the charts when Hank Cochran walked in his office with a few lines scribbled on a scrap of paper. Hank had played several songs for Owen that day, and after they listened to the demo tapes, he happened to mention an idea he was working on, a song titled "I Fall to Pieces."

"Hank was such a funny guy when he was pitching songs," Owen recalled with a grin. "He was like an Oriental, very humble and bowing when he'd leave. One day he showed me the beginning of 'I Fall to Pieces,' and I told him I liked the idea and to let me hear it as soon as it was finished." Hank enlisted the help of Harlan Howard, and when the two finished, they took it back to Owen. "I first took it to Roy Drusky," Owen recalled. "But he thought it was too weak for a man to sing. He said he didn't think a man would sing a line like 'I fall to pieces,' but he did think about cutting it. Then during the session a songwriter brought in a song he liked better. I also pitched it to Brenda Lee. She turned it down, too. Then I pitched it to Patsy, and she turned it down! I think she thought if it wasn't good enough for Roy and Brenda it wasn't good enough for her."

Owen was determined that one of his artists would have a hit with the song, so he made a deal with Patsy. If she'd cut "I Fall to Pieces," she could pick any song, and he'd cut it on her whether he liked it or not. The song she found had been written by Freddie Hart, and was titled "Lovin' in Vain." Patsy still didn't like "I Fall to Pieces" and only learned it for her show after it was such a big hit that people started requesting it.

"People get 'I Fall to Pieces' confused with 'Crazy,' " Owen explained. "I didn't even realize that she didn't like 'Pieces' until after she had her car accident. She came in one day and said, 'Owen, I ain't going to record any more.' I was stunned, and asked her why not? She said, 'I had such a hard time getting a hit and I don't even like that ol' song. I like 'Lovin' in Vain' a lot better!' *Sweet Dreams,* the movie about Patsy, started people thinking it was 'Crazy' she didn't like. I consulted on the movie, and told them that wasn't the song. They never did show me the whole script. She was sold on 'Crazy' from the beginning.''

Yet Patsy presented Hank Cochran and Harlan Howard with gifts as a thank-you for her hit: a ring and a money clip for Hank and a silver ID bracelet for Harlan. And she took out a small ad in the *Music Reporter* that read: "I've tried and I've tried, but I haven't found a way to thank so many wonderful people for so much. Thank you and bless you. Gratefully, Patsy Cline.''

It almost came to an end on June 14, 1961, when Patsy was involved in a near-fatal collision on a rain-slick street in Nashville. She was coming back from buying the materials to mend one of her stage costumes when a car attempted to pass another and hit Patsy's car head-on. Patsy went through the windshield and over the hood of the car. When she arrived at Madison Hospital, she had massive facial injuries, a dislocated hip, cracked ribs and a broken wrist. She'd also lost a lot of blood.

Another misconception furthered by the movie involves Patsy's stay in the hospital. In *Coal Miner's Daughter*, Patsy Cline's husband sneaks beer to his wife in the hospital. That never happened. "I get sick of reading some of the stuff they write about Patsy's hard living," Owen said. "Minnie Pearl and I were talking about Patsy one time and she said she'd never heard Patsy use the kind of language some of the books and articles attribute to her. She was a strong-willed woman, and she could use colorful language. But she didn't use gutter talk and she wasn't trashy.''

Patsy's recovery was long and painful. By the time she was able to record again, eight months had gone by. "I Fall to Pieces" had been a pop and country hit and Owen was determined to find a song that would keep her at the top of both those charts. Once again, Hank Cochran walked into his office with a song. This time it was "Crazy,'' written by a friend of Hank's, a Texan named Willie Nelson.

"We tried to cut 'Crazy' over and over,'' Owen said. "Maybe that's where this legend [started] about her not being able to 'get' the song because of the way Willie Nelson sings, which is often ahead or behind the beat. But I have no memory of her saying anything about Willie's singing when she heard the song. The reason it took a longer time to record was that she was still recuperating from her accident.

"Her ribcage was just too sore for her to really sing, and there was one note she had problems with. But we got the tracks down, and I finally said, 'Patsy, let's quit. You're beating yourself up and wasting money. It's your money, too, since you're in the black with us!' She was reluctant, but she went home. In two weeks we went back in and she did 'Crazy' in one take.

Hank Cochran brought Patsy another hit, one he pitched as soon as he finished writing it. "I got a smash for you," he hollered into the phone. "Cut the BS and come on over and play it for me then," Patsy laughed. The song was "She's Got You," and Patsy loved it so much that she started calling people up on the phone and singing it to them. Owen Bradley loved it, too.

For the next couple of years, Patsy and Owen looked for and found the hit songs she needed. Her final session was held on February 7, 1963. She recorded Harlan Howard's "He Called Me Baby," Chuck Seals and Ralph Mooney's "Crazy Arms," Harlan Howard, Wynn Stewart and Skeets McDonald's "You Took Him Off My Hands" and Henry Barnard, Henry Thurston, Lois Mann and Morry Burns's "I'll Sail My Ship Alone." "He Called Me Baby" was a top-20 single the following year. Almost four decades later, she's still outselling many contemporary country artists.

OWEN THOUGHT THE answer to Patsy's continued popularity was threefold. First, he said, once she was out from under the Four Star deal, she recorded great standard songs that appealed to both country and pop fans. Next, her song styling ability was extraordinary. "When you hear Patsy Cline, you don't just hear a song," he said. "You hear her life. That's the mark of a great artist."

The third reason Owen thought Patsy lasted the way she has is her untimely death. "If Patsy Cline had been recording when she was sixty, it might have been different," he reflected. "In the minds of the listeners, Patsy is still thirty years old, and that doesn't take anything away from her talent. She still sings as good as she ever did, better actually, since we have the technology to enhance records now. Over the years, I've remixed Patsy's records every way imaginable to come up with new packages, and every day there are new people discovering her."

What would have happened if Patsy hadn't died in that plane crash on March 5, 1963? A lot of people speculated that she'd have been a pop singer, but I don't think that's so. Owen told me that the biggest disagreements he and Patsy had involved her wanting to record western- or cowboy-type material, while he knew she could make the crossover and have far bigger sales with the pop-flavored arrangements. When Patsy died she and Owen were working on two songs: the bluesy "Can't Help Lovin' That Man" and Bill Monroe's bluegrass standard, "Uncle Pen." They stood at opposite ends of the musical spectrum.

COUNTRY SONGS HAVE their beginnings in hundreds of ways. Sometimes a line uttered by chance is such an obvious hook that a song is born then and there. Bud Lee had forgotten his wallet one day when he and his friend DeWayne Blackwell were at a Nashville watering hole. When the bill came De-Wayne chided Bud, asking him how he planned on settling up. "I've got friends in low places," Bud joked. "Friends in Low Places" became the first single from Garth's groundbreaking *No Fences* album, and a CMA Song of the Year.

Some writers read novels to get ideas, others are avid movie-goers and still others find inspiration in the news. When Vince Gill read about the 1996 drive-by shooting of twelve-year-old Adriane Dickerson in the parking lot of a Nashville supermarket, he composed the heart-wrenching "Pretty Little Adriane," a Grammy winner in 1998. Television, too, inspires. Bobby Braddock once watched a TV show about a pistol passing through many hands, often bringing tragedy. The show hit Bobby particularly hard, and he talked to Rafe VanHoy about using the same concept for a song about a pair of wedding rings in a pawnshop. They took the song to Billy Sherrill during a George Jones and Tammy Wynette session, and Billy snapped it up. In 1976 "Golden Ring" became one of George and Tammy's biggest hits.

In one case a song was born out of necessity. Faron Young was involved in a car wreck in 1970 that nearly tore out his tongue, and put an end to one of country's most auspicious careers. The doctors sewed the tongue back together, never once believing that the operation would succeed. "The doctor told me that the only reason he stitched it back on was so I'd still have a tongue when I woke up," Faron said. "He was positive the surgery wouldn't take. But in a couple of days the color started to come back, and we knew I had a shot at saving the tongue." Faron underwent several more surgeries that kept him from recording for nearly a year. And even when the tongue healed, Faron was left with a slight lisp.

"When I went in to cut I was as nervous as I'd been the first day I ever walked into a recording studio," he recalled. "I didn't know if I'd ever have a hit again."

Fortunately, he'd been talking to a songwriter named Jerry Chestnutt, who wanted to write a song expressly for Faron. "I told him I had trouble lisping and if he wanted to write me a song to stay away from words that started with 's'."

Jerry went back home and wrote "It's Four in the Morning." It held the #1 spot in the country charts for two weeks and brought him back into the pop charts for the first time in nearly ten years.

Willie Nelson is often inspired by real life; he may not report the exact event that prompted the song, but you can bet there's a story behind every tune. In the case of "What Can You Do to Me Now?" when he sat down to write with Hank Cochran, Willie'd just had a bad run of luck: his wife divorced him and he'd wrecked four cars and a pickup truck. The two men wrote the song and the very next day Willie's house burned down.

"It didn't end there," Willie once told me. "The song became the title cut on the album, and when my record label sent a promotional copy to my manager he opened it up and found a Waylon Jennings record inside."

What can you do to me now? A lot, as it turned out.

I'M NOT A songwriter, but if I were, I'd probably be working on a song called "Till Death Do Us Part" right now. My inspiration would have been the story of Dr. Thomas Frist and his wife, Dorothy. A founder of the Hospital Corporation of America, Dr. Frist was a well-loved Nashville doctor known to make house calls long after other doctors gave it up. He was also very much in love with his wife; the couple was inseparable, and an inspiration to anyone who ever questioned true love.

Thomas Frist was a humorous man and when he died in January 1998 his pastor told how he'd written his own eulogy. It seems that Dr. Frist once attended a funeral where the pastor droned on and on about the dearly departed. After the service Dr. Frist returned to his home and phoned his own pastor, the Reverend K. C. Ptomey.

"Too many ministers talk too long," Dr. Frist told his friend. "All I want you to say at my funeral is 'He loved God. He loved his family. He loved the practice of medicine.' And then you sit down."

Dr. Frist didn't have it his way on January 7, 1998, because too many friends and admirers showed up at the memorial, a joint service for Thomas and Dorothy. Both were eighty-seven years old when they died three days apart. Dr. Frist died at home on a Sunday afternoon, and his wife, hospitalized following a fall, died on Tuesday. They say she didn't know her husband had passed away.

I wonder.

NOTE: Dr. Thomas Frist left a million-dollar bequest for the Country Music Hall of Fame's new building in downtown Nashville.

13

DOLLY AND FRIENDS:

AT TOOTSIE'S ORCHID

LOUNGE

We've got this little girl who just graduated from high school, and she is really good," Pearl Butler exclaimed. "Would you use her on your television show?"

Carl and Pearl Butler introduced me to Dolly Parton, fresh off the bus from Sevierville, Tennessee, and bursting with talent and ambition. She had some great champions in the Butlers, who had a number of hits on Columbia Records, including 1962's "Don't Let Me Cross Over," which stayed at the top of the charts for eleven weeks. Long before Dolly came to Nashville, they'd heard her singing on the *Cas Walker Farm and Home* show on WIVK Knoxville, and convinced Jimmy C. Newman to let her sing on his portion of the Grand Ole Opry.

I told them, "Sure, bring her on." Dolly bounced onto the set brimming with energy and announced that she was going to sing a George Jones song, "You Gotta Be My Baby." She took a bouncy, up-tempo approach to the song that told me she'd be a breath of fresh air to Nashville's early risers. It was my first introduction to the woman I think is the most extraordinary, larger-than-life star I've seen in my forty-plus years in the business. Dolly seems to be capable of succeeding at anything she sets her mind to.

That's why it came as a big surprise when the ABC television show she hosted in the mid-'80s went nowhere. Dolly says it was doomed from the beginning, because the show's producers tried to revive the old-style variety show with a Carol Burnett approach. Dolly is Dolly; she knew her audience didn't want to hear her singing Broadway show tunes, they wanted Dolly Parton music. Dolly has a great grasp of her persona; it's too bad the show's producers didn't.

Dolly had some strong words about her variety show in particular and television in general in her 1994 autobiography, *My Life and Other Unfinished Business:* "There are very few talented and truly creative people in television; the rest of them tend to hang on to their coattails. They're harmless enough if they are simply 'along for the ride,' but they can all too often actually drag the talented person backward."

She said she didn't know at what point the producers knew the show was bombing, but that at some point along the way they brought in "every old fart in Hollywood" to try and fix it. Somewhere in the middle of all the meetings and personnel changes, Dolly Parton got lost in the machinery. They should have turned the show over to its star, and allowed her to slip back into herself, the way she did on the segments they filmed on location. These were among her favorites, and I had the opportunity to participate in one of them.

DOLLY WANTED TO give her viewers a taste of what Nashville had been like when she arrived in 1965, so she assembled a group of us who had been with her before she was a star. Carl and Pearl Butler had both passed away when Dolly taped her television show in Nashville, but she invited a lot of the characters from her past; in addition to me there were Uncle Bill Owens, Fred Foster, Jimmy C. Newman, Curley Putnam, Faron Young, Bill Phillips, Buck Trent, Porter Wagoner, Bill Carlisle and Johnny Russell.

We had no script, and no agenda. Dolly just wanted viewers to "eavesdrop" on a bunch of music people hanging out in Nashville, and where better to do it than at Tootsie's Orchid Lounge? Tootsie's back door faces the Ryman Auditorium's back door, so Opry stars who were so inclined could slip across for a cold beer between their sets. Naturally all the songwriters hung out there to pitch their songs.

Tootsie's, which had formerly been called "Mom's," opened in March 1960 under the proprietorship of Mrs. Hattie Louise Bess, affectionately known as Tootsie to her customers. It was just plain old Tootsie's for a year or so, until Hank Cochran and Harlan How-ard wrote a song about the place and titled it "Tootsie's Orchid Lounge." Hank was on Liberty Records at the time, and while the song didn't chart in *Billboard*, it got some play around town so the name stuck.

Dolly loves Tootsie's for its history and its atmosphere. If you look on the walls sooner or later you'll find photos and autographs—and even some bounced checks—of Nashville's finest singers and songwriters. When we gathered for Dolly's taping Buck Trent owned up to the fact that he'd once bounced a check for two dollars at Tootsie's. Buck played with both the Bill Carlisle Show and Por-ter's Wagonmasters, and is noted for popularizing the electric banjo, an instrument built like a steel guitar and designed by steel man Shot Jackson. Once Buck got famous, Tootsie hung the bounced check up on the wall.

Dolly asked Fred Foster, the owner of her first record label in Nashville, Monument, to explain how he used Tootsie as an unoffi-cial A&R person.

"Tootsie was sort of the Queen Bee for the Opry stars," Fred said. "Plus she was a surrogate mother to the starving young artists and writers that came to town. When people first came to town, Tootsie's was where they'd come, and she got to hear everybody first. I got on to the fact that Tootsie was a good talent scout pretty quick. Sooner or later, the people that Tootsie really liked made it big, so I started paying attention to who she liked and who she didn't. If Tootsie liked them, I'd try to sign them. I missed a couple but I got a couple. I got Willie Nelson and Kris Kristofferson because Tootsie championed them."

Tootsie didn't like any foolishness, and when she got ready to close up shop, you better be ready to leave. Every night at midnight Tootsie would blow a whistle, and if you didn't get out she stuck you with a hat pin.

Faron Young recalled that one new hopeful in town panicked the first time he heard Tootsie announce closing time.

"One night she blew her police whistle, and there was a new guy in town who didn't know the rules," Faron explained. "He was in the restroom when she blew the whistle, and he came running out yelling, 'What is it, a raid?' We said, 'No, that's just Tootsie closing.' 'Hell,' the fellow said. 'I poured all my pills down the commode!' "

DOLLY'S SONGWRITER PARTNER and uncle, Bill Owens, visited Tootsie's on a regular basis, as Dolly explained. "Uncle Bill used to call me from down here, and of course, he was usually drunk," she laughed. "He'd call and say,'I got one of our songs cut!' One song Uncle Bill pitched was the song of the year that year. Bill Phillips had a hit record off a song we wrote called 'Put It Off Until Tomorrow.' "

Bill "Tater" Phillips had started out recording duets with Mel Tillis on Columbia Records in 1959, after Mel helped him secure a publishing contract with Cedarwood Publishing. Two singles made it to country's top-20, but for the next several years Columbia couldn't chart him. In 1964 Bill signed with Decca, and in '66 he released "Put It Off Until Tomorrow." Dolly sang backup on the song and very soon folks around Nashville started calling Decca and asking for the name of the harmony singer. "That song really started it all," Dolly reflected.

SONGS GOT PITCHED all the time at Tootsie's; some were good and some were not. Porter told us about one songwriter and his pitch.

"I have this song that will make you all kinds of money," the songwriter said to Porter. "I guarantee you it will be the number one song of the year. It is a gold standard."

"Well, go ahead and sing it," Porter said.

The guy looked around and shook his head, "There's too many people. Step outside with me."

"Nah, I don't want to," Porter said.

"It'll be worth your dime, I'm not kidding," the guy insisted.

He finally wore Porter down and the two stepped out back in the alley.

The songwriter reared back and started to sing: "Just Molly and me and baby makes three. We are happy in my green heaven . . .' "

"Are you crazy?" Porter asked. "That is the same as 'My Blue Heaven.' "

"Yeah, but people are into money now!" The guy said. "It's a whole new approach."

Porter told another great story, one that started out at Tootsie's and involved Mel Tillis. Porter had finished playing the Opry one night and Mel met him at Tootsie's for a beer before they took off on a late-night fishing expedition. They had a couple of brews and moved into something stronger, the "uppers" so many of us took back in the '70s.

"There was a lot of pill-taking in that time," Dolly said, shaking her head. "People were traveling around in cars and buses and people took these pills to stay awake."

"I never took 'em," Faron shot back. "I was too hyper."

"You loved to drink that beer, though, Faron," Dolly laughed. "That's why we have so many stories about you."

"Faron drank and we got the brain damage," Bill Phillips added.

Porter went on with his Mel Tillis story. "Yeah, we threw back a couple old yeller's. Those were kind of 'Don't get scared pills' if you are going fishing in the middle of the night."

Mel bought a case of beer and put it in the car, and the two left for Old Hickory Lake. They drank beer all the way to the lake, finally pulling up to the boat dock a little after midnight. Porter pulled the boat into a cove he knew to be a good fishing spot. It was so still that not even a leaf rustled. It was also very dark.

"Now, Mel is a wonderful man and he's not afraid of anything except the dark," Porter said. "It was so dark out that you could hardly tell if your eyes were open or closed."

Finally Mel whispered, "It sure is quiet in here, isn't it, Chief?"

Porter says he knew right then Mel was going to get spooked.

"It ain't too bad," Porter answered.

"Have you seen them stars falling?" Mel asked.

Porter shrugged it off. "I haven't paid any attention to it."

"I've counted seven falling stars since we've been in this cove," Mel said uneasily. "I've got a bad feeling about tonight."

"Mel, it's going to be all right," Porter said. But he decided he better get the boat out to where it was a little lighter, and pulled back out to the main channel. All of a sudden the whole eastern seaboard lit up.

"I swear it looked like a million Roman Candles going off in the atmosphere," Porter laughs. "The Army was setting some stuff off, but of course, we didn't know that at the time. Mel took one look at that and started throwing beer out of the boat."

"What's the matter with you?" Porter asked.

"It's the end of time!" Mel shouted, and kept on pitching beer cans in the lake.

"Stop throwing away the beer, Mel," Porter commanded. "Hell, that's nothing."

"Please, Porter. Don't cuss no more," Mel said as he threw the last brew out of the boat. "We're in enough trouble already."

CURLEY PUTNAM WROTE Dolly's first hit, "Dumb Blonde," and that night at Tootsie's he told the star he wanted to make sure she knew one thing: "I didn't write that song because I thought you were a dumb blonde, Dolly," Curley assured her. "Dumb you are not. The song says, 'Just because I am blonde don't think I'm dumb. Because this dumb blonde ain't nobody's fool.' "

"Had you had a few beers from Tootsie's when you wrote that for me?" Dolly kidded.

"Probably." Bill laughed.

"When did you write "Green Green Grass of Home?" Dolly asked Curley. "I know Porter had the first big country record on that and then Tom Jones."

"The latter part of 1964," Curley said. "It was about the time you and Bill signed with Tree. I was trying to find myself and my dreams while you were starting to find yours. You and Bill both. I didn't have any luck plugging your songs back then because you had just started writing. We all had a lot to learn about songs, even myself."

"The ones that were worth recording did get cut sooner or later," Dolly laughed. "But we had a lot of junk songs too. Anytime you are a songwriter you have a lot of songs that nobody would ever record."

Curley reminded Dolly that her early recordings on Monument

were more pop than country, and Fred Foster clarified his decision-making process regarding Dolly's direction.

"Ray Stevens just flipped out and said that Dolly was a pop singer," Fred explained. "Since I thought you could do about anything, I let him try to cut you pop. Then you came to me one day and said, 'If you want me on this label, I'm gonna sing country music!' I agreed and 'Dumb Blonde' was the first song we recorded."

They followed that with "Something Fishy," which charted in the 20s, and several other songs that didn't chart. In 1967 she signed with RCA. Fred Foster laughs about it now, but at the time it hurt him.

"I've been wanting to tell this story for a long time," Fred said with a grin. "I played a golf tournament out at Henry Horton State Park not long after Dolly left Monument. I was lining up my three wood hoping I could get to the top of the hill, when I heard a woman screaming. I looked up and here came Dolly Parton roaring down the hill in Porter's chrome-bumpered, fox-tail-decorated golf cart. I tried to figure out which way she was going and jump out of the way, but every time I jumped one way she swerved right at me. When I finally gave up and stood still, Dolly went roaring right by me. She got the cart back in control and drove back to apologize. I said, 'Wasn't leaving me bad enough? You have to try to kill me too?'"

JOHNNY RUSSELL EASED up his chair about then and told Dolly that one of the reasons he loved being around her was that she liked to eat. He is also a very big guy who hasn't missed many meals in his life. Johnny's written classics including "Act Naturally" and "Let's Fall to Pieces Together," and he recorded for RCA at the same time Dolly was newly signed to the label.

"One time RCA sent us to Chicago to perform at a convention," Johnny recalled. "They fed us at rehearsals and they fed us at the show. Later that night a bunch of us got together and ordered room service in Dolly's room. We ate everything we could find. The next morning we went down and had a big buffet breakfast at the hotel. When we got to the airport, Dolly went to the coffee shop, ordered a strawberry waffle and ate every bit of it except for one bite, which she gave to me. Later we were walking down the hall on the way to the plane, and a very shapely girl was walking right ahead of Dolly and me. Dolly said, 'What do you think of that, Johnny?' I said, 'That is pretty nice.' So Dolly started walking really fast and got in front of me and started swinging her hips back and forth. After she finished her little strut, she came back to me and grinned. 'What did you think of that?' she asked. I said, 'Well, Dolly, I think I just found that strawberry waffle.' "

HANK COCHRAN AND Harlan Howard once told Johnny Russell he'd never make it as a writer in Nashville because didn't hang out at Tootsie's. "Tootsie would never give me anything free to eat," Johnny explained. "That was one reason I never hung out here, and aside from that, I didn't drink, take pills or chase women. That's probably the reason I wrote all those sad songs."

"And that's the reason you'll probably live to be a hundred," Porter threw out, then cracked: "Or at least it will seem like it."

Johnny Russell told one on Faron, too. "One time I did come in here and lost fifteen dollars to Faron Young playing shuffleboard at a dollar a game. Faron got to feeling sorry for me and insisted I keep my money. Later, when I walked back over to the Opry, he asked somebody what I did and who I was. They said, 'Oh, he's got a Jim Reeves record out that's sold over three million records.' Faron ran across the alley to the Opry and asked for the fifteen dollars back!"

Talking about Faron reminded Bill Carlisle of the story of Faron and the Wild Man. "Faron and I played a date down in Florida together and on the way back we kept seeing these signs that read: 'Wild Man in Rattlesnake Pit.' Faron insisted we see this attraction, so we stopped at this old tent and bought two tickets. The man who sold us the tickets said it would be just a few minutes until showtime and sent us down a little hall inside the tent to wait. Finally a voice boomed out telling us to enter, and when we went inside the room, there was the guy who sold us the tickets, wearing a wig and picking snakes up and shaking them with his teeth. There was a diamond-back in the cage, but a glass partition separated the phony wild man

from the rattler, and Faron spotted it. He kept pointing at the rattler and yelling, 'Hey, you—pick up *that* snake and shake it.' The
guy finally leapt up at the glass where Faron stood and shook a
snake at him, yelling 'Grrrr.' So Faron yelled back, 'I'll Grrr you,
you phony so-and-so!' The guy ripped the wig off, came around
front and threw us out. So you can honestly say that Faron Young
has even been kicked out of a snake pit!"

SINCE DOLLY HAD wanted some reminisces about some of Nashville's
great "characters," I asked if anyone had a Stringbean story. String
was an Opry favorite with his crazy costumes, banjo picking and
funny sketches. Stringbean had one very dangerous habit, and it
ended up costing him his life: he loved to pull a wad of money from
his overalls and flash it around. Because of that, the rumor started
around town that String kept large amounts of money at his house.
Every time I saw him pull out wads of cash or heard rumors about
his stash at home, I worried.

Finally, on November 10, 1973, as String and his wife arrived
home they were accosted by burglars and shot to death. Ironically,
String's stash was finally located in 1997 when a fireplace in his
former home was torn down. What is estimated to have been thousands of dollars was found moldy and in shreds behind the bricks.

String took chances flashing money, but he didn't do it because
he had a death wish. Fred Foster remembered a time when Ray
Price and Stringbean were touring together, traveling in Ray's limousine. "Ray was running a little late for this date, and was doing
over a hundred miles an hour," Fred said. "Stringbean was sitting
in the back, and he was nervous. Finally he didn't want to create
too much of a disturbance and he leaned up and tapped Ray on
the shoulder real soft and said, 'Chief, do you think you could slow
down a little? I'd rather have people say 'String is late' than say 'the
late String.' "

Porter remembered how String kidded everybody about what a
great banjo player he was: "One night he came out of the Opry and
he came down to me real serious and said, 'Juice, you know what?
I am going to have to quit playing so good on the Opry. Earl Scruggs

and Grandpa Jones are stealing me blind. I go out and play an original lick and I'd hear it back three times the next night!' "

PORTER TOLD ANOTHER funny story about the days when he and
Dolly played the Opry together. Back then the Opry didn't have any
kind of crowd control, and fans would be standing out in back waiting for autographs. That caused a problem when a star had to get
right on the bus to make it to a show halfway across the country the
following night.

"Dolly and I came out the back door one night and I told her,
'We're going to have to go straight for the bus or we're not going
to make tomorrow's date,' " Porter said. "This one woman was waiting right on the steps of the Opry. 'I've got to get y'all's autograph,'
she yelled. But there were four or five hundred people out there,
and I knew we couldn't even start signing autographs or we'd never
get gone. I said, 'Look we can't sign your autograph. It wouldn't be
fair to these other people, and we don't have any time.'

" 'Just sign mine,' she insisted.

" 'That wouldn't be fair,' I repeated. 'All these other people are
here. We can't just sign one.'

"That woman followed us all the way across the parking lot and
other people behind her all the way till we got to the bus. Finally
when we got to the bus she shouted:

" 'I didn't want y'all's autograph anyway. I voted for Conway
and Loretta.' "

GRANDPA JONES, ANOTHER legend who died in 1998, was one more
great character in country music. Grandpa had already developed
that old-timer persona that *Hee-Haw* fans loved way back in the mid-
1930s when he was a young entertainer. The story goes that a singer,
Bradley Kincaid, joked that banjo picker Louis Marshall Jones
walked as slow as an old grandpa. Fred Foster remembered the time
that Grandpa bought a new Cadillac.

"Grandpa had never had a new car that had intermittent windshield wipers," Fred said. "It was raining on the day he picked the

Cadillac up from the dealers, and on the way home he turned the wipers on. They went one wipe and stopped. The windshield would cover up with rain and Grandpa couldn't see. So he turned them on again. One wipe and stop. He went about three traffic lights, then slammed that Cadillac up in park, got on the hood and started moving the wipers back and forth shouting, 'No, like this!' "

DOLLY WOUND UP the taping by talking about the closeness of the Nashville music community. "I really think what is so great about Nashville is that we are one big family," she mused. "We aren't always a happy family—there have been some unhappy times—but through it all, everybody has stuck together."

Porter said he believed that the reason so many great songs were born here in Music City had to do with that closeness. "I remember years ago when all these famous writers that we have been talking about, Willie Nelson, Kris Kristofferson, Curley Putnam, Bill Carlisle, Johnny Russell, were turning out one great song after another," Porter said. "People shared ideas with each other. There is not any one person brilliant enough to come up with all the great things it takes to make this business go. I think it's a combination of all these great minds working. I know I've seen guys help somebody else; maybe one writer had a great song finished except for two lines and another writer would help him finish it. More often than not the guy who added the lines didn't even want a financial share of the song. He knew that the next day somebody might help him finish one."

Porter paused a minute. "That's what this songwriting community is about."

His comment reminded me of when Art Satherley said all those years ago that this music is made possible by the stories, the dialects and the rural heritage. That's what makes it America's music.

HERE'S A FOOTNOTE about how television works. They shot about an hour that night at Tootsie's. When the show aired, they showed about a minute of it.

GATOR BAIT

NOBODY WOULD HAVE dreamed that the young man gazing up at a Marine recruiting sign in 1942 was only thirteen years old. He was nearly six feet tall, weighed over 150 pounds and had a well-muscled physique. And nobody questioned him when he signed up, saying he was seventeen years old, had a sixth-grade education and was ready to fight in World War II. That boy (who had only gone to the second grade) went on to fight with the Marines at Iwo Jima and Okinawa. Somewhere along the line, his fellow soldiers whispered among themselves, questioning the fact that Fred Segrest never seemed to need a shave. But by the time his superior officers started harboring the suspicion that Fred might have lied when he said he'd been born in 1926, it was too late. They were in the Pacific, securing Guam.

After the war, Freddie left the Marines with a stack of medals and a black belt in karate. He started working odd jobs in California, singing at local clubs when he could get the work, trying to make it to Nashville and a recording career. No stranger to survival, he often slept in ditches along the way to Tennessee, sometimes covering himself in dirt to stay warm. Eventually he took a job as a roadie with Hank Williams. By 1959 Fred Segrest was going by the stage name of Freddie Hart, and was signed to Columbia Records. He spent years trying for that elusive hit, first breaking into *Billboard*'s charts in '59 with "The Wall," which made it to #24. Still signed to Columbia Records, he went on to have some chart success in 1960 and 1961. He was without a record deal from '61 to '65, when he signed with Kapp Records. Still, the breakthrough hit never happened.

In 1970 he moved to Capitol Records and released four marginally successful singles in quick succession. By 1971, Capitol had already canceled his contract when they reluctantly released what would have been his final single, a self-penned tune called "Easy Loving." The song took off like a rocket and became one of the biggest songs of the year, spending two weeks at #1 in country and hitting the top-20 in pop.

You can bet the boys at Capitol tracked Freddie down with a contract and a pen in hand when that happened. Freddie went on to have a big string of hits into the mid-1980s, and retired from music happy, successful and rich. It's a true country music rags-to-riches story, but one with a twist. Freddie didn't just start out poor. He started out as gator bait.

Freddie was born on December 21, 1926, in Lochapoka, Alabama, one of fifteen children in a poverty-stricken family. The Segrests later moved into the swamp land on the Georgia/Florida border, and it was there that Freddie got his first taste of the survival tactics that would serve him as well in the music business as they did in a world war.

"One way we tracked gators back then was to use somebody as 'gator bait,' " Freddie once told me. "When I was about four years old I accepted a bet with some older boys, and they started using me as gator bait. What they did was this: they strapped me into a halter and had me hold onto a piece of raw meat. Then they'd pull me along in the water and the gators would smell the blood from the raw meat. Gators are bottom dwellers, you see, and something had to attract them to the surface. The older boys are there to trap them the minute they get close to the 'bait,' which, in many cases, was me. It wasn't all that dangerous. At least, I never got hurt."

A lot of guys heard about Freddie's war record and karate expertise and tried to start fights with him when he played the clubs in their towns. I'd be willing to bet they would have backed off if they knew the story of four-year-old Freddie and Gator Bait.

NOTE: Jerry Reed's song "Amos Moses" was inspired by Freddie Hart's gator bait story.

14

THE DRUMMER
IS A RUMMER AND CAN'T
HOLD THE BEAT

The group of psychics conducted seances regularly, usually about once a week at one or the other's New York homes. They were a respected organization, not given to publicity or attempting to profit from their extrasensory gifts. One night in 1967 they glimpsed a pale figure with what looked like a large white light around its head, appearing in the room for a moment, then vanishing, a reticent apparition that left as swiftly as it had come. Several weeks later the figure appeared again, stronger this time, in clear enough view to see that the light surrounding his head was a white cowboy hat. For a moment, it seemed he would speak, but then, as before, the spirit moved on. The members wondered about the man who had nearly spoken, but it would be three more years before they learned who he was, and the significance of his visit.

PEOPLE HAVE TRIED to prove or disprove the concept of "life after death" for centuries, with well-known figures such as Edgar Cayce and Houdini promising in vain to send word back from "the other side" after they died. One celebrity came through on such a promise, according to music icon Merle Kilgore, who tells one of country music's strangest stories, a tale involving the legendary Johnny Horton's premonition of death, and a mysterious message delivered to Merle ten years after Johnny died.

The year was 1960. Merle Kilgore was riding high in his career back then, releasing back-to-back hits with "Dear Mama" and "Love Has Made You Beautiful" as a solo artist on Starday Records, and penning Johnny Horton's 1959 hit, "Johnny Reb." Horton, after struggling through most of the 1950s trying to find his niche in country music, hit upon his trademark "saga song" approach when, in 1959, he recorded "When It's Springtime in Alaska (It's Forty Below)," then followed it with his monster hit, "The Battle of New Orleans," which stayed at *Billboard*'s #1 spot on the country charts for ten weeks, and at pop music's top spot for six weeks. Merle ran into Johnny at a show in Spring Hill, Louisiana, the last week of October, and according to Merle, here is what Johnny told him:

"Merle, the spirits have told me to bring you my guitar," Johnny said. "I will probably die within the next ten days, and I've been instructed to tell my friends good-bye, and to give you this guitar. Don't sell it, though, keep it and loan it out to museums. I'm going to play Austin, Texas, next week, and I'm afraid that's where it will happen. I've been told that a drunk is gonna kill me."

Although both men believed in psychic phenomena, Merle was shocked at the fatalistic prediction, wondering if the singer's concerns could have been caused by the fact that Johnny was married to Billie Jean, Hank Williams's widow, and he was playing the club where Hank had played his last paying gig.

"Do you have to play the show?" Merle asked.

"Yes," Johnny said. "The deal's been made. I have to go, and I'm afraid some drunk is gonna take a shot at me onstage. But before I do, I want to do like Houdini did and give you a code. I want to try and reach you from the other side, just to prove that it's there."

"All right, Johnny, let's have it," Merle said, finally.

"The drummer is a rummer and can't hold the beat."

Merle repeated the statement back to Johnny.

"Remember that, Merle. Write it down a hundred times if you have to, but just don't tell anybody about it. No one can know except you and me. That way, when I get word back somehow, you'll know there is another side, and that I'm there, I'm okay and waiting on you there."

Merle was grim, but he nodded, promising to remember the lines. For the next week and a half, Merle was troubled, a state that proved justified when, on November 5, 1960, Johnny Horton was killed in a car wreck. He'd played the show in Austin with no incident. According to his manager, Tillman Franks, Johnny was elated, thinking he'd somehow cheated his own prophecy of death. Then, as he traveled home, a drunk college boy drove head-on into Johnny's car, killing the singer instantly. A drunk had killed him after all, and on the night he'd feared.

"It's hard to get back from the other side," Merle told me. "I know, because it took Johnny almost ten years to find a way to do it."

Seven years passed, and unbeknownst to Merle, Johnny Horton contacted a group of mediums in New York. At first they only saw the faint figure of a man, but over the next year and a half, he returned several times, becoming stronger and stronger at each sighting. Finally he spoke to the group:

"Tell Merle Kilgore . . ." the ghostly figure began. "Tell Merle it's Johnny Horton."

Not one person in the group of psychics and mediums was a country music fan, so the name meant nothing. The man in the cowboy hat came back several more time, but what he said was gibberish, and the psychics just filed it away under "unanswered questions." Then, nearly ten years after Johnny Horton's death, one of the psychics indulged in an earthly pleasure, baseball, and tuned to radio station WJRZ in Hackensack, New Jersey, which regularly played country music, but also broadcast the New York Mets games. The fellow had barely settled back in his chair when the game was called on account of rain. Before he could get up to change the dial, a deejay named Bob Lockwood came on the air and said, "I just got back from visiting my old friend Merle Kilgore, so I'd like to dedicate something to him—a song he wrote for the late Johnny Horton. 'He fought all the way, Johnny Reb, Johnny Reb.' "

The psychic couldn't believe he was hearing the two names his group had heard several times over the past few years: Johnny Horton and Merle Kilgore. He telephoned Lockwood at WJRZ, who put him in touch with Kilgore. When he located Merle by phone, the medium explained about the cowboy in the white hat who had instructed the group to contact him. "We didn't have any idea who you were or how to find you," the man said.

"Did he have any message for me?" Merle said, a chill running over him as he thought back all those years ago to his last conversation with Johnny.

"Yes, but it made no sense," the psychic said. "He said 'The drummer is a rummer and can't hold the beat.' "

"I believe in ESP," Merle says. "And there have been other times in my life that I've witnessed unexplained phenomena. But this event proved to me that there is life after death, something I always believed on a religious level, anyway. But this was factual proof to me, because I had never told another soul that line."

There are other stars Merle Kilgore has seen display extraordinary amounts of ESP. George Jones, according to Merle, once correctly predicted the exact amount of money he would win in one day at a dog track: $3,000.

Merle told me about an odd experience that happened soon after he first met Elvis Presley in 1954 at the *Louisiana Hayride*. "Elvis was wearing a pink jacket, with black and white shoes, and you could tell that the white had been painted over pink," Merle laughs. "He must have decided the pink and black shoes were too much and tried to paint over them. He asked me if I knew Tibby Edwards, a little Cajun guy who wore real flashy rhinestone suits and had a couple of regional hits back then. I said sure, I knew him, and we went to Tibby's dressing room and the three of us talked a while. Elvis and I got along right off."

When Pappy Covington, who was running the artist service bureau for the *Hayride,* saw that Merle had met Elvis, he asked him to do a couple of tour dates with him. At that time, Elvis's band, the Blue Moon Boys, consisted of just Scotty Moore on guitar and Bill Black on bass. Merle agreed to go along, but in the car driving to the next show, Elvis began to intimidate him.

"Elvis was driving, but he kept staring at me when he should have been looking at the road," Merle recalls. "I didn't know what to make of him. Once I'd seen his show and the reaction of the fans, I knew he was a superstar waiting to happen. I thought maybe he could sense my nervousness around him and it was upsetting him, so I finally asked him if anything was wrong.

" 'Aw, man, there's something I've been wanting to ask you ever since I met you back at the *Hayride*,' Elvis said.

" 'Well, ask me!' I answered.

" 'You're gonna think I'm crazy, but what's your mama's name?'

" 'My mama's name is Gladys,' I answered.

" 'I knew it,' he said, and slapped his knee. 'My mama's name is Gladys! I never knew anybody else whose mama's name was Gladys!'

" 'Me neither,' I said.

"Well, Elvis and I got along just fine after that, and he used me on every show he could after that. All because I had a mama named Gladys."

But Elvis was no "Mama's Boy" when things got tough, as Merle soon found out. "We were playing the NCO Club at the Red River Arsenal in New Boston, Texas, right outside of Texarkana," Merle recalls. "It was New Year's Eve, and the club was thick with cigarette smoke, which bothered Elvis since he was a nonsmoker. He went outside on the porch to get some air, and some drunk corporal came up and started in on Elvis. He was mad that his girlfriend had said Elvis turned her on. Elvis was real polite, and said, 'I'm so sorry, man, I never meant to . . .' and the guy swung at Elvis and knocked him off that porch. Well, that night I saw why they called Elvis the Hillbilly Cat, because his body never touched the steps as he went to the ground. His legs and arms kept him from hurting his back as he went down, and the minute he got to the bottom, he sprung back up, just like a cat. He raced back up the stairs and whacked that guy. D. J. Fontana and I were standing on the porch, and we jumped back to get out of the way of the fight. After some noncommissioned officers came and broke it up, D.J. said the only casualty was him, because I jumped so fast I stepped on his feet and mashed his body to the wall! But the thing is about Elvis, he sat down and cried when they drug that soldier off. It hurt him that he had to fight. But it was also instinctual for him to defend himself and do it well."

Hank Williams Sr. is one that many credit with having ESP. Members of his band, the Drifting Cowboys, still talk of getting a "Hank-Alert" while driving down the road, long before electronic devices could alert speeders of highway patrol cars. "Better slow down 'cause there's a police car right up around this corner," Hank would say. And sure enough, there would be a police car, right where he'd predicted it would be.

Loretta Lynn is another star who believes she knows what happens after death: you come back. Loretta has even been hypnotized and taken back into past lives, including one in which she was married to an Indian chief, one where she was a man living in New York City, and another where she was the mistress of King George II of England. In this story, Loretta comes to a bad end when the King dies and his best friend chokes her to death.

When I interviewed Loretta for *On the Record* in 1997, she hesitated when I asked her about her belief in reincarnation, reminded, perhaps, of past problems she faced after speaking candidly on the subject. Over twenty years ago, Loretta told me she'd talked openly about reincarnation on David Frost's show, only to face recriminations from her fans. "I got hundreds and hundreds of letters—you wouldn't believe the mail I got. They told me I wasn't right, and was goin' to go to you-know-where!" Loretta personally answered those letters, and explained that she could find no place in the Bible that said there was or was not such a thing as reincarnation. She attempted to explain her belief in natural terms. "I explained to them that the grass dies in the winter and comes back in the summer," she said. "Leaves drop in the fall and grow back in the spring."

Loretta has never sidestepped the fact that she believes in ghosts, or that she believes her house is haunted. As she pointed out in her autobiography, *Coal Miner's Daughter,* her home at Hurricane Mills, Tennessee, sits on land that once saw a Civil War battle, where nineteen Confederate soldiers were killed and buried. One night Loretta and Mooney's son, Ernest Ray, awakened in the middle of the night and saw a ghostly figure dressed in a Confederate uniform hovering at the foot of his bed. On another night Loretta was operating a Ouija board that spelled out the name "Anderson." Almost immediately, she said, the table rose up and crashed violently to the floor, breaking into pieces. "The next day I learned that the original owner of the house, James Anderson, was buried right near the house," Loretta wrote in her memoir. "We never tried talking to him again."

Like Carl Perkins, Loretta believes she was visited in the studio by a star who'd passed on, her close friend Patsy Cline. "Years after Patsy died, I decided to try and record an album of her songs," Loretta says. "I was in the studio with Owen Bradley producing, and I couldn't do anything right. I was either above the pitch or below it every time I opened my mouth. Finally I told Owen we'd better give up and try it again sometime. But just as I started to leave the vocal booth, I heard a voice that said, 'You turn around!' I stopped dead in my tracks and looked around, but nobody was there. So I said, 'Well, Loretta, you better turn around!' I went back to the mike and told Owen to just start rolling tape and not stop. We ran through every song and I only missed a few of the notes that time."

There was another time, too, a date in Las Vegas, when Loretta came down with "Vegas throat" from the dry climate. The one part of her show that she feared was her Patsy Cline medley, with its big musical range, and when she walked out on stage, she considered dropping it from the show.

"Then I looked out and saw her," Loretta said. "It was Patsy Cline—or so I thought—dressed in her spandex pedal pushers and wearing those little elastic shoes she loved. She looked me straight in the eye and said, 'Yes you can. I'm ashamed of you!' Patsy was always saying that when I said I couldn't do something: 'Yes you can. I'm ashamed of you!' Was it Patsy? Well, I don't know. But I do know there's a lot of things in this world that we can't explain."

SAMMY KERSHAW HAS stories that can't be explained, unless, that is, you believe in guardian angels. Sammy has good reason to believe in miracles and ghosts and guardian angels, because he's been visited by an angel and it saved his life. It happened in 1980, when Sammy and his then-wife were living in Antlers, Oklahoma. Sammy had just turned twenty-one, and although as a member of the noted Louisiana musical Kershaws, he'd been performing music since he was a child, he'd given it up to work a series of day jobs. There weren't many opportunities in Antlers, but since it was his wife's hometown, the two stayed on while Sammy attempted to find a way to earn a living. Noticing that one amenity the town lacked was a dry cleaner, he took out a bank loan and opened a dry-cleaning establishment.

"We worked long hours," Sammy says. "We usually arrived some-time between three and four o'clock A.M., and didn't leave until late at night."

The exhausting schedule took its toll, and the two eventually divorced. Not surprisingly, Antlers lined up on the side of the home-town girl. "I didn't have any friends left," Sammy admits. "So I was still broke, a long way away from my family, working those awful hours trying to make the bank notes, with no social life and personal support system. Plus, I'd really cared about my wife. The more I worked, the more in debt I was, and the worse everything got. I was even getting behind in my work. Every day I'd walk by a pile of clothes to be cleaned, and the pile just kept getting bigger. I wanted to just pack up and leave town, but I felt I couldn't walk away from the business and the bank note. I wanted to kill myself, but didn't know if I'd have the guts."

One morning Sammy woke up and knew he had the guts. He was very calm about it, feeling no self-recriminations or fear. He simply took the shotgun he'd used only for duck hunting and drove to the store in the wee hours of the morning. He calmly went in back to the store's boiler room, found an old paint can and sat down on it, propping the shotgun between his legs. He inserted a stick just over the trigger and put the gun barrel in his mouth. Just as he was about to use his feet to push the stick forward and pull the trigger, the store's front door buzzer rang alerting him to a customer arriving long before opening time.

"I couldn't put some unsuspecting customer through my sui-cide," Sammy says. "So I propped the gun in the corner, planning to come back the minute I got rid of them. I didn't even put the safety back on the shotgun. It was sitting there waiting for me to do what I had to do. I walked past the stack of dirty clothes, which was about five feet high by then, and into the front of the store.

"There stood a woman who looked like she was in her early six-ties. She wore glasses, and although her face wasn't familiar, I felt like I knew her, or had known her at some time in my life. My imme-diate thought was that she was lost and wanted directions, because of both the early hour and the fact that she didn't have a purse or any clothes to leave with me."

"May I help you?" Sammy asked.

"No," the woman said. "I just stopped by to see how you were doing."

The moment the woman spoke, Sammy says an overwhelming feeling of being at peace came over him. But since he didn't know her, her personal inquiry was confusing. "To see how I was doing?" he asked, to make sure he understood her properly.

She nodded, and they spoke a few minutes about nothing in particular. Sammy says it was just small talk, and he has no memory of the specifics of the conversation.

Finally she said, "I have to go now. I just wanted to make sure you were okay."

Sammy stood, almost in a trance, and watched her leave the store. When the door closed behind her he rushed around the counter and hurried out onto the street just behind her. But the street was empty.

"There were no cars anywhere," Sammy recalls. "Not in the parking lot, not in the street and not in the little market on the corner. There was nothing open, so she couldn't have walked anywhere. She had disappeared, and standing there in what seemed like a deadly silence, I felt like I was the only person on earth. I stood there in this *Twilight Zone*-like atmosphere, then went straight back to the boiler room, unloaded my shotgun and walked out back to my car. I drove home, packed my belongings and left for Louisiana. In some strange way, the woman had turned everything around, and I knew that I was meant to live, and to go home to my family. I left the cleaners for the town to figure out. For the first time in months, I believed my life was worth more than any store."

In the seventeen years since that incident, Sammy has never again seen the woman who kept him from taking his life, but he has thought about her often. "I know she was my guardian angel," Sammy says with conviction. "And while I have never seen her or actually talked to her again, there have been many times I felt her spirit and she's helped me get through something. At times I've wondered if she's the spirit of my grandmother, my mother's mother, who died when I was a child. But my grandmother was always tough on me. She never let me get away with anything and would tear me up if I did something wrong. You don't know how those things work, you just know they do."

He moved back to Kaplan, Louisiana, to live with his mother, widowed when Sammy's father had died of lung cancer ten years earlier. He noticed some construction going on down the street, and when he stopped by to inquire about work, he learned that a country radio station was being built, almost in his mother's backyard. "I filled out an application and left a tape of my speaking voice, and became the first disc jockey on the air when the station opened," Sammy says. "Two and a half weeks later I was singing with a band."

Working at radio encouraged Sammy to try to get his music career up and running again, and his new band, named Blackwater, toured in Louisiana, Texas, Wyoming, New Mexico and the Dakotas. He released several well-received singles on small independent labels, but nothing caught fire, and he eventually took a job as a supervisor, overseeing the remodeling of WalMart stores throughout the United States. In 1990 he talked with friends in Nashville, and decided to try again for the stardom that had thus far eluded him. He found management, who set up a showcase in Music City, and began learning a long list of songs they believed would impress industry executives. Two more trips to the "twilight zone" awaited him before he signed his recording contract.

"I took off from work on the night before my showcase, and started driving to Nashville," Sammy recalls. "I was exhausted, and about twenty miles south of Jackson, Mississippi, I fell asleep at the wheel. The truck went straight into the guardrail on a concrete bridge, and by all rights, should have flipped over into the river below. If that had happened, I'd have been finished. But it rolled to a stop, and I got out to see the damage. The whole right side of the truck was demolished, yet none of the wheels were locked, and the truck was all right to drive. Once again, I had this feeling of being the only person in the world when I stood beside that truck and understood what could have happened. The only other presence I felt was of a spiritual nature."

When Sammy finally made it to the Opryland Hotel in Nashville, he slept a few hours, then went to rehearse with the band his managers had put together for the show. Rehearsal was a disaster. Not only did Sammy not know all the lyrics to the songs they were playing, the band hadn't even listened to the tape they'd been given. "I'd listened to the songs on earphones a lot," he says. "But it was while I was working at WalMart, and I must not have paid good enough attention, because I didn't know them." An hour or so before the show, Sammy told his managers, "This ain't gonna work. This is the chance of my lifetime, the thing I've worked twenty years for, and I've gone and blown it." Then he went back to his hotel room to shower and dress for what might have been his golden opportunity for a record deal.

He went back to the Opryland Hotel's Stagedoor Lounge just before showtime, only to find a total of six people in the room: his managers, Mercury Records executives Harold Shedd and Buddy Cannon, and two waitresses. He walked over to the side of the room and knelt down beside his guitar case thinking, "This is a terrible way to go down." But when he opened the case and started to take the instrument out, he had a shock.

"I looked down, and saw my father's face staring back at me. A big old tear slid down my face and onto the image of my dad. Then as plain as day, I heard his voice saying, 'Everything's gonna be all right, son.' Now, when my dad was alive, he was just as hard on me as my grandmother had been, so when he said things were all right, I had to believe him. I picked up the guitar, walked the four or so yards up to the stage, and when I stepped up on stage, and turned around, the room was full of people."

Sammy Kershaw put on quite a show that night. The band never missed a note. And when he finished the last song, he got a standing ovation and an encore. He played "The Race Is On" and the crowd went wild. He signed a record deal with Mercury's Harold Shedd the next day, with Buddy Cannon as his producer.

When Sammy and I talked about this experience, I asked him if he'd ever wondered if the crowd was real, or somehow planted in his mind to help him do a rousing show. He said he didn't know, but he did know that the face and voice of his father were in that room. He's continued to have psychic experiences, too, one of which involves a promise to God.

"When I signed the record deal, I made a promise to the Lord," Sammy says. "I promised to always sign autographs with a 'God Bless' just as a small reminder of how much we owe the Lord. I did it for several years, but as my career took off, I thought I was too busy to do it and started just signing my name. I was off the top-ten for the next two years. One day I was sitting on the bus, signing autographs and wondering what had happened to my career, and it hit me that I hadn't kept my promise to God. I went through the photos and added God Bless, and never stopped. The very next single cracked the top-five."

The most recent encounter Sammy'd experienced when we spoke had occurred just a few weeks earlier. He was plowing a field on his tractor, when he had the sudden urge to call country television personality Lorianne Crook. "I'd been on *Crook & Chase* in January of '97," Sammy says. "That's the last time I'd seen Lorianne, and I don't think I've ever talked to her except during interviews or events. But I knew I needed to talk to her, and called my office and asked them to see if they could find her. They called back and said she was taping a show so they'd given her my pager and cellular numbers. She called a couple of days later and I told her that there had been no reason I needed to talk to her, except that nagging feeling that something was about to happen. Lorianne told me her husband, Jim Owens, had suffered a slight stroke later in the day on the afternoon I'd tried to find her."

Deborah Allen's paranormal experience was the result of her longtime admiration for Sarah Vaughn. Deborah, who later recorded for several labels, including Capitol, RCA and Giant, was singing at Opryland when she was chosen to appear with Tennessee Ernie Ford on his 1974 tour of the Soviet Union. The tour had a stopover in Chicago on the way back home to Nashville, and Deborah used her night in the Windy City to catch Vaughn in concert at a local nightspot. She noticed that a young comic named Freddie Prinz was opening the show, but the news didn't excite her. It was Sarah Vaughn Deborah wanted to see. Once she arrived at the club, Deborah began devising a plan to get backstage and convey her respects to the legendary vocalist. Her years of experience in the entertainment business served her well, and she wound her way through the theater's back halls and stairways to the dressing room area. A young couple passed her on a staircase, and she admired the huge painting of Marilyn Monroe the man carried.

"We're on our way to see Freddie Prinz," the man said. "Are you waiting to meet him?"

"No, I'm hoping to meet Sarah Vaughn," Deborah explained.

At that, the couple offered to introduce Deborah to Freddie, and she could ask the comic to arrange an audience with Ms. Vaughn. Freddie Prinz did just that. Deborah was ushered into a small dressing room, where her idol sat watching a show on a small black-and-white television, one foot propped up on a chair. There was a hole in Vaughn's stocking, and her toe poked through.

"I took in the whole scene and thought it was so cool," Deborah recalls. "I thought, 'This is the blues. This is jazz. This is backstage!' "

She went back to her seat, and watched Freddie's performance, followed by Sarah's headline act, where Vaughn even dedicated "I Remember April" to Deborah. "She referred to me as 'Debby,' " Deborah says with a laugh. "I wouldn't have let anybody else get away with that."

Deborah again went backstage after the show, and it was during this visit that she became better acquainted with Prinz. "We were just buddying around," Deborah says. "There was no romance involved." When Deborah moved to Los Angeles to become a regular on Jim Stafford's television show, the friendship between Deborah and Freddie grew. "I was hanging out at comedy clubs like the Improv and the Comedy Store with Jim Stafford," she says. "And we kept running into Freddie."

Freddie was by then filming *Chico and the Man* and he offered Deborah a role as an extra in several episodes, although, he added, her southern accent would preclude any spoken lines. Deborah's parents came to visit and she planned to introduce them to Freddie at a lunch the following day, after which they would be his guests at a taping of the show.

That night Deborah had a nightmare. "I dreamed I saw a hand reach under a pillow, and take out a gun," she says. "The dream frightened me so much I woke up, shaking. I didn't have the feeling that anything was threatening me, though. It was just an awful fear of what had happened when the hand took that gun from under the pillow."

The next morning was a dismal dark and rainy day in Los Angeles, and when Deborah's boyfriend awakened, she told him of the dream, and how scared she'd been. The morning news brought terrible news about her friend Freddie. He had shot himself in the head the previous night, taking a gun from under his pillow, and turning it on himself.

"I believe we were on the same wavelength that night," she says. "I think Freddie was thinking about the fact we were supposed to see each other the next day, and he knew he was not going to be there. According to the newspaper, he shot himself moments before I awakened from the dream."

AND NOW FOR a personal note:

When Skeeter Davis and I got a divorce in 1964, I bought a house on Shy's Hill in the Green Hills area of Nashville. Shy's Hill is located on the site of the Confederate left flank during the Battle of Nashville, where so many Confederate soldiers perished in December 1864. Many of the Confederates didn't even have shoes to wear in the frigid weather, yet they fought bravely until finally the Union army was able to move troops in behind the line. One soldier later wrote that the shot was so thick a snowbird couldn't have flown through it. When the line collapsed from Shy's Hill to Peach Orchard Hill, the Battle of Nashville was lost.

My house sat on the site where those frozen young men made that stand, and although I often thought about it, I never considered the fact that the place might be haunted until one freezing December night in 1965. Up until then I had always left one window open to let in fresh air, even in cold weather. But that night the wind was too strong and the temperature far below freezing, so for the first time my house was locked up tight.

I went to bed as usual, and during the middle of the night I had a violent dream that someone was breaking into the house. I sat up in bed but heard nothing, so I pulled the covers up tighter around me and lay back down. Suddenly a freezing wind passed over me, leaving the bedroom cold as ice. Yet the window I'd closed was still locked tight. You can make of it what you will, but I've wondered many times if it was the spirit of a young, cold Confederate soldier seeking shelter. I'd never be the one to say it wasn't. Nor would I be the one to discount the other stories told in this chapter. Not me.

HAIRDRESSER TO THE STAR?

BARBARA MANDRELL HAD just turned thirteen the winter of 1961 when she left on a package tour with Johnny Cash, George Jones, Don Gibson and Patsy Cline. Patsy and Barbara were roommates, and since they didn't always have first-class accommodations in those days, the two usually had to share not only a room, but a double bed. Barbara told me she was not easy to sleep with.

"You know how kids are, Ralph," she laughed. "They twist and turn and grab the covers. One night I woke up and heard Patsy whispering, 'Uh, Barbara, would you mind moving over just a little?' I realized I was laying right on top of her!"

Patsy was a great touring partner for the young girl, mothering Barbara, taking her shopping and out to lunch. She even allowed the thirteen-year-old to style her hair. "Patsy went to a beauty shop in some town and had her hair done. She just hated it, but it was too late to get it redone. So I said, 'Patsy, I can comb your hair. I even cut my mother's hair.' Can you imagine that, Ralph? If a thirteen-year-old offered to style my hair I'd say, '*Sure* kid . . .'

"But she went along with it, and even liked the way I combed it. For the rest of the two-week run I was Patsy Cline's hairdresser."

15

HILLBILLY MUSIC?

One of the things that has aggravated me through the years is to hear country artists called "hillbilly singers." There are country artists who good-naturedly refer to themselves as "hill-billies"; Faron Young used to call himself a hillbilly and Marty Stuart wears the label with pride. But usually the hillbilly tag is used with contempt. I remember Eddy Arnold telling me about going to a big package show in New York City back in 1948. Eddy stood and waited while the pop singers checked into their rooms at an elegant hotel. When his turn came, he stepped up to the desk.

"Do you have a reservation for Eddy Arnold?" he asked.

The desk clerk checked his list. "Oh, you're the hillbilly singer," he said. "You aren't staying here." Then he gave Eddy directions to a much lower-scale hotel in another part of the city. Eddy was a major star by 1948. His single "Anytime" had spent nine weeks at the top of the country charts and become a top-20 pop hit. But he was just another hillbilly singer to the hotel clerk.

"Redneck" is still another handle I don't like. The Reverend Will Campbell, author and longtime civil rights activist, agrees. In 1997 he spoke at the third annual International Conference on Elvis Presley and addressed the fact that many academics considered the meetings absurd. An entire conference about a redneck? Preposterous. Reverend Campbell began his speech saying, "If we are to academize Elvis Presley, there is one word and concept that must be dealt with at the outset. That word is 'redneck.' It must be dealt with because it is an ugly word, an invective used to defame a proud and tragic people—the poor, white, rural, working class of the South; a word used often to berate Elvis Presley and his people because the word is used as a synonym for bigot."

Reverend Campbell hit the nail on the head. Labels like "hillbilly" and "redneck" are almost always used in a condescending or scornful tone. I'm sometimes reminded of Dorothy Kilgallen's 1961 column in the *New York Journal,* when she so angered Patsy Cline by portraying country performers as poor white trash. That was Ms. Kilgallen's welcome to the Opry stars coming to perform a landmark show at Carnegie Hall that November. Along with Patsy, the lineup included Jim Reeves, Marty Robbins, Faron Young, the Jordanaires, Bill Monroe, Grandpa Jones, Tommy Jackson, Minnie Pearl and the Stony Mountain Cloggers, the "hicks from the sticks" as one column read. During one of her concerts, Patsy suggested that in reality, Dorothy was the Wicked Witch of the East. Kilgallen also took a shot at Elvis, labeling him nothing but a "hillbilly from Tupelo" in one column. Chet Atkins told me that it amused rather than angered Elvis, though.

The hillbilly name stuck until 1949 when country music pioneer Cliffie Stone convinced his record label, Capitol, to adopt the name "country" music. Cliffie, who passed away in January 1998 at the age of eighty, went on to play a big role in the development of country music in Southern California. He had a well-rounded career as a musician, singer, comic, deejay, music publisher, producer, record executive and author. Key to the careers of artists like Tennessee Ernie Ford, Merle Travis and Ferlin Husky, Cliffie was inducted into the Country Music Hall of Fame in 1989. Thanks, Cliffie. Thanks to you, it isn't the Hillbilly Hall of Fame.

Hicks. Rednecks. Hillbillies. The story of how country music got tagged hillbilly began in the spring of 1924, when Joe Hopkins stopped in Tony Alderman's Galax, Virginia, barbershop for a haircut, spied a fiddle hanging on the barbershop wall, and stayed for a hoedown. Joe, a railway express agent from nearby White Top Gap, came to town on a weekly basis to play and sing at his brother Jacob's medical clinic. The Hopkins brothers, Doctor Jacob, Joe and

Al, who served as the hospital administrator, firmly believed in the restorative powers of music, and over the years, people around Galax had come to agree with them.

Tony and Joe decided to start a band, and with brother Al they formed a trio that quickly made a name for itself throughout the region. Another local musician, five-string banjo player John Rector, had already made one record in New York, and was hoping to make another trip east. Not only did Rector think the combination of the brothers Hopkins, Alderman and himself could outplay any band currently on the show circuit, he also had a private agenda. Rector was a storekeeper, and needed to travel to New York to buy his fall stock.

The group recorded first for Victor, but the sessions came to nothing since the band was so spread out in the studio they couldn't hear each other playing. A year later they again set out for New York's recording studios, this time to work with Ralph Peer at Okeh. On the way the four men stopped by Joe and Al Hopkins's home in Washington, D.C., where, according to music historian Archie Green, former North Carolina state legislator John Hopkins listened to their plan with interest and some amusement.

"What do you hillbillies think you'll do up there?" he asked with a grin.

There in the Hopkinses' well-furnished home, the hillbilly handle was just a joke among friends. And so, after the Okeh sessions were complete, when label executive Ralph Peer asked the name of the band, Joe Hopkins said, "We're nothing but a bunch of hillbillies from North Carolina and Virginia. Call us anything you want." With the same amusement and good spirits displayed by the elder Hopkins, Peer called his secretary and told her to sign up "The Hill-Billies."

Tony Alderman was not so amused as he made the trip back home. The term "hillbilly" was not exactly flattering in polite circles. As far back as 1900, the New York Journal had described a hillbilly thus: ". . . a free and untrammelled white citizen of Alabama, who lives in the hills, has no means to speak of, dresses as he can, talks as he pleases, drinks whiskey when he gets it, and fires off his revolver as the fancy takes him." No one in the band even remotely fit those qualifications.

Back in Galax, Tony was still considering sending a wire to Peer and asking for a name change, when he ran into the man who taught him to play fiddle in the first place, Ernest "Pop" Stoneman. Pop was also an Okeh recording artist and a man of stature in southern musical circles. When he heard about "The Hill-Billies" Pop just laughed. It sounded like a catchy little name for a Virginia band.

In their earliest form, the folk songs that evolved into modern country music reflected the basic human need for something safe and familiar: an honest longing for solidarity. Much of the music evolved in the South. The settlers who entered this country through ports in the Carolinas faced a very different world than their Ellis Island counterparts. Northern immigrants intermingled with people from many countries, and whether they liked it or not, the cultures influenced each other. The South remained more isolated, with an agrarian economy; the earliest interest the South held for Europeans had, after all, been its tobacco-raising potential. As settlers spread out through the Southern regions of the United States, small pockets of population tended to burrow into the hill country and live out their lives with minimal contact with the outside, or urban, world.

The folk traditions brought from England, Scotland and Ireland, which were the basis for what we call American country music, were not exclusive to the South. Those same ballads could be found in settlements thoughout the New World. But in population pockets throughout the South, fewer outside influences touched the art form, and it retained a purity there as nowhere else.

It's possible to look on an isolated group in two ways. The first and most obvious is to view the population in terms of its lack of education or sophistication, its high illiteracy rate, the absence of modern amenities and seemingly slow social progress. Another way to see these pockets of population is as simple, untouched and proud keepers of their ancestors' culture. The people who took European folk traditions and turned them into America's music are all of the above.

The folk ballads dated back to medieval times and mysticism, religion and basic human survival were the primary themes. The songs often contained references to violence, natural disasters, religious experience, retribution and, always, death; the heritage of the Middle Ages remained even when settlers rewrote the old ballads to reflect their new circumstances or experiences. In a 1944 interview with the *Saturday Evening Post,* Art Satherley, the man who founded Columbia Records' country and folk division, explained: "The country people, these so-called hillbillies, are tremendously sensitive people, with deep emotions. Whereas the sophisticated city person likes these humbug boy-girl love songs, with everything pretty-pretty, the mountaineer is a realist. His songs deal with loneliness, misery, death and murder."

People write and sing about things they know, so as the folk traditions spread throughout the United States, the music picked up regional adaptations. Coal miners sang coal mining songs. Pioneers traveling in wagons took folk melodies and revised the words to include Indian attacks and starvation and broken-down wagons. In the West, cowhands sang to their herds and wrote what is now called "cowboy poetry." In often lengthy verse, these men held forth on topics from nights on the range to notorious outlaws and prostitutes to their love of Mom and hopes for a family. From Texas to California, Spanish influences were felt. Through all of America, certain themes are constant. Love won and love lost is the most common, whether it simply addresses a light longing for another or takes a dark turn to revenge and murder when love goes bad. Disasters, both natural and man-made, make great topics for country songs, and every American generation has produced odes to everything from train wrecks to coal mine cave-ins to the *Titanic* to the Gulf War.

It's a shame that this great music is often looked down upon as a stepchild of the industry and derisively called "hillbilly music." In the early days of the recording industry, few lived up—or down—to the name. The first two men to record country music were not hill people from isolated regions of the South, but westerners. In 1922, two years before The Hill-Billies recorded for Okeh, Oklahoma-born Henry Gilliland and Texan Eck Robertson recorded what are thought to be the first genuine country records ever made. Eck Robertson had knocked around for years playing traveling medicine shows, and Henry Gilliland billed himself as one of the most famous Indian fighters of the old West. The two had been slated to play a Civil War veterans' reunion in Virginia when on a whim they decided instead to go to Victor's New York offices and get themselves recorded. Gilliland was wearing a Confederate uniform and Robertson was outfitted in cowboy garb when they walked into the Victor company.

Henry Whitter, a Virginia cotton mill worker who called himself "the world's greatest harmonica player," saved his money, traveled to New York, and set up a meeting with Ralph Peer, the record executive who would two years later name the genre. When word slowly spread through rural America that a cotton mill worker could get an appointment with a record man in New York, many more began to save a bit each week. Another early figure, Georgia-born "Fiddlin' " John Carson, had worked as a racehorse jockey, a house painter and a cotton mill worker. And Vernon Dalhart, who had the first million-seller in 1924 with "Prisoner's Song," was a Texas native, but vocally trained at the Dallas Conservatory of Music, aiming for a career in light opera. So to label the music—and the artists—as "hillbilly" is misleading.

THERE ARE STORIES in this book from and about a lot of the people who made Nashville music the success it is today. Some came from the hills, others from small towns, still others from great urban centers. More than a few of today's stars have college degrees tucked in their guitar cases. What they share isn't a "hillbilly" personality, it's a love of this wonderful, earthy music sometimes called white man's blues.

LAWNMOWER MAN

EDDY ARNOLD WAS the Country Music Association's first Entertainer of the Year and one of the first to be inducted into the Country Music Hall of Fame. He has also sold over eighty-five million records. But Eddy grew up poor and as a consequence he is very tight with his money. I don't want to say my friend Eddy is cheap, but . . .

Eddy used to own a lot of property in Madison, Tennessee. One of his properties was leased by a big Buick dealership; they paid a lot of money every month to sell cars on Eddy's land. One day Eddy went down to that dealership and bought a new Buick, one equipped with neither air-conditioning nor a radio. A friend of his asked him why in the world he'd buy a brand new car without air-conditioning, especially here in the South.

"It's those extras that get you every time," Eddy said.

Eddy also cuts his own grass, even though he is over eighty years old. One day he was dressed in his old work clothes and mowing his lawn when a woman pulled into his driveway. When she hailed him, Eddy turned off the mower and went over to see what she wanted.

"I have a yard about this size," the woman said. "What do you get for cutting this one?"

"The lady of the house lets me sleep with her," Eddy deadpanned.

16

MONUMENT:

FOSTER'S MAVERICK

LABEL

Fred Foster had only recently moved Monument Records and Combine Publishing from Washington, D.C., to Nashville in 1960 when Wesley Rose invited him to lunch with a group of industry leaders. Wesley, the son of Acuff-Rose founder Fred Rose, managed one of Monument's biggest acts, Roy Orbison, and Fred Foster often disagreed with Rose regarding Orbison's career. That made the lunch invitation all the more sweet; Fred thought it was a "welcome to Music City" event.

He arrived to find Wesley, Hubert Long, Lucky Moeller and several other old-timers seated around the table. Before he could even look at the menu, Wesley spoke.

"What do you have against Nashville?" Wesley asked sharply.

"Why, nothing," Fred stammered. "I love this town. That's why I moved here."

"We think you're trying to destroy it," Wesley swept on. "You're making all kinds of rock records, race records—this is the country music capital of the world in case you forgot."

Fred was also making country records, but he decided not to argue about it. "Wesley, I believe there's only two kinds of records. Good ones and bad ones." And he put his napkin on the table and left.

About a week later Fred got a call from Owen Bradley, arguably the most powerful man in country music.

"Let's have lunch," Owen said.

Oh man, Fred thought. *Here we go again.* But since Owen was the big man in town, he agreed.

Fred hadn't even picked up the menu when Owen spoke.

"I understand you've met the Old Guard," he said with a sly grin.

"I guess I have," Fred said.

"Don't pay any attention to 'em," Owen went on. "You keep doing what you're doing—making great records."

IT WOULDN'T BE fair to talk about the Nashville Sound of the 1960s and 1970s, and the growth of Nashville as a recording center, without taking a look at the contributions of Fred Foster and Monument Records. At one time or another Monument was home to artists ranging from Orbison, Billy Walker, Jeannie Seely, Larry Gatlin, Boots Randolph, Billy Joe Shaver, Billy Grammer and Tony Joe White to Ella Washington, Little Milton, Roscoe Shelton and Joe Simon.

Fred signed both Dolly Parton and Kris Kristofferson to their first recording contracts, and he had his friend Willie Nelson on Monument—for about fifteen minutes. That signing has got to be one of the funniest signing scenarios in the history of Nashville.

Fred had been a fan of Willie Nelson's from the first time he heard him sing, but since Willie was on Liberty Records at the time, there was no way to sign him to Monument. One day Willie called and told Fred that he was off Liberty and looking for a label. "Come on over," Fred said. "I'll have your contract ready!" Willie signed with the label the same week that pop singer Lloyd Price ("Stagger Lee") signed, and that's where the story gets messy.

"I told Willie that I was going to take out full-page ads in *Billboard* to welcome them both to the label," Fred recalls ruefully. "They were so different that there certainly wouldn't be any competition between the two. The guy who was putting the ads together was a huge Willie Nelson fan, and he wanted to do a fancy ad, using purple to indicate royalty. The color kept running and he asked me if we could hold Willie's ad for the following week. I said 'Okay,' and called Willie. Well, everybody knows how tough it can sometimes be to track down Willie Nelson. I left messages all over Texas. Sure enough, on Monday morning Willie ran out and got a *Billboard* and his ad wasn't there. Lloyd Price's ad was, though. Willie thought I wasn't sincere about the deal, went out and got drunk and decided to sign with RCA. By the time I finally found him and explained what had happened, it was a done deal. RCA would have sued him, so I agreed to cut him loose.''

Willie and Fred remain close friends to this day, and they often laugh about the great *Billboard* fiasco and Willie's fifteen minutes on Monument.

I'M SORRY THAT there isn't a video to go along with this book, because I'd like people to meet Fred in person and feel the full impact of just how much he loves music. He's a sincere man who I believe treated his writers and artists as fair as or more fairly than anyone ever has in this town. Nashville politics meant nothing to him. The idea of cashing in on an artist's hard times was something that never occurred to him, and believe me, that's happened throughout the years in this business. Willie Nelson sold away the rights to ''Family Bible'' and ''Night Life'' for enough money to feed his family. When Kris Kristofferson came to Fred during a tough time, Fred could probably have had him over a barrel contract-wise. But as you'll see in this chapter, he played fair. I have a lot of respect for Fred Foster, yet another man who deserves his rightful spot in the Country Music Hall of Fame.

I FIRST MET Fred in 1953 when he was managing Del Wood and the two stopped by WAGG in Franklin, my third radio job in the short span of two and a half years. (Young disc jockeys move around a lot for a little more money.) I'd only recently been hired away from WNAH in Nashville to be a staff announcer and disc jockey at WAGG; it was a move I relished since as a junior jock at WTPR in Paris, Tennessee, I didn't get to do any interviews. I learned about pecking orders when the legendary Carter family visited me at WTPR, my first radio job. A senior disc jockey pulled rank and got the interview. Of course, the truth is, I'd only been there a few weeks and had no interviewing skills, so it's not surprising someone else got tapped to talk to the Carters.

So it happened that my first on-air interview was with Del Wood, the Grand Ole Opry's ragtime pianist who'd had an instrumental hit with "Down Yonder" in 1951. I had no way of knowing that over the next couple of decades, the young man with her would become one of the most vital and influential men in Music City.

Fred's managing an Opry star is one of those strange show business stories that sound like they were scripted for Hollywood. Fred Foster grew up in rural Rutherford County, North Carolina, surrounded by a music-loving family fond of front porch "play-downs," or jam sessions. When Fred's father died, the teenage boy tried to manage the family farm for several years, finally moving to Washington, D.C., where his sister lived.

He soon met a local entertainer named Billy Strickland, who introduced him to the music scene in Washington, and the two began writing songs together. To pay the rent he took a job in a record store and it was there that he met Del Wood.

Fred took his responsibilities seriously, considering it his job to educate people about songs, singers and musical roots. If a customer requested Frankie Laine's version of "Hey Good Lookin'," Fred insisted they hear the Hank Williams original as well. One day Del Wood happened into the store while in town promoting "Down Yonder." Fred didn't know who she was at first, and gave her the full roots and records treatment. Del loved it, introduced herself, bought a pile of records and asked Fred for his business card.

"Oh, I'm not high enough on the food chain to have a business card." Fred laughed.

"You should be," Del said.

About a month later Del contacted the young go-getter and asked him to manage her. "Are you kidding?" Fred asked, astonished. "I can't manage myself!"

Del persisted, enlisting the aid of her husband, and the two finally convinced Fred that while he had no real connections or contacts at the time, those were things he could make. What they needed was a go-getter who knew music.

"Del, I think you must be missing a board in your loft," Fred said.

"But I'll give it three months and see if it's something I can do."
Exactly three months later, Fred explained to Del that although he
believed he belonged in some facet of the recording industry, management wasn't his forte.

He stayed in Washington, D.C., where he worked for a succession
of record companies over the next few years. In 1958 he took a job
with J&F Distribution in Baltimore, and he was given a mission: create a pop division for London Records. Fred didn't last long with
J&F, since they refused to understand the importance of the emerging rock 'n' roll music. Fred explained in no uncertain terms that
they couldn't compete against Elvis Presley, Chuck Berry, Little
Richard and Fats Domino with safe, soft pop vocalists. "These are
the guys who are eating radio up!" Fred protested.

"If you think you can do any better on your own, go do it," an
executive named Walt McGuire said.

"I'll do that," Fred retorted.

AND SO IN August 1958 Fred Foster launched Monument Records
(named in honor of the Washington Monument) and Combine
Publishing with his life savings of $1,200. The first thing he needed
was a hit; it came through a pesky neighbor.

"A guy who lived upstairs in my apartment building was always
trying to get me to listen to his homemade recordings of sing-downs
and hootenannies," Fred recalls. "They were hard to listen to because they were poorly recorded and a lot of the music was bad, so
I'd resist as long as I could. But once when I went up and listened
a song jumped out at me. It was called 'Done Laid Around' and I
thought it had potential if parts were rewritten. My neighbor told
me it was an old public domain folk tune so I set to work on it. The
first thing that had to go was the title. I rewrote the chorus, added
a third verse and called it 'Gotta Travel On.' "

Fred called Billy Grammer, a member of Jimmy Dean's band, and
asked him to record the song, then phoned Chet Atkins in Nashville
and asked him to hire a band. By this time Chet was running RCA
Records and wasn't really in the business of being a session leader,
but he knew and liked Fred so he accommodated him. They recorded three tunes at RCA's Studio B, "Little Victor," and when

the sessions were complete, Fred had $80 left. He returned to Washington, D.C., and called Walt McGuire in New York.

"You told me to do better and I did," Fred said. "I'm in Washington making acetates right now."

"I'll take the shuttle," Walt said without hesitation.

McGuire knew Fred had recorded a hit, and tried to convince him to put it out on London Records. But Fred held out; "Gotta Travel On" became the first release on Monument Records, and Monument became the first of the London-distributed independent labels. Monument's debut release, a nineteenth-century British folk song rewritten by a North Carolina farmer-turned-big-city-record man, recorded by a member of Jimmy Dean's band in Nashville, became an international country and pop smash. Then Fred turned around and wrote "The Shag," recorded it on a guy named Billy Graves, and started a teen dance craze.

IN 1960 FRED moved Monument Records to the city where he recorded: Nashville. By this time he had several more artists, not the least of which was a Texas boy named Roy Orbison. Roy had recorded for Sun in Memphis but when he didn't break as fast as Elvis Presley, Carl Perkins, Johnny Cash and Jerry Lee Lewis, Sam Phillips cut him loose. Chet Atkins recorded some sides on him, but when he sent them to RCA's New York office the label turned them down.

Roy's manager, Wesley Rose, called Fred as soon as he learned that RCA had turned down Chet's session. Fred signed Roy immediately.

Chet once told me that when he produced Roy that old intimidation factor worked against them. "Roy later said that he believed we should have been able to make hit records," Chet said. "But he admitted that I made him nervous during the sessions. It was different—more laid back—when he went over to Fred at Monument."

Fred agreed that Roy was very unsure of himself in the early days. "The first session I cut on Roy got off to a bad start because Wesley forgot to tell him we started at ten o'clock A.M.," Fred recalled. "So I had the band there and Roy was a no-show. By the time we got him out of bed at the hotel and to the studio, he was very flustered about the mistake. And he was so shy that it was hard to get him to sing up over the band. We were recording two-track, and there wasn't any question of overdubbing. I used every kind of echo known to man and Gordon Stoker singing in unison with him on that first session.''

Nothing came of those first songs, except, perhaps, a lasting bond between Roy Orbison and Fred Foster. Once Roy relaxed, the hits started to come: "Only the Lonely," "Blue Angel," "I'm Hurting," and the first #1 pop single: 1961's "Running Scared." Once the mutual trust was formed, it had taken just a year to make the shy Texan a star, a singer's singer.

"Whenever we had a new Roy Orbison record, Elvis would call Monument and order several hundred singles at a time," Fred said. "Then he'd pass them out at his own shows, or take them to disc jockeys and say, 'Want to hear the greatest voice in the world?' You couldn't ask for a better endorsement.''

The strange thing was, Wesley Rose didn't seem to grasp just what he had in Roy. Once during an early session Roy asked if he could add strings, and Fred located four violinists, substantially raising costs.

"Why are you wasting your money on strings?" Wesley asked.

"The song needs them and Roy wants them," Fred said.

"Do you really think this guy's gonna make it?" Wesley asked.

"Sure I think he is," Fred answered, stunned at the seeming lack of confidence Rose displayed. This was Roy Orbison's own manager and song publisher.

Wesley shrugged. "He's not all that good-looking, especially when you compare him to guys like Fabian. I don't think he can compete.''

Fred was flabbergasted, and furious. "With friends like you, Wesley, Roy ain't gonna have to look hard for enemies. And anyway, it's my money.''

FRED ALWAYS THOUGHT in terms of the global market, and with Roy he hoped he had a worldwide star. The "Running Scared" session convinced him that he did. "Roy's high notes on 'Only the Lonely' were all in falsetto," Fred explained. "Then on 'Running Scared' we had this arrangement that started out with just a rhythm guitar and built up to strings, horns, guitars, drums and eight voices. The note at the end was the G above high C, and with the track so full you couldn't hear Roy when he went into the falsetto. I asked him to try and hit it full voice, and Roy said, 'Fred, I'm not Mario Lanza.' I finally got him to try by assuring him I'd erase it off the track if he couldn't do it. I didn't even tell the musicians that he was going for it. We started the song and it was a killer take, just magic. Then we come to the end, and Roy hit that note full voice. I'm surprised the musicians didn't just lay down their instruments. Harold Bradley's eyes widened and he stood up, still playing his guitar, but with his mouth wide open. Roy never again doubted himself, and I knew I had a star who could combine opera, blues, country and soul. He could sell records anywhere in the world.''

THE FIRST TIME I saw Roy Orbison play a show was in 1962 when he shared the bill in Montgomery, Alabama, with Bobby Vinton and my then-wife, Skeeter Davis, who was flying high then as a country star. One thing that stands out in my memory is the mob scene the teenage girls in the audience created when Bobby Vinton arrived. The other is Roy Orbison's lack of movement on stage. Roy belted out his hits, and even with the screaming audience members, he didn't react but just stood there wearing sunglasses and sang his songs. Fred told me why Roy turned from "entertainer" to singer.

"Roy tried to put together a show that was more than just his vocal performance," Fred said. "He told some stories and jokes and moved around on stage. But he was using Bobby Goldsboro's band back then, and once when he missed a flight connection he arrived at the venue so late that Bobby told all his jokes. Roy didn't know it, and got up and started telling the same stories the audience had already heard. There was dead silence, and Roy was mortified. He decided right then that his voice was going to have to be enough to carry the show. And it was more than enough.''

I asked Fred about the trademark sunglasses, and it turned out that the Montgomery show was the first time Roy wore them on stage. "Roy had sufficient vision problems that he had to wear glasses all the time," Fred said. "I thought he should get something different than the big round tortoise shell ones he usually wore, and we designed those straight-edged, flat-topped black-rimmed glasses that became associated with him. We got six regular glasses and six sunglasses in Roy's prescription. The guy who made them up for us actually trademarked them as 'Cat Glasses' and made a fortune. Roy accidentally left his regular glasses on the airplane going to Montgomery, and had to wear the sunglasses at the show. The publicity it generated was so big he decided to make them a part of his image."

Roy went on tour in England in 1963 opening for a band who'd had some success on the Continent: the Beatles. The British kids couldn't get enough of Roy, and his international success story was ensured on that trip. The Beatles loved Roy and his music, and the feeling was mutual. Not so with the next British band on tour with Roy. In 1964, just as the Beatles were making history in the United States, Roy returned to tour with another British band gaining in popularity: the Rolling Stones.

Roy and the Stones boarded a small charter plane to travel from London to Paris, where they would begin the second leg of their tour. When a storm blew up while they were over the English Channel, the light aircraft was tossed about, putting everyone in serious danger. Mick Jagger made his way to the front of the plane and grabbed the stewardess's microphone: "This is your Captain, Jim Reeves," he said. "I'd like to introduce your First Officer, Cowboy Copas and your stewardess, Patsy Cline."

Roy was thunderstruck. Nashville was reeling from the death earlier that year of Jim Reeves, and wounds still hadn't healed from the loss of Patsy Cline, Cowboy Copas and Hawkshaw Hawkins; all had died in air crashes. Then Mick took it one step further and began shouting at God.

"God, can you hear me? If you're such a big guy, knock us down! Just knock us out of the sky!"

Almost always quiet and soft-spoken, Roy didn't say a word until the plane landed safely in Paris. Then he walked up to Mick and said: "You'll never ride in the same airplane as me again. Don't speak to me. Don't even come near me."

He left the plane, went to his hotel, got on the telephone and repeated his sentiments to the tour promoter. They finished the tour, but the tension remained thick.

"Roy was a very spiritual guy," Fred explained. "So in addition

to the bad taste of what Mick said, Roy considered the whole mono-
logue blasphemy.''

Fred told me some interesting trivia about Roy Orbison. For one
thing, Roy loved movies. The first time the two went to New York,
Roy dragged Fred to five movies in one day. He loved the fact that
in New York you could go to movies starting in the morning. Another thing I found interesting was that Roy was a history buff. He
studied two time periods in particular: World War II and the Old
West. "You could ask Roy Orbison about any World War II battle,
or any obscure gunfight in El Paso and he could tell you exactly
what happened.''

One day in early December 1963, Willie Nelson walked into Fred's
office and said, "I know it's awful late in the day, but I just wrote a
Christmas song I want you to hear, 'Pretty Paper.' '' Fred loved it,
picked up the phone and called Roy in Europe where he was touring.

"I'm overnighting you a demo," Fred said. "If you like the song,
call and tell me the key.''

The next afternoon Roy called with a key. Fred got Bill Justis to
do an arrangement, they cut the track and Fred was on a plane to
Europe the following day. When he arrived, Roy was sick, but even
with a temperature of a 103, he nailed the song in one take. Fred
flew back, pressed the records and released the song to radio. It had
been about a week since Willie Nelson had written it. When Willie
heard it on the radio he again stopped by Fred's office. "So that's
how it's done," he said.

I asked Fred how "Pretty Woman" came about and he said that
Roy's first wife, Claudette, inspired the song. It seems that Bill Dees
came to Roy's house to write one afternoon, just as Claudette was
going shopping. Roy asked his wife if she needed any money and
she said no, she didn't.

"Don't you know that pretty women don't need money?'' Roy
laughed. Then the two men looked at each other and said almost
in unison: "Pretty Woman.''

They finished the song and brought it to Fred the next morning.
"It was a great song, with one problem," Fred recalled. "The last
verse went like this: 'You're not the only fish in the sea. Go on, walk
away from me.' I said, 'Roy, that's too negative. Just because she
doesn't fall all over this guy doesn't make her any less pretty, and

that's the point of your song.' Roy just shook his head and said, 'I don't know how I let that slip by!' He rewrote the final part of the song and it was a smash."

I've always thought that the arrangement of "Pretty Woman" was outstanding, but Fred said there wasn't an arrangement when they went in to cut the song. "Roy's initial thoughts were to arrange the song along the lines of 'Only the Lonely,' " Fred said. "But we really needed a driving song, so he started working the rhythm out there in the studio. Jerry Kennedy was playing guitar on the record, and he came up with the idea of playing it through with one guitar, then adding a second guitar, and finally a third. Also, Roy wanted his road drummer to play on the record along with Buddy Harmon. I knew the road guy wasn't getting to play as much as he'd like, so to pacify him I had him double with Buddy and the result was that hard-driving beat."

Another "accidental" arrangement happened with "Yakety Sax," the classic Boots Randolph release that *Billboard* called the "world's largest selling instrumental." It was all because the water fountain behind the piano at "Little Victor" studio had malfunctioned, and the repairmen had left some copper tubing on the floor. "I picked up one of the tubes, and for some unknown reason put it on the piano bench," Fred recalled. "Bill Purcell was playing a rhythm pattern and the tubing made an interesting sound bouncing on the bench beside him. I thought, 'I wonder what would happen if I put another tube there?' We knew, however, that the bass note wouldn't match up with the copper tubing bouncing around, and so we got some paper towels from the bathroom and muted the bass. *Billboard* wrote in their review: "Multi-harpsichord rhythm track. Scintillating."

Fred told me that Boots sold more records for Monument than Roy Orbison, and I found that fascinating. If you'd ask almost anyone who they thought was the biggest seller, I'd wager they'd pick Orbison.

TO ME, KRIS Kristofferson has always been one of the most enigmatic of Nashville's characters. We didn't get many Rhodes Scholars in town, especially ones who take janitor jobs at record labels, as Kris did when he came to town. He'd come here after turning down a first chair professor position in English Literature at West Point, which would have made him the youngest colonel in the army not commissioned on the battlefield. When he first walked into the Monument Record offices, he was having boot problems.

"Bob Beckham ran Combine Music for me," Fred explained. "We had a deal where he could sign writers for a certain amount of money without checking with me, but if they needed a bigger weekly draw, both of us had to be involved. He phoned me one day and said he wanted to sign a guy named Kris Kristofferson but he wanted twenty-five dollars more a week than our usual deal. I told him to bring him over. Kris walked in, nervous as a cat at a dog show, with the sole of his boot torn halfway down.

" 'The first thing we better do is fix that boot,' I said, and put a big rubber band around the boot to keep it from flapping. Kris loved that, and I guess he saw immediately that we weren't exactly formal.

"I always had writers sing me four songs, since I knew anybody, talent or not, could luck up and write one really good one but probably not four. About halfway through the second song I thought, 'Boy I hope I'm not hallucinating because this guy is great!' When he finished I told him I'd sign him to a writing contract on one condition. That he also sign a recording contract and make records for Monument.

" 'Man, I can't sing,' Kris said. 'I sound like a frog.'

" 'Yeah, but a frog that can communicate,' I answered.

" 'Well, if you're crazy enough to offer me a record deal, I'm crazy enough to take it,' Kris said."

ABOUT THREE WEEKS later Kris came to Fred's office and told him that paying him his weekly draw was throwing money away. "I'll let you out of the deal," Kris said. "I can't write. The well's run dry."

Fred could see that something was troubling Kris, and asked him what it was. Kris hesitated and finally explained that he was having money problems. "I owe more money than there is in the world," he said.

"How much is that?" Fred asked.

"I don't even know," Kris said.

So the two put a pencil to it, and finally figured out that Kris owed around $13,000, much of it for his children's doctor bills. Fred co-signed a loan, upped Kris's weekly draw, and vowed to come up with an idea to help him get rid of his writer's block.

"Your well's not dry," Fred said. "The bucket just isn't hitting the water right now."

Several days later, Fred was in the office of songwriter Boudleaux Bryant, with whom he was planning a trip to Mexico City to record the symphony. Boudleaux had an office in the Monument building, and Fred had been in and out several times that day checking on trip details. Boudleaux had just hired a new receptionist named Barbara McKee, and at one point, he kidded Fred.

"I don't think you're coming in here to see me, I think you're coming in to see Bobbie."

"Bobbie?" Fred said.

"The receptionist. Bobbie McKee," Boudleaux answered.

"Right, haven't you heard about me and Bobbie McKee?" Fred said. By the time he got back to his office he had the idea. Kris wrote the song "Me and Bobby McGee," insisting on sharing writing credit with Fred. The writer's block was not merely broken, it was shattered. Within a week Kris brought in two more songs: "Help Me Make It Through the Night" and "Sunday Morning Coming Down."

On hearing his two latest efforts, Fred wryly commented, "I guess the well wasn't quite dry after all, was it Kris?"

Kris attended a church service with his friend Connie Smith and was inspired to write the song that became his biggest solo hit, "Why Me." Fred was knocked completely back by the power of the song, but wasn't sure about putting it on the otherwise secular album they were recording. "At the end of the session I suggested we record 'Why Me' and see how it came out," Fred recalled. "Kris's wife, Rita Coolidge, and Larry Gatlin sang harmony. It was a tremendous recording, and after Kris went back to L.A., I decided to add the Jordanaires and put the song on the album. When I told Kris about the Jordanaires he said, 'Man, I feel like Ricky Nelson!' We were distributed by Columbia at the time, and Danny Pinkart, their Atlanta promotion guy, told me a great story about breaking the song. Danny was shaving one morning when the head of CBS, Clive Davis, called him. Now Clive Davis is probably the greatest record man that's ever lived so a field guy getting a personal call from him was something. 'Danny, I read in your weekly report that Kris Kristofferson's 'Why Me' is getting some airplay in Marietta, Georgia.' The guy stammered. 'Yes sir.' He didn't even know Clive read those reports. 'See if you can't expand on that in some other Georgia markets,' Clive said. Well, Danny was so excited that Clive Davis had called him personally that he ran out to his car and got halfway to his office before he realized he'd only shaved half of his face! He broke the song big in Atlanta. It sold over six hundred thousand copies and is still the biggest-selling single in the history of the Atlanta branch. That kickstarted everything, and it became a number one country hit nationally."

One day when Fred was in New York, Clive asked him to come to his office and listen to a song that the late Janis Joplin had recorded shortly before she died. "I'm having trouble with my A&R department," Clive said. "I'd like your opinion on a mix."

"Well, that's not really fair," Fred said. "You've got a multitrack tape around somewhere and you're going to play me a two-track mix. I won't know what's on all the tracks."

"You'll be able to tell," Clive answered. "They tell me the guitar is too loud."

"Oh, sure," Fred said with a shrug. "I can tell you that."

The intro kicked in and Fred sat there thinking that it sounded like the same chord progression as "Me and Bobby McGee."

"Then that voice came in with 'Busted flat in Baton Rouge,' " Fred recalled. "I thought 'Oh, man!' I knew she was a great rock singer but I didn't realize she could sing as soulfully and gently as she did on that song. I told Clive I couldn't help him on the mix. The record had just shattered me. After the song was over, it took me a while to get myself together. And I kept thinking Clive would never sign a new distribution deal with anybody as unstable as me who couldn't even comment on a mix! Finally I said, 'Anybody touches that mix, you break their arms.' Clive smiled and said, 'That's exactly what I think.' Then he picked up the phone and told his staff to release the record as it stood. There'd be no remix. That night I called Kris and told him that it wasn't a record, it was an experience. Kris heard it once and the experience was so potent in light of her death that he couldn't listen again for a long, long time."

MONUMENT HAD TWO of my favorite records of all time: "Christmas Guest" by Grandpa Jones and "I Just Wish You Were Someone I Loved" by Larry Gatlin and the Gatlin Brothers. Fred told me that Grandpa discovered the basis for "Christmas Guest" among some old books of public domain poetry he discovered when he was touring in Germany.

"The National Library should have as good a poetry collection as Grandpa Jones," Fred said. "I've never seen anything like it, and I also have seldom heard the emotion put into a song that Grandpa put in that recording."

Larry Gatlin came to the label through Kris Kristofferson and Dottie West. "I was at the studio recording a Billy Walker album one day when Kris and Dottie stopped by with an artist's tape. They had some young kid with them, but he stayed in the background and I thought he must be their driver. I listened to the voice on the tape and said, 'Bring this guy to the office tomorrow. I'll get a contract ready.' Kris pointed to the kid and said, 'There he is. His name's Larry Gatlin.' "

HIS DECISION TO offer Dolly a deal was just as swift and sure as were the Kris Kristofferson and Larry Gatlin signings. Fred signed Dolly when nobody else in town would give her a chance.

Billy Graves, who'd recorded "The Shag" for Monument, was working at Capitol Records under Ken Nelson. "Billy went out on one tour with 'The Shag' and when he got back he told me he hated being a star," Fred laughs. "So he decided to get into A&R." When Ken turned down Dolly, Billy called Fred. Once again, Fred asked the singer/songwriter to sing four songs. When she finished he said, "I'll have the contract drawn up tomorrow."

"I don't know why you even listened to me," the astonished Dolly said. "Everybody in town has turned me down!"

"I'm not everybody in town," Fred said.

But then he offered her a warning. "Dolly, you're very different, and you'll have to understand going in that there will be people who don't like your voice. There'll be critics who won't accept you at first."

"That's all right," Dolly said. "I just want *somebody* to like me."

There was criticism, too. Her vibrato irritated some, and she worked to tone it down. I didn't mind it; after all, Kitty Wells had that vibrato and it didn't hurt her at all. Luckily for country music, enough "somebodies" liked Dolly's music.

Fred wrote some prophetic liner notes on her first album. He compared her to Jean Harlow and Marilyn Monroe and predicted that in addition to a successful recording career, Dolly Parton would one day be a great movie star.

"A *movie star?* You are the craziest fool I've ever met!" Dolly said when she read the notes.

In Chapter Thirteen, "Dolly and Friends: At Tootsie's Orchid Lounge," I touched on the time when Dolly left Monument and signed with Porter's label, RCA. When I got together with Fred privately, I asked him how that whole thing was handled.

"It wasn't handled," he said, shaking his head. "Not well anyway."

"Were you just a nice guy and let her go where Porter wanted her?" I asked.

"I sure didn't feel like a nice guy," he answered.

Here's how it came down: Dolly's original contract with Monument expired just before Porter signed Dolly as a regular to his television show. Fred sent her a new one with a royalty increase and other benefits. She called and thanked Fred, telling him how happy she was with the contract. "I'll sign it," Dolly promised. In the meantime, Fred and Dolly started recording her next album, and one day Dolly excitedly told Fred that Porter Wagoner was auditioning her to replace Norma Jean. The next thing Fred knew, Dolly was hired for the *Porter Wagoner Show* and Porter wanted a meeting to discuss Dolly's promotion.

"I'll have our promotion people go wherever you and Dolly tour," Fred said. "They'll take her around to the radio stations separate from you and RCA. We'll work with you however you want."

"I'm gonna need forty-five hundred deejay copies of each single," Porter said. "What's my price?"

"Whatever they cost me."

They talked a bit more, all very cordial, or so Fred thought. Then a few days later Fred was working at a studio on 7th Avenue North in Nashville, and got a call from Dolly.

"Can you have lunch with Uncle Bill and me at the Downtowner?" she asked.

Fred thought she was bringing him the signed contract. But they'd no more than sat down when Dolly told him that she couldn't re-sign with Monument.

"Porter says RCA won't let us do duets if I'm on Monument," she said regretfully. "I just hate it but I don't know what else I can do."

"I hate it, too," Fred said, suddenly lacking in appetite.

"You aren't mad are you?" Dolly asked, nearly in tears.

"I better go," Fred said. "It's best we don't talk about this right now."

He went back to the studio, crushed. He knew that the fact that they'd already started on a new album could legally bind Dolly to another contract, but he also knew he wouldn't press the issue. If she was being pushed from one side, he wouldn't add more pressure on her. Fred's lawyers hit the fan over his decision.

"It's a matter of intent," they said. "She's already recording with Monument. You can force her to stay."

"No, I can't do that," Fred said. "I *won't* do that."

"I was devastated," Fred said. "It was like if your wife walked out on you. I had so many plans for Dolly. I knew she could be a huge star—records, movies—you name it, she had the talent."

As you read in the Tootsie chapter, Fred and Dolly stayed friends in spite of what happened. I have to say that a lot of record executives wouldn't have been as nice about it. They'd have tied her up whether Porter liked it or not. But, to paraphrase what Fred told Dolly when he gave her the chance to make records: he's not like everybody in this town.

My hat's always been off to real record men like Fred Foster.

"REMEMBER ME?"

I'M A BIG fan of actress Katharine Hepburn, so when Theodore Bikel appeared on *Nashville Now* to promote *Fiddler on the Roof,* I was anxious to hear his experiences working with her. Theodore made his film debut in 1951's *The African Queen,* after director John Huston saw him perform in a London play called "The Love of Four Colonels." The invitation to appear in a film with Bogart and Hepburn thrilled him; learning that neither were on "star trips" delighted him.

"Humphrey Bogart was a very warm and genuine person," Theodore said. "He had a crusty facade that was all an act that you saw through quickly. Katharine Hepburn lacked any star pretenses. She peddled around on her bicycle, and when we shot scenes on the water, she would paddle about in a small boat handing out flasks of rum or brandy. It was an unforgettable experience."

Theodore Bikel went on to a distinguished film and theater career after that auspicious beginning, including receiving an Oscar nomination for supporting actor in *The Defiant Ones* in 1958 and creating the role of Captain Von Trapp in the original Broadway cast of Rodgers and Hammerstein's *The Sound of Music.* He was living in New York in the late 1960s, and had just finished installing central air-conditioning when the phone rang and a voice from his past asked him if he would give the air-conditioning firm a good reference. The woman identified herself thus:

"Mr. Bikel. My name is Katharine Hepburn. I wonder if you remember me?"

17

OLIVIA NEWTON-JOHN:

NEW BEGINNINGS

I didn't agree with the brouhaha following Olivia Newton-John's Female Vocalist of the Year win at the 1974 Country Music Association awards show. It seemed like half the people in Nashville were mad that what they considered an "outsider" had snared the top prize for women, over Loretta Lynn, Anne Murray, Dolly Parton and Tanya Tucker. A group even broke from the CMA for a while and formed their own short-lived competitive organization, ACE, the Association for Country Entertainers.

It seemed to me that it was a slam at the country disc jockeys who were playing her records, and that included me and virtually every other country deejay in America. Her 1973 U.S. debut, "Let Me Be There," was a top-10 hit in both country and pop, as were her two 1974 releases, "If You Love Me (Let Me Know)" and "I Honestly Love You."

After all, country artists did handstands when they crossed over and made a splash in the pop charts, so why shouldn't Olivia—or anyone else—cross the opposite way if the song fit our format? Moreover, Olivia hadn't been known in this country long enough to have been typecast. According to Olivia, two of the 1974 nominees went out of their way to be publicly supportive of Olivia and her Female Vocalist title: Loretta Lynn and Dolly Parton. Loretta, especially, knew what it felt like to be the new "girl singer" in town, and have others question whether the proper dues had been paid. It had been Patsy Cline who stepped to the fore on Loretta's behalf, and Loretta was now repaying that debt in a way.

WHEN I INTERVIEWED Olivia for *On the Record* in 1998 she told me she had never seen a broadcast of the show since she'd been in England touring at the time. I had a clip of the show ready to roll, and we both laughed when Roy Acuff announced the winner: *Oliver Newton-John.*

I asked Roy one time how it had happened and he reminded me that he'd tried to get his fellow presenter, Chet Atkins, to read the name, and Chet refused. "It was because Chet didn't want all the girls out there to know he had to wear reading glasses," Roy explained. "I couldn't see the name very good even with my glasses."

Olivia learned about the clamor over her new title months later. "I was touring at the time," she reflects. "So it took the news a while to catch up to me. I think my manager withheld the story from me for quite a while to spare my feelings. But while I did understand why it would be a bit peeving to see some Aussie woman come along and win, I do think it opened even more doors for country artists to cross over to pop."

I have to admit that I got sick of hearing "Let Me Be There." Not only was it playing nonstop on the radio, but also, every female singer who came on my morning television show that year wanted to sing that song. But I never tired of hearing Olivia sing, and she sings just as beautifully now as she did twenty-five years ago.

In November 1997, Joy and I attended the Operation Smile concert in Nashville. The funds raised at this annual event go to help rebuild children's faces deformed by accident or birth defect. One of the night's highlights was when Olivia and Vince Gill sang "You're the One That I Want." And Vince even danced, although according to Olivia he balked at the idea at first. "Vince came to me during rehearsal and said he couldn't dance," Olivia laughed. "I said, 'Would it be okay if I just pulled you along?' He agreed, so that's what I did. I grabbed Vince by the collar and hauled him around the stage."

Her interest in Operation Smile is not surprising, since Olivia is so involved in charity work that people in Australia sometimes compare her to the late Princess Diana, calling Olivia their own "Princess of Hearts." She's currently working for a Children's Bill of Rights and she works tirelessly for environmental causes. One of the ways she's raised funds for her work with environmental groups is by donating a portion of the royalties received from her 1993 children's book, *A Pig Tale*.

"I like pigs a lot," Olivia said. "And one day I mentioned to my son that I was annoyed at the way people disrespected pigs. You know, they'll refer to some despicable individual as 'such a pig.' So I said we should start referring to despicable people by saying, 'Oh, they're such humans!' My son liked that and started writing a little story about a family of pigs. Much later, I attended an AIDS fund-raising dinner in New York and sat next to an editor at Simon and Schuster who liked the idea, and asked me to write it in rhyme. It's all about a pig family who recycles."

Born in Cambridge, England, Olivia moved to Australia at age five when her father, Brinley, was named the Master (Dean) at Ormond College in Melbourne. Academia was an important element to both sides of her family; Olivia's maternal grandfather was Nobel Prize–winning physicist Max Born. Yet Professor Born discouraged Olivia's mother, Irene, from pursuing an academic career. "My mother would have been a wonderful teacher," Olivia said. "She is very intelligent and wanted to study science. But for some reason, my grandfather didn't encourage her along those lines."

He did encourage music, though, and Olivia's mother remembers many times that Born, his friend and colleague Alfred Einstein and other family members gathered with violins and cellos at the Born home to play classical music.

Born, whose Nobel Prize was for his work in quantum physics, which led to the splitting of the atom, left Germany as Adolf Hitler was coming to power. "He read *Mein Kampf* and got the family out immediately," Olivia explained. Born always feared the misuse of the scientific knowledge he and Einstein helped unleash. "My mother and I were watching television when the first news reports of the Three Mile Island incident occurred," Olivia recalled. "Mother turned pale and said, 'That's exactly what my father feared.' "

The name Newton-John is a combination of her father's surname,

John, and his mother's maiden name, Newton. It caused some confusion at least once, when a Las Vegas hotel manager mentioned to a well-known comic's manager that his client would be on the bill with Olivia Newton-John. "My guy doesn't work with trios," the comic's representative said.

The first record Olivia's father ever bought her was Tennessee Ernie Ford's *Gather 'Round,* which included a song that became one of Olivia's favorites, "Old Blue." She's always had a love of folk songs like "Banks of the Ohio," which had moderate success in America, and was a big hit in England. She played this song a lot in her live shows, because as she explained to me: "It's only got about three chords, and that's about all I can play on the guitar!"

It always mystified me that the British people could identify with songs about American places, like the Ohio River. I asked Olivia if she thought they were interested in the places, or just liked the music. She thinks it's because of the tie to old Celtic folk songs. "I don't think I ever understood just how violent a lot of these old folk songs are until much later," she laughed. "They have all these lines like, 'I held a knife against his breast.' "

Olivia won a talent contest in Australia at age fifteen, one that included a trip to England where she performed on the *Johnny O'Keefe Show,* a British program much like Dick Clark's *American Bandstand.* Her mother came with her, and when opportunities to perform kept cropping up, the two stayed on. Olivia and a friend, Pat Carroll, formed a pop duet, singing and dancing in numerous clubs in London. They made their own costumes, with Pat constructing the garments and Olivia adding the handwork that made them distinctive.

Pat ended up marrying writer/producer John Farrar, of the British group called The Shadows, who would later become Olivia's producer and write many of her hits. Olivia continued a solo career and in 1971 got an amazing break when she was invited to tour with British superstar Cliff Richard. In 1970 she became a regular on his television show. Olivia continued to have hits through the 1970s, charting for the last time (to date) in country music with 1979's top-30 "Dancin' Round and Round." Some of her hits were "Have You Never Been Mellow," "Please Mr. Please," "Let It Shine" and "Come On Over."

*   *   *

IN 1978 A chance meeting with a film producer who was looking for a female lead for his musical, *Grease,* led Olivia to a successful career in films. We talked about *Grease,* which was set for a twentieth anniversary rerelease in 1998. "I can't believe twenty years have gone by," Olivia said. "I guess the lesson there is to enjoy every day, because all of a sudden you'll turn around and two decades are gone."

Olivia aced out stars including Ann-Margret and Marie Osmond through a chance meeting with the film's producer. "Helen Reddy, who is a fellow Aussie, invited me to a dinner party in Los Angeles," Olivia explained. "I sat opposite Allen Carr, who was looking for someone to play the role of Sandy. I didn't even know about *Grease* and spent the whole night clowning around, as usual. Allen decided I was perfect for the part, but I was not convinced at all. I asked him for a screen test, so we could make sure I was capable of playing the role. There were actually two roles to be played, Sandy One and Sandy Two. I thought I could carry off Sandy One, the good girl. But I didn't know about Sandy Two, the wild one. The day I dressed in my leather pants, curled my hair and sprayed it and put on all the make-up, a lot of the guys working on the crew didn't recognize me! They started whistling when I walked through the set."

Grease has become an American classic, and I asked Olivia if she had a theory as to why. "The music is fun and the characters are cartoon-like, larger than life," she speculated.

In 1980 Olivia had the opportunity to work with the legendary Gene Kelly in the musical *Xanadu,* which resulted in a #1 pop hit, "Magic." For this film, she not only had to learn to tap dance, but to roller-skate. "You can imagine how nervous I was when I knew I'd be dancing with Gene Kelly," she said. "I'm not a trained dancer. I have to practice every step. And the roller-skating proved a real problem. I fell and cracked my tailbone, so I had to sit on an ice donut between every take!"

Olivia has won countless awards throughout her career. One of the most exciting was her first Grammy, in 1973, the first time a singer from outside the United States won the top female vocalist award. Other high points include the 1978 OBE award (Officer of the Order of the British Empire) presented by the Queen of England. She's also made a Command Performance for the Queen (with Paul Hogan, who actually started his career as a comic in Australia) and was a guest star on the *Silver Jubilee Television Show,* honoring Queen Elizabeth II's twenty-fifth year of reign.

In 1984 Olivia went into partnership with her old friend and duet partner, Pat Carroll, and founded a clothing company called Koala Blue, opening their first store on Melrose in West Hollywood. The business eventually expanded into fifty-five countries.

By this time Olivia was a mother, so throughout the remainder of the decade, Olivia concentrated on her daughter, and on her clothing company. Then, in 1992 her world began to crumble. Her father was diagnosed with cancer and Koala Blue filed for bankruptcy.

Olivia hadn't toured for nearly ten years, but she gamely agreed to get back out on the road. She was just beginning rehearsals for her first major concert tour in ten years when she discovered a lump in her breast.

Although a mammogram turned out negative, Olivia was still concerned enough to request a needle biopsy. That, too, had negative results. But Olivia hadn't been feeling her usual energetic, positive self, and she feared there was something the tests had missed. A complete biopsy was finally performed, but her husband withheld the results because that same week, Olivia's father became very ill with cancer.

She visited him in Australia, hoping to return after her tour. When she came back to L.A., she had a full biopsy, then went on a short trip to rest and recover. The day she got home, she replayed messages on her answering machine and heard her doctor's voice requesting a callback. In the meantime she received word that her father had passed away.

"I knew then that it was cancer," she said. "I had the surgery and began eight months of chemotherapy, all the while worrying that I'd let people down by canceling the tour. Finally I had to come to terms with putting grief over my father's death and concerns about the tour on the back burner. I had to concentrate on getting well."

Concentrate she did. Like Naomi Judd, Olivia made a concentrated effort to learn how to deal with catastrophic illness. She read, meditated, drew on faith and gathered a support system around her.

She learned to visualize the healing process by picturing her dog stalking cancer cells in her body and systematically gobbling them up. And she learned she had strengths she didn't know existed, and courage to face down cancer and win. Even the chemotherapy, which scared her more than the initial surgery, was something she could face.

"I was so afraid when they put the needle in me that first time, that I really thought I was dying. But then I came through it. I learned something very important: cancer is not always a death sentence. I'd always thought it was. The minute I heard someone had cancer, I thought they were dying. But that's not true. In some ways the experience enriched my life. I know that sounds odd, but it has helped me grow and understand my priorities. I'm grateful for every day."

Today she often gives talks to women's groups, talking about her own experience, counseling other cancer survivors. "It's so important to have support from women who have gone through this," she said. "When I first started chemo, my doctor gave me the names of two women who had come through it, and I relied so much on them. It was as if I could see down the road when I, too, would be well."

OLIVIA CAN NOW help others look down the road to wellness, because she has beat cancer. "I don't even use the word 'remission'," she explained. "It makes it sound like the cancer might come back." And in conjunction with her return to health, Olivia is returning to country music. In 1997 she returned to Nashville and began work on a new album for MCA Records. *Back with a Heart* was released on May 12, 1998.

"I don't relate to pop music anymore," she told me during our *On the Record* interview. "And the camaraderie in Nashville is something I've always loved, something that made me feel welcome." I asked her what country artist she'd like to tour with, and she didn't miss a beat: Vince Gill.

There is—and always has been—room for more than traditional country music in Nashville. Owen and Chet proved that years ago. Patsy Cline proved it. And my next chapter is devoted to a woman who possibly proved it more than anyone else: Brenda Lee.

GEORGE BUSH:
COUNTRY FAN IN THE WHITE HOUSE

PERHAPS MORE THAN any other United States Chief, George Bush focused the nation's attention on Nashville and country music. When I interviewed him at his office in Texas, he expanded on his feelings about one artist in particular: Roy Acuff. "I knew Roy long before I met him, because I've loved country music for a long time. I think he was probably the first musician I remember from the days in Odessa and Midland, Texas, back in the late forties and early fifties. He was the 'Dean' of country music back then. Then I had a lot of contact with him over the years when I got into public life. Roy was a sound thinker politically. He was a great American and a good friend."

George Bush has always been his own man, whether it was standing up for his political decisions or for the music he loved. President Bush was sometimes accused of using country music as a political tool, to make himself seem—as his friend Jimmy Dean once joked—"less stuffy and more accessible." It is an accusation that angers him.

"A lot of the sophisticated Beltway pundits would have had the American people believe that my love of country music was an affectation. That I was trying to be a good-old-boy and get people in the South to vote for me. I've always loved country music, and it burned me up to hear people accuse me of using it. They always want you to fit a mold. Yes, I grew up in the East, and yes I was privileged and given a lot of things. But I spent years listening to country music in little clubs in Texas, and this music is in my heartbeat. But that is something the cynics would never see. I say, the hell with 'em."

I agree. The hell with 'em.

18

B R E N D A L E E :

L E G E N D S A M O N G U S

Brenda Lee is one of the funniest people I know. If she hadn't been busy selling over a hundred million records on her way to rock and country legend status, she could have had a great career in stand-up comedy. Brenda is especially good at Phyllis Diller routines:

"My mother-in-law is so fat she wore gray one day and an admiral boarded her. When she wants a salad we just pour oil and vinegar on the lawn and set her out to graze."

But most of her humor is directed at herself. Her size is one of her favorite gags. One day she told me that like many people, she'd started to shrink as she got older. "I'm down from four nine to four eight now," she said ruefully. "Before long I'm just gonna be a grease spot in the hall."

Brenda's size gave her a leg up in the Japanese record market, she says. After years of selling gold and playing standing-room-only concerts in Japan, Brenda was talking to a promoter and asked why he thought she had so many fans in the country. "Well, aside from your singing, it's because you're so little," he explained. "You're as short as they are." Brenda shared the sentiment, too. "It's not all that great, living life at armpit level," she said with a sly smile. "So every time tall people get to bugging me, I catch a plane to Tokyo."

I once played Brenda a recording of the following radio interview I did with Pat Boone:

ME: "Pat, you must have an introduction for the little girl that your father-in-law, Red Foley, discovered."

PAT: "We used to call her the tennis ball when we watched her on Red's show in Springfield."

ME: "Why?"

PAT: "Because she seemed about as big as a tennis ball. Then her hair was sort of fuzzy. She was just a little girl with a voice like a female moose."

ME: "I'd like to hear Brenda's reaction to that comment!"

PAT: "What I meant was the volume of her voice. It was so big. This big booming voice coming out of this little girl."

After the tape finished, I laughed and said to Brenda: "Fuzzy hair, tennis ball, voice of a moose—and he was trying to be nice!"

"Now Ralph," she said. "I'll bet he wouldn't call Dolly Parton a moose!"

That's Brenda. She never takes herself too seriously.

I'M SURE THE staff at Emory University Hospital charity ward just saw the baby girl born to Ruben and Grayce Tarpley on December 11, 1944, as another child born to poor parents in wartime America. I wonder if years later any of them ever turned on a television and saw Little Miss Dynamite, or purchased an album featuring Brenda Lee, one of the biggest-selling stars in the history of recorded music.

Brenda's father wanted to name her Hortense, but luckily Grayce won out, and the baby girl was named Brenda Mae, nicknamed Mae Pop for a flower found growing wild in Georgia. She began singing while still a tiny tot, able by the time she was three years old to voice the lyrics of any song she heard. The family was too poor to have either a television or a radio, but Brenda discovered music anyway. She loved the Hank Williams songs her mother sang around the house, and the gospel songs she heard in church each week. But she was extremely partial to one song, "My Daddy's Only a Picture," performed by both Eddy Arnold and Mahalia Jackson.

She started winning contests at an early age, too. Her older sister, Linda, entered her in a school talent contest before she was even a student, and Brenda won a box of peppermint candy for her efforts. She was invited to become a regular on a local radio show, *Starmakers Review,* and her performance of "Hey, Good Lookin' " on Atlanta's *TV Ranch* secured her a regular spot on that show as well. Brenda's first paying job netted $30, for an appearance at a Shriner's Club luncheon. Getting paid to sing soon became of paramount importance to the young girl.

Brenda's father, a former semipro baseball player and construction worker, died in 1953, and the next few years were hard for the family. Grayce's small income working long hours in a cotton mill could not have fed and clothed the family were it not for Brenda's singing jobs on the weekends. Both mother and daughter were perpetually exhausted.

In 1955 Grayce married Jay Rainwater, who took a job at the Jimmy Skinner Music Center in Cincinnati and moved his new family to Ohio, where Brenda began performing with Skinner on his Saturday morning radio shows. But Jay Rainwater soon wanted to return to Georgia and moved the family back to Augusta, where he opened a record store. In Augusta, Brenda crossed paths with two men who had major influences on her career. First, Brenda began singing at WRDW Radio on a show hosted by Charlie "Peanuts" Faircloth, a man who would later introduce her to two of the most important men in her career. And when she started performing on WJAT-TV's *Peach Blossom Special,* the show's director, Sammy Barton, dubbed her Brenda Lee. "Sammy said 'Lee' was easier to remember and easier on the eye in promo materials," Brenda explained.

Brenda's musical tastes were expanding all the time. Now that the family had a radio and a phonograph, the young vocalist was listening to the people who would become major influences: Edith Piaf, Judy Garland, Bessie Smith and Billie Holiday. But she also loved country music, and it was a country star who helped her secure a recording contract.

In 1955 Brenda made one of the best decisions of her young life when she turned down a $30 gig for a radio station in Swansboro, Georgia, to attend an Augusta performance of one of her favorite country stars: Red Foley. Dub Allbritten was managing Red, and Charlie Faircloth badgered him into introducing his child prodigy singer to the star. Red reluctantly allowed Brenda to sing, and later explained that he stood transfixed, chills running up his spine at the power of the voice and the professional stage demeanor.

Red and Dub immediately signed Brenda to appear on Red's *Junior Jamboree*, a once-a-month version of the *Ozark Jubilee*. It was her first nationwide television performance, and it led to performances on other national shows, including *Perry Como* and *Steve Allen*.

"My mom and I would get on a bus every Friday after school and ride all night long to get to Springfield, Missouri," Brenda recalled. "I'd rehearse all day and tape the *Junior Jamboree* that evening. Then we'd get back on a bus and go back home."

Finding Brenda a record label proved more difficult than Red and Dub had anticipated, since many label executives were reluctant to sign a child. The last label the two men visited was Red's own record company, Decca, where Paul Cohen signed her in May 1956, after hearing her sing once.

Three months later Cohen took Brenda into the studio where they recorded "Jambalaya," "Your Cheatin' Heart," "Doodle Bug Rag," "Christy Christmas" and "Bigelow 6–200." The label released "Jambalaya," backed by "Bigelow 6–200," the next month, promoting their new artist as Little Brenda Lee, age nine, three years younger than her real age.

"I remember the players from that first session well," she says. "Grady Martin never smiled, and I was just terribly afraid of him. It's funny, because he became a great friend, but at first I thought he was fearsome. Of course, all the players were looking at me like they were thinking, 'Oh boy, here we are with this kid.' Bob Moore hit a bad note on his bass during that session and I stopped singing and said, 'The bass player played a bad note.' Bobby bristled and said, 'I did not.' So they played it back and sure enough, he was off. The guys got a big chuckle over that."

"Jambalaya" didn't survive the charts, and the age deception later caused much confusion, according to Owen Bradley, who ultimately became the prime force in her recording career. "I remember one birthday party she had where they made three cakes just to catch up and set the record straight," Owen laughed. "It took me a long time to figure out just how old she was!"

Decca then tried to launch Brenda with the two Christmas songs, but even with the holidays looming, the singles stiffed on the charts. Luckily, the chart problems didn't stop Brenda's concert draw. She played her first Las Vegas date that December, and went out on a tour with some of country's biggest stars, including Patsy Cline.

"The promoter of the tour ran off with the money, and that left my mother and me high and dry," Brenda recalled. "We couldn't even eat, let alone get back to Nashville. When Patsy realized what we were up against, she packed us up in her car, bought us food, paid our hotel bills and got us home. She became like a big sister to me."

I reminded Brenda that Patsy's reputation was a bit saucy, and asked if she ever saw that side of her.

"Patsy gave as good as she got," Brenda explained. "She believed you had to stand up for yourself, and not prostitute your beliefs. She always told me to not take things too seriously, just to try to be professional, to show up on time and do your job. She also said to be appreciative of what was given to you through the business.

"I'd say that in the very best sense of the term, Patsy Cline was a good broad. I loved her so much I named my daughter Julie after her daughter. I'd have named her Patsy except Loretta beat me to the name when she had her twins!"

Paul Cohen decided to give Brenda more of a rock edge and teamed her with Milt Gabler, who had produced Bill Haley's "Rock Around the Clock" for Decca two years earlier. Backed by the Ray Charles Singers, Brenda recorded her first chart single, a pop gospel song titled "One Step at a Time." Another song recorded at the session, "Dynamite," didn't chart, but gave Brenda a nickname, Little Miss Dynamite.

In 1957 Brenda's parents moved to Nashville, officially signing Dub Allbritten as her manager. To protect her financial future, Judge Beverly Briley made Charlie Mosley, an accountant and the co-owner of Ernest Tubb's Record Shop, her legal guardian. Due to the Jackie Coogan laws, Brenda's money was put into a trust until she was twenty-one years old. And it was a considerable amount of money, too, because even without a released album, Brenda was reportedly making $34,000 a month! But there was a downside to this situation: Brenda may have been a big star, but she was still living poor.

"We lived in a trailer park on Dickerson Road in Nashville," she says. "The trailer we had was terrible, two rooms and an outside toilet. We lived there until 1960. They allocated my mother $75 a week and that had to support me, my mother, my sister and brother and half sister."

Brenda attended Maplewood High in Nashville for two years. She was well-liked at school, serving as class president, editor of the school newspaper and cheerleader, along with her friend Rita Coolidge. I told her I would have thought she was too short to be a cheerleader.

"I tried out for the basketball team first," she said with a quick grin. "When they laughed at that I decided that cheerleading was the only way I could be part of the sports program. We wore white bucks with the bobbie socks rolled down. I wore double socks so the tops would be thicker. And our skirts came clear down to the rolled-up socks. We must have looked amazing!"

There is only one bad memory Brenda has of her school days: algebra. "I made good grades until they threw algebra at me. I flunked it and they sent me back to general math. That was a big humiliation in my life."

Brenda's mother Grayce, while no stage mother, did have good instincts about her daughter's career path, and she was determined to allow her as close to normal a childhood as was possible under the extraordinary circumstances. Owen Bradley told me that Grayce often asked Brenda to sing a song again, even after her producer felt she'd nailed it. And he admitted that Grayce's instincts were usually right.

BRENDA STAYED IN Nashville public school until her last two years of high school, when the family finally moved to Los Angeles so she could star in *Two Little Bears* with Eddie Albert, Jane Wyatt and

Jimmy Boyd, who'd had a hit with "I Saw Mommy Kissing Santa Claus."

"I went to Hollywood's Professional School in Los Angeles the last two years of high school," she says. "The school was a riot. They had two shifts, one from eight A.M. to twelve P.M., and another from twelve P.M. to four P.M. You could be right in the middle of a test and a casting agent would come in the classroom and say, 'We need an eight-year-old with blond hair and blue eyes.' And if you fit the bill, you just left. A lot of us went to the school. I was in classes with Mickey Rooney Jr., and we had our graduation party at Ryan O'Neal's house. I graduated with his brother, Kevin. I showed up in my bobby socks and poodle skirt, only to find that Ryan had hired two strippers to perform as a present to his little brother! Luckily, I told my friend I thought we should leave and we did, because they got raided."

BRENDA FIRST APPEARED on the Grand Ole Opry in December 1957, sharing the bill with Elvis Presley. Brenda sang "Jambalaya" and "Bill Bailey Won't You Please Come Home," and Elvis, in town to meet with Colonel Tom Parker, performed "Blue Moon of Kentucky" and "That's All Right." I'd always heard that Brenda and Elvis forged a friendship that night that lasted until his death in 1977.

"We were friends in that I knew I could always talk to him, or see him if I wanted," Brenda explained. "He gave me his phone numbers at Graceland and Los Angeles. But Elvis had so little privacy, I never wanted to infringe on it. The strange thing is that the week before Elvis died, I'd been on a plane with Ginger Alden and happened to mention that my youngest daughter, Jolie, loved Elvis. I said I'd love to get Jolie a scarf autographed by Elvis, and Ginger said she'd send one. Two days after he died I received the scarf in the mail."

I also asked Brenda about the night the two performed on the Opry. The photos I saw showed him to be wearing a tuxedo, which seemed an unlikely costume for the King. Brenda says when he got to the Opry, he was told his attire was not appropriate. Elvis ran down to Mallernees Men's Shop and bought a tux.

*   *   *

PAUL COHEN MOVED to Coral records in 1958 and he turned the Nashville operations of Decca over to Owen Bradley. Part of his job involved producing Brenda Lee, now fourteen years old.

In May 1958, Owen put Brenda in his renowned Quonset Hut studio with his A-Team musicians: Floyd Cramer on piano, Hank Garland and Grady Martin on guitars, Harold Bradley on electric bass and Bob Moore on stand-up bass, and Buddy Harmon on drums. The first session produced no hits, but when they returned in October, they recorded a song called "Rockin' Around the Christmas Tree," which went on to become one of the top-10 Christmas songs of all time.

The song was written by Johnny Marks, whom I had known from his many visits to Nashville. He also wrote "Rudolph the Red-Nosed Reindeer." I interviewed him a number of times, and he once told me that he sent Decca twenty-five of his best works, but the only one they kept was a Christmas song: "Rockin' Around the Christmas Tree."

"People think I only write Christmas songs," he said.

But it's like Harlan Howard once told me: better to write a standard than a hit any day.

Brenda says when Owen played her the songs, that was the one she liked. Paul Cohen applauded the choice, because he felt Brenda needed to record a Christmas song.

"When the holidays roll around, labels start thinking they ought to make Christmas records," Owen said with a grin. "So we did. But the demo was just Johnny playing a piano, there wasn't anything rocking about it. We made up the entire arrangement in the studio. That was the Nashville Sound at its best, when everybody was being creative. The problem was that Brenda still wasn't having chart success, so the label didn't press enough records or promote it big. If you want a big seller you've got to have the distribution, press up a half million copies. I guess we sold five thousand copies that first year. It didn't chart until the following year, after she had hits with 'Sweet Nothin's,' 'I'm Sorry' and 'I Want to Be Wanted.' They've done pretty well with that Christmas record over the past thirty years."

I asked Owen if he'd been reluctant to record a child, and he laughed: "I was glad to record *anybody* in those days. And once you worked around Brenda a little, you stopped thinking about her as a child."

EARLIER IN HER career, searching for a way to propel Brenda to stardom, Paul Cohen asked Owen to record a collection of pop standards for the European market and the result was an album titled *Grandma, What Great Songs You Sing*, released in France in conjunction with a 1958 European tour. Excitement grew on the continent when rumors started flying that Little Miss Dynamite was really a thirty-two-year-old midget.

"Dub Allbritten started that." Brenda laughed. "We'd sent my promo pictures to France, with me in my little dress and crinolines, my Mary Janes. They kept writing and asking for more current photos. When Dub realized that they thought I was much older, he decided it would be fun to play it up. Dub had been a wrestling promoter and like Colonel Parker, he had a circus background. It was a natural for him."

That tour marked the beginning of a love affair between Brenda and European music fans. They have remained among her most loyal throughout her career, a phenomenon Brenda says reflects the European love of rockabilly and respect for music history. From Europe, Decca sent Brenda on to Brazil, where the press translated Little Miss Dynamite to The Explosive Girl. Japan, too, was a prime market. But that all-important success in the United States eluded her.

THEN, IN AUGUST of 1959, Brenda and Owen heard the song that would change all that. "Dub and myself and Brenda were out on Old Hickory Lake, in a little boat that had a thirty-five-horsepower engine on the back," Owen explained. "I'd brought a tape recorder and we were listening to tapes, and all of a sudden we heard a hit, 'Sweet Nothin's,' written by Ronnie Self, a friend of Brenda's from the *Ozark Jubilee* days."

"Sweet Nothin's" was released in February 1960 and it made it to top-5 in the pop charts. Not long after it hit, Elvis Presley called

Brenda at her office and asked for an autographed copy of the single. "It's my favorite record out right now," he said. Brenda's first #1 pop record, "I'm Sorry" (also written by Self), was released in June 1960 and stayed at #1 for three straight weeks, beating out even Roy Orbison's "Only the Lonely."

"I'm Sorry" remains Brenda's biggest-selling single, and it garnered her a Grammy nomination and a gold record.

For little Brenda Lee, 1960 was a life-altering year; after struggling five years for a hit, she arrived in a big way. Following "Sweet Nothin's" and "I'm Sorry" came hits with "That's All You Gotta Do" and "I Want to Be Wanted." And for the 1960 Christmas season, Decca rereleased "Rockin' Around the Christmas Tree."

Brenda decided it was high time to get her family out of the Dickerson Road trailer, and petitioned the court for enough money to buy her mother a house. "Charlie Mosley looked at the house and the financial papers, and finally agreed to the purchase. The house only cost fourteen thousand dollars, but considering the red tape involved in our buying it, you'd have thought it was the Taj Mahal."

I WASN'T ALLOWED to play any of these records on my all-night show at WSM. They had strict rules about what we could play, and pop or rockabilly records were forbidden on a country show. I remember once when Buddy Holly stopped by the station I had to apologize to him because we didn't have any of his records. I couldn't have played them even if he'd brought one with him. Buddy was very cordial about it, though, and seemed to understand that it was station policy over which I had no control. "Oh, that's okay," he said. And he just sat there and talked for an hour or so.

The programming setup was very strange back then. From 6:00 A.M. to 7:00 P.M., WSM played soft pop music à la Nat King Cole and Perry Como. From 7:00 to 10:00 P.M., classical music, a favorite of WSM president Jack DeWitt, was programmed. I came on with my country show right after the 10:00 news, and I often led the show off with Flatt & Scruggs playing "Shuckin' the Corn." I've always pictured a symphony lover sitting by his fireplace, sipping a brandy and listening to the news, forgetting what came next. I'm positive "Shuckin' the Corn" wasn't pleasing to the classical ear.

Brenda wasn't thinking in terms of what charts she would hit. She was simply looking for good songs. "I trusted Owen," she says. "I don't know why, but from the very beginning I knew he would look out for me musically. I just wanted to get good songs and sing them the best I could."

Since Grayce still had small children at home, she couldn't always travel with Brenda, so manager Dub Allbritten kept a close watch on the young girl out on the road. "Dub didn't have any children," Brenda laughs. "Maybe that was why he was so protective. He'd lock me in the hotel room because he was so afraid someone would knock on the door and I'd let them in. Years later I asked him what would have happened if the hotel burned down! He said the thought hadn't occurred to him."

One night during a European tour, Dub locked Brenda in her room and headed off to bed. Unbeknownst to him, it was the hotel's practice to put a hot water bottle in each bed. He crawled into bed and his foot hit the bottle, which was not smooth like the standard hot water bottles, but ridged, making Dub believe an animal was in the bed with him.

"I heard a big commotion from the next room, but there was nothing I could do to help because I was locked in," Brenda laughs. "Dub said he jumped out of bed and tried to beat the animal to death with a coat hanger. It kept on gurgling there under the cover, so he grabbed a pillow and tried to smother it. The more he fought with it, the more it gurgled. I thought it was hysterical when he started telling me about it the next morning."

There's another great Dub Allbritten story that happened years later, during the blackout in New York City. Brenda, her husband Ronnie Shacklett and Dub were in New York, staying on the seventeenth floor of a hotel. They got back late that night and retired to their rooms. Dub had been having some eye problems and was feeling less than a hundred percent. Brenda was napping and Ronnie was showering when the lights went out. Ronnie stumbled from the shower to open a curtain, thinking the street lights would help some. The entire city was black. Within a couple of minutes they heard Dub shouting and banging on their door.

"Let me in," he cried. "I've gone blind!"

On one trip to England Brenda became acquainted with an unknown band named the Silver Beatles who toured with a singer named Tony Sheridan. Brenda began working with the Silver Beatles, John, Paul, George and Ringo, at a famous German night-spot called the Star Club. They were playing the songs that they later made famous, and Brenda knew they were headed for stardom.

"They were crazy, those boys. But I loved them and I loved their songs. They were fabulous. It was amazing to listen to them do a whole show of songs they'd written and each one was better than the last! And as crazy as it sounds, I liked their irreverence. I took back a little demo tape and a picture and tried to get Decca to sign them. I wish I had the tape now, it would be worth a fortune since one of the songs was 'I Want to Hold Your Hand.' I think the people at Decca didn't like their sound and couldn't get past their haircuts, which was one of the things I loved about them. I was used to working with European acts who dressed up, so the look didn't phase me. That was in 1962, and they exploded in Europe the following year."

ONE OF HER British fans asked his mother if she would invite Brenda to sing for him. The fan was Charles, Prince of Wales, and he convinced his mother, Queen Elizabeth, to request a Command Performance. Also on the bill were Americans Bob Newhart and Lena Horne and British performers including comic Tommy Cooper and singers Cilla Black, Cathy Kirby and Millicent Martin.

Brenda soon learned that there are a lot of rules connected with singing for the Queen of England. First, the royal aides told her she mustn't look at the Queen while she sang her song, "All the Way."

"She'll be seated in a box to your left, but don't look," one gentleman admonished. Brenda had no idea how she'd manage that, but she said she'd certainly try.

The next potential source of embarrassment was the curtsy she was expected to give at the end of her performance. "I had a knee injury from a skating accident, and I just knew my knee would go out if I tried to curtsy," Brenda said. "I had on a long dress and asked them if I couldn't curtsy with my good knee since nobody could see. That was vetoed."

The stage was set up with a revolving Rolls-Royce convertible in the center. As soon the curtain came up, a driver was supposed to open the door and Brenda was to emerge. When the time came, the door stuck. The entire crowd waited while the man pulled and pulled. No luck. Finally, while the musical introduction was playing, Brenda could see no alternative. She hiked up her gown, climbed out over the top of the door and took the microphone.

"I walked on stage and my eyes fluttered to the left, and there was the Queen of England ablaze in about eighty million dollars' worth of jewels! How in the world was I going to keep from looking at her?"

Brenda did keep from looking directly at the Queen, and she even made it through her curtsy. But backstage she was advised that if she was to be presented to the Queen she must be wearing gloves.

"You may not touch the Queen's skin," the aide cautioned.

Brenda had no gloves. "I have never been accused of being feminine," she laughs now. "I'm too much of a tomboy to own fancy gloves."

Backstage at the Command Performance, Dub Allbritten was not amused.

"You don't have any gloves with you?" He frowned.

"Did you tell me to bring gloves?" Brenda responded.

"You won't be able to meet the Queen," Dub said, running around frantically backstage. "This is terrible."

"Let's run out and buy some gloves," the enterprising Brenda suggested.

"Nothing's open," Dub said.

All of a sudden a dancer from one of the acts sharing the Command Performance walked by and Dub noticed she was wearing long gloves. "Dub walked right up and asked her if I could borrow them," Brenda says. "They were so long on me that they came up to my shoulders and the hands were so much bigger than mine that I was afraid the Queen would shake my hand and get nothing but a fist full of glove. If the Queen noticed my outsized gloves she didn't react. She said 'My son Charles is your great fan, and it was at his request that we invited you to sing for us.' "

ONE OF BRENDA'S favorite recollections is of meeting Judy Garland. "I was fourteen years old and set to follow Judy in the main room

at the Sahara Hotel in Las Vegas," she says. "I was scared to death
to be following Judy and although I desperately wanted to meet her,
I was also scared at the prospect of it. It was like the experience
would be too thrilling or something. I went to see her show the last
night she played and she was wonderful. But I chickened out and
didn't go backstage. Somehow she got wind of the fact that I wanted
to meet her, and the next day I received a message from one of her
representatives. Judy invited me to meet her and her daughter, Liza,
who was about my age, down by the pool.

"When I got down there, she turned out to be one of the kindest
and most gracious ladies I've ever had the privilege to meet. She
talked about the fact that she, too, had started in show business
when she was a child, and told me she understood the pressures of
having a career so young. She asked me if I was nervous about headlining in Vegas for the first time. When I admitted that I was terrified, she gave me a pep talk."

"It'll be okay, so don't worry about it," Judy told Brenda. "You
just get out there on that stage and do what you normally do. This
is no different than anywhere else you play. Get out there and sing
your songs, and the audience will love you."

Brenda told me that Judy Garland's taking the time and effort to
bolster a young girl's confidence is one of the favorite memories in
her entire career. "It was one of those rare moments when you
know you are in the presence of greatness," she explained. "I wish
now I'd have asked her for her autograph. But I felt she was too big
a star for me to ask it."

Brenda crossed paths with one artist long before he was a star:
Elton John. "While I was on a European tour in the late 1960s I
bought a record by an English artist I'd never heard about," she
recalled. "I loved the music, and wondered why Elton John
wasn't a household name. A couple of years later he exploded
with 'Your Song.' "

In 1972 Elton John played a concert at the Municipal Auditorium. Brenda didn't pull any strings, as she easily could have, to get
choice seats; she and Ronnie stood in line and bought their tickets
like everyone else. How Elton John knew she was there is a mystery,
but about halfway through the show he introduced his current hit

thus: "I wrote this next song for a hero of mine: Brenda Lee. Brenda, would you please stand up?"

"I almost fainted," Brenda says. "Ronnie and I had been sitting there, bopping along to the music and having a great time. I had no idea he knew anything about me or that I was in the audience. And I certainly had no idea that he wrote 'Crocodile Rock' for me!"

Throughout the 1960s Brenda turned to primarily pop-flavored recordings, then in 1970, Decca urged her to work with another producer. She declined, and instead took some time off to reevaluate her career. She wasn't yet thirty years old. "I didn't think there was a place for me in music any longer," she reflects. "Publishers were not pitching me their best songs, and my career seemed stalled. I decided I'd rather not release bad records, so I stopped recording."

Brenda's career has country bookends. She started out with Foley in country music, took time off to make rock history, then in 1971, Brenda and Owen made the decision to come full circle, back to country music where she had started. After a string of moderately successful chart records, they recorded a Kris Kristofferson song, "Nobody Wins," at Bradley's Barn, and the song became a top-5 hit.

Her biggest "comeback" chart hit came in 1974 with "Big Four Poster Bed," and she also had hits with "Tell Me What It's Like," "The Cowgirl and the Dandy" and "Broken Trust" with the Oak Ridge Boys. In 1984 Brenda and George Jones had a top-20 hit with "Hallelujah, I Love You So."

This body of music alone would have been enough to ensure Brenda's place among music's legends. But as Owen said when Brenda was inducted to the Country Music Hall of Fame, her contribution to the genre is in part because she proved that more than country records could be successfully produced in Nashville. Through the years of adulation, Brenda remained one of the most stable individuals imaginable.

Owen credited Brenda's home life and devotion to family as one of the things that kept her steady through a world-renowned career.

Brenda had gone on a few double dates when she met Ronnie Shacklett in 1962, but she'd never gone on a date all on her own. "I was ready to start dating at twelve," she laughs. "But Mother wouldn't let me. She was very strict about boys. She was like Dr. Jekyll and Mr. Hyde when it came to my seeing boys. Plus, I worked all the time. Consequently, when I got married, I'd never been to a drive-in movie. Never been to a circus. Ronnie took me to my first drive-in movie after we were married. I'd always heard about what people do at drive-in movies, but we just watched the film. Mother shouldn't have worried. Ronnie's so straight that if he had a mirror over the bed he'd probably just shave in it."

Brenda first saw Ronnie at the Nashville fairgrounds coliseum at a Jackie Wilson concert. "I was there with a couple of girlfriends, and all of a sudden I spotted him. I told my friends that I thought he was cute, and it turned out one of them knew the guy Ronnie was there with. As trite as it sounds, I sent him a note, that said 'My name is Brenda and here's my phone number.' "

Ronnie wasn't a follower of music and had never heard of Brenda Lee, even though at the time she had the #1 record in the world: "All Alone Am I." He waited a couple of weeks and called her for a date. At some point early in the courtship he mentioned to his father that he was taking out a girl named Brenda Lee. Ronnie's father was thunderstruck. He knew exactly who she was and in fact, was a big fan. "I always tell people I married Ronnie for his father," Brenda jokes. That was in October 1962, and despite objections from Dub Allbritten and Brenda's mother, Grayce, they married the next April.

I asked Brenda why the two objected. Did they think Ronnie was after her money?

"Oh, no," Brenda laughed. "I couldn't touch any of my money. Ronnie's family had the money. As a matter of fact, I might have married him for *his* money. My mother just thought I was too young, and Dub feared I'd get pregnant and stall out my career. A year later, when I did get pregnant, Dub said, 'You can't have a baby, you're booked!' "

Brenda and Ronnie's honeymoon was somewhat unconventional. "We didn't tell anybody we were going to get married, because we didn't want anybody to try and stop us," she says. "Ronnie fainted during the blood test and the doctor looked at me and said, 'Well, does that give you a clue?' I said, 'Revive him! He's going to have it whether he wants it or not!' We finally got to the church, got married, and left for Gatlinburg for our honeymoon.''

Brenda doesn't know how it happened, but a reporter in Gatlinburg got wind of the fact that Brenda Lee and her new husband were spending their wedding night in a local motel, and he camped out beside their door. It was April, and it was still cold in that part of Tennessee.

''We were scared to make any noise! The guy was right outside the door.'' Brenda laughs. ''And we got to worrying that he'd freeze to death sitting out there so finally Ronnie went out and asked him if he needed a blanket. Ronnie and I watched *Perry Mason* on television—we were big fans of Lieutenant Tragg. I said to Ronnie, 'Is this what happens on a honeymoon?'

''He said, 'I don't know, I've never been on one.' ''

Ronnie Shacklett is six foot four, and because of the height difference Brenda says they stopped dancing as soon as they got married. ''I was very personal with Ronnie's navel,'' she says, laughing. ''We try to make friends with couples where the husband is short and the wife is tall so we can go out dancing.''

Brenda is always poking fun at her culinary and homemaking efforts. She's actually a good cook, but it wasn't always so. ''We ate at Ronnie's mother's house for the first four years we were married,'' she laughs. ''They always set a plate for us because they knew we'd show up.

''Ronnie once had a terrible cold and put some Vicks VapoRub in a pan on the stove so he could heat it up later to inhale. I thought the Vicks was lard and used it to season the cabbage. My father-in-law ate it and never knew the difference between that and my usual cooking. I once tried to cut up a chicken and ended up with twenty-eight pieces. That was my first chicken and my last. I can make peanut butter and jelly sandwiches. As long as you don't have to put it in the oven, I'm safe. I'm pretty good with soup, though. Campbell's. Just zip off the top of the can and heat it up. Ronnie lost a lot of weight when we got married.''

Once when Brenda was on my radio show, I asked her about cooking for the holidays. Here's what she said:

RALPH: Do you cook the Christmas dinner?

BRENDA: Are you kidding!?

RALPH: We haven't talked about your culinary arts this time.

BRENDA: I'll just say this, if anybody is going to cook a turkey, take the insides out. That advice is for all the young married ladies that just got married. You do take those bags out.

RALPH: You cooked a turkey one time?

BRENDA: Yeah. And when Ronnie carved it, there was one of those little innards bags inside.

RALPH: You left all that in?

BRENDA: Sure I left it in. Nobody told me to take it out.

RALPH: What did Ronnie say?

BRENDA: He got a strange look on his face because we had his mother and dad over and all his relatives. So we all went out and ate.

RALPH: You didn't stay there and eat it?

BRENDA: Are you kidding? It was terrible! This year I bought everything assembled.

Brenda's bad driving is another source of Shacklett family legend. Over the years she's totaled four cars, a parking meter and a gas station. The parking meter, she simply ran over. The gas station was a little more difficult.

"I was filling my gas tank at the local filling station and got distracted," Brenda says. "I went in and paid for the gas, came back out and completely forgot that the nozzle was still in the tank. So I pulled out and started driving away, and the whole pump pulled out of the ground and gas started spewing everywhere. We're just lucky nobody was standing around smoking. I can't even imagine what it cost when Ronnie got the bill for that. I got so I wouldn't even tell him. They just phone him from 'You Smash 'Em, We Fix 'Em' and say, 'She's here again.' "

When Ronnie and Brenda bought a farm a while back, Brenda

was quick to remind him that field work wasn't her idea of a good time. "I told him that my hands were made for charge cards, not hoeing," she laughed. "Ronnie loves farm work—he just eats it up. He's one of those athletic out-of-doors types." Brenda paused and added, with a wink: "I'm pretty sure that fresh air makes you sick."

Brenda is always getting mistaken for other stars, and she takes great delight in going along with the individual who's uttered the faux pas. She's also a self-confessed yard sale freak, and one day she was sorting through some items at a sale when two elderly women approached her. "They were adorable," Brenda recalls. "They were ahead of me in line and loaded down with stuff they bought. When they were almost to their car one of them turned around to me and said 'Hey!' Well, I thought they wanted me to help them with their packages, so I put my stuff down and went over to them."

"Theresa Brewer! You look wonderful," said one of the women.

"Why thank you," Brenda said, taking several of the packages from the woman and walking along to the car.

"We bought 'Put Another Nickel In' and 'Ricochet Romance,' " the other woman exclaimed.

"Well, I am so proud you did that," Brenda smiled, and put the packages in the car.

"Now Theresa, you take care of yourself and we'll be watching for you on TV," one said as they buckled up.

"Okay," Brenda said, and waved good-bye.

One time Brenda and Ronnie were sitting at the Nashville airport when a small child lagging behind her parents noticed Brenda and stopped dead in her tracks. When the child's mother turned to urge her to hurry, the little girl pointed at Brenda. "I was flattered," Brenda said. "I told Ronnie, 'Look, that little girl knows who I am and she can't be more than three years old.' "

Ronnie looked at the girl and shook his head. "She must be pointing at the window. She's too young to know who you are."

The girl continued to point, and Brenda said, "No, I tell you she recognizes me. Isn't that amazing?"

Just then the little girl walked up to Brenda and spoke to the tiny singer with the curly red hair: "Hi, Annie!"

Ronnie laughed so hard he almost fell off his chair. Brenda just smiled and said, "Well, hi, honey!"

*   *   *

IT'S DIFFICULT TO be around Brenda and remember that this woman has sold over a hundred million records. A hundred *million!* Consider the following:

- Brenda is credited with more double-sided hit singles than any other woman in the history of pop music.
- She consistently charted in more categories (pop, rock, easy listening, country and R&B) than any other female in the history of recorded music.
- During the 1960s Brenda was the top charted female act and fourth overall charted act, outdistanced only by Elvis, the Beatles and Ray Charles.
- She ranks #9 in "Most Consecutive Top Ten Hits of All-Time."

BRENDA'S TOO NORMAL to have done all that. Too regular. Too much the bright, funny lady who might live next door to you and ask you over for coffee, to joke about her cooking, her driving, her honeymoon. If there's an ounce of "staritis" in her, I've never seen it. It's as though, unlike so many legends, she sailed right through it all unscathed and unaffected. Owen Bradley was right about her family: Grayce was part of the reason for her balanced nature, as was Ronnie Shacklett, Dub Allbritten and Owen Bradley.

Owen, in particular, became a father figure to her, and they were close friends until the day he died. It took every ounce of strength she could muster to accommodate a wish Owen had expressed to his wife and son: that Brenda Lee sing "Peace in the Valley" at his funeral. The emotion must have been fierce, because in addition to her feelings for Owen, Brenda's first mentor, Red Foley, had the hit with this song back in 1951 and it remains one of his signature songs.

I asked Brenda if there was one moment in her career that stood out more than any other. People have asked me the same thing and I've never come up with a good response. Brenda thought about it and finally said: "Probably when I knew I had a career. We released so many records in the United States that didn't do diddly-squat in the first years. Keep in mind that I started when I was five years old. 'Sweet Nothin's' hit in 1960, when I was sixteen, eleven years after I started singing professionally. When we got that hit, I knew I had a career. That was the moment.''

It reminded me of an old show business saying: there's one Cadillac that counts the most, and that's the first one you buy.

DOLLY AND BARBARA—
BATHING TIPS

DOLLY PARTON USES hill country humor in most of her favorite stories. Take the one about how the eleven Parton kids used to have to bathe in the hills.

"In the summer we'd bathe in the river," she says with a sly grin. "In fact, us Partons left a ring around the banks of the Little Pigeon River. But during the winter we had to wash up in the house. We'd use a wash pan, and wash up as far as possible, and then down as far as possible. Then when my brothers left the room, we'd wash possible."

BARBARA MANDRELL DIDN'T grow up in the backwoods where out-of-door toilet facilities are common. She was raised in California, but when she and her family went on a tour of military bases during her early teens, she didn't flinch at the makeshift bathing accommodations set up between two Quonset huts. "Mother and I were so happy to get a shower," Barbara recalled. "During much of the trip we had to use pails of soapy water and take sponge baths. We were lathering up in these small roofless tin buildings, when we heard some muffled noises coming from up above us. We looked around but couldn't see anything. But just when we rinsed off and wrapped up in our towels we realized that a group of men was peering over the wall at us. We screamed and a guard came running. Of course the men scattered before he could see them to make any identifications.

"Now the funny thing is, my mother is the straightest woman, the most perfect lady, I have ever met. But she took it in stride. She just grabbed towels around us and ducked out saying:

" 'Well, we came over here to entertain the boys, and I guess that's what we've done!' "

C O L O N E L   T O M   P A R K E R :

H O W   M U C H   D O E S   I T

C O S T   I F   I T ' S   F R E E ?

I've never seen such divergent death notices as when Colonel Tom Parker died in January 1997. They ranged from labeling the Colonel a liar, a cheat and the man who ruined Elvis to calling him funny, shrewd and scrupulous even in a handshake agreement. You get two different versions from men with whom the Colonel worked pre-Presley, too. Eddy Arnold has told me on several occasions that he liked and respected Tom Parker. Hank Snow, on the other hand, called him ". . . the most egotistical, obnoxious human being I have ever had dealings with."

Snow, who helped convince the Presleys to sign with what he assumed was to be Hank Snow/Colonel Tom Parker Management, later learned that the Colonel had cut him out of the deal, and never got over it. I phoned Hank and asked him if he'd talk to me about Tom Parker, and after a couple of minutes of dead silence on the line, Hank said: "Ralph, I hated Tom Parker. I'm not sure he didn't hate me, too."

"Hank, I thought you two were partners at one time," I said.

"I thought so, too," Hank said. And that was his final word on the subject.

COLONEL PARKER WAS a throwback to the old carnival pitchmen; that's how he started and how he finished, living for the art of the deal. You had to admire his chutzpah. When, for example, he began negotiating with Hollywood moguls about Elvis's film debut in *Love Me Tender,* he asked for $100,000. When told by one aghast executive that Jack Lemmon didn't even get a hundred grand for a picture, the Colonel puffed on one of his Cuban cigars and said, "Well, maybe Jack needs a new manager."

There's another great movie story. It seems a producer told the Colonel that Elvis would need to be at the studio by 5:00 A.M. to be ready to start shooting. "Would you inform Elvis of this?" the producer asked.

"I will inform him," responded the Colonel. "But for a little more money I'll go get him up and see to it he arrives."

The Colonel was always angling for a little more money. Hubert Long told me that the Colonel said if he wrote his memoirs, he was going to sell Purina the middle two pages for a dog food ad. He didn't think it was cheesy, just a moneymaking opportunity.

Another example of his carny personality involves the sort of hotels he preferred. The Colonel had become used to some specific, old—and just a little seedy—hotels while he booked shows throughout the South. Even with Elvis being a big star, he hated to change his pattern. So one night in Mobile he booked himself and Elvis into a less-than-fashionable place, where it turned out Elvis didn't have air-conditioning. Elvis called downstairs and asked the woman at the front desk to send up a fan.

"I don't have time to fool with you," she said abruptly. "Don't you know that Elvis is in town!"

The Colonel had a lot of imagination and he stayed close to the street. His job was to create an aura around Elvis, to make him look like an even bigger star than he was. In the early days he'd let it slip where Elvis was recording, then alert the press that hundreds of teenage girls were mobbing the studio. That's smart marketing as far as I'm concerned.

Former RCA promotion man Gaylen Adams once told the *Atlanta Constitution* how Colonel Parker cooked up a scheme to publicize Elvis's film *Tickle Me.* He ordered 350,000 feathers to attach to promotional photos he was selling. On receiving the order, he complained to the supplier that he'd been shorted by 50,000. The man was stunned that the Colonel had counted them, and said as much.

The colonel didn't lie, he just asked: "Don't you count everything you buy?" He got his extra 50,000 feathers, and jacked the price of the photos from the usual $4.00 to $8.00, thereby making the extra feathers amount to a tidy profit.

Nobody should be surprised at the way the man's mind worked; after all, some credited him with inventing the foot-long hot dog. The trick was, he made them by slicing a hot dog down the middle and covering up the skimpier yet longer dog with sauerkraut. It's no stretch, then, to imagine how his mind worked when he noticed young men at Elvis Presley concerts grumbling when their girlfriends bought "I Love Elvis" pins for a dollar. Easily solved. Just have the same number of "I Hate Elvis" pins manufactured and sell them to the disgruntled boyfriends. And when asked how he could in good conscience take 50 percent of Elvis's earnings, the Colonel didn't miss a beat: "He takes fifty percent of my earnings."

I don't know why people give a damn about that 50 percent the Colonel took from Presley. Carl Perkins told me he never once heard Elvis complain about it, and if it was all right with Elvis, it ought to be all right with everyone else.

THE COLONEL WAS a great fan of *Nashville Now* and had visited the show some years back. He didn't want to be interviewed, though, so I simply introduced him from the stage. In 1994 I wanted to talk with him about the possibility of doing an in-depth, in-person interview with me, and our mutual friend, booking agency owner Buddy Lee, gave me his Las Vegas phone number. Buddy, I'm sorry to report, is yet another friend that passed away in this winter of 1997–98.

I called the Colonel and while he declined a lengthy interview, he talked with me for quite a while. His responses to my questions showed the Colonel to be as sharp and sassy as ever.

He told me, for example, that the first act he ever managed was pop star Gene Austin. Gene is a cousin of country singer Tommy Overstreet, and I commented:

"So that's how you know Tommy Overstreet."

"That's how he knows me," the Colonel clarified.

*   *   *

HE WAS A promoter up to the day he died. When I talked with him he'd just finished promoting the Wayne Newton show and was gearing up for Bill Cosby.

"You're consulting the Baron Hilton in Vegas?" I asked.

"Yes, but I don't have a contract. The last time I had a contract with them it would have to be fifteen years or so ago. I didn't hear from them when the time was up so I wrote them a nice thank-you letter and said if they ever needed me to call. I got a letter back right away. It said 'Perish the thought of you ever leaving this team.' And I've been with them ever since without a contract."

"They must think a lot of you," I said.

"They know that I do a job," he said confidently. "I've had offers far better financially since those new places went up but I stayed with the Hilton. It's like the artists moving from record company to record company. See, when I started Elvis, my deal was with Sam Phillips, but once we moved to RCA we stayed there. All these artists go with one record company a while and then another one, four or five different ones. With Eddy Arnold it was RCA and Elvis was RCA and we had all kinds of offers from other companies but I stayed with them. They handled our tour. You move around too much and you finally get wore out."

He was quick to reveal both his role with the Hilton and the fact that he was still a powerbroker in the business. "I don't book the acts," he explained. "The hotel books them and puts together their promotions—billboards and all. I do the extras, the radio spots and posters, that kind of thing. I handled Ricky Van Shelton for Buddy Lee when Ricky played the rodeo here. I've been doing George Strait for the past four years. I got George the connection for that movie, *Pure Country,* with Warner Brothers. I'd been telling him for years that he ought to make a movie, and he'd always say, 'No, Colonel, I'm no actor.' I said, 'Well, you ought to try.' So a couple of years ago I got Irv Woolsey together with Jerry Weintraub. So when George was in the press he said, 'It's the Colonel made it all happen.' "

Golden words to the Colonel's ears. And true, too. He did make

a lot of things happen. Back in the mid-1950s a lot of show promoters and bookers "set up office" in WSM's lobby. I remember when
I first came to WSM, all the stars' mailboxes were down at one end
of the hall. It was a huge station, built to accommodate live radio
shows with audiences of up to three hundred people. Many of the
old-time promoters received their mail there, or simply hung
around to wheel and deal with the Opry acts. The Colonel wheeled
and dealed with the best of them, and wound up managing both
Eddy Arnold and Hank Snow, two of the biggest acts in country
music. I asked him who was the first country act he booked.

"Clyde Moody. I booked some dates for him. Then I had the
Carter family, Mother Maybelle, June Carter. I kept them working.
I even had June Carter with Elvis for some dates. I started with Eddy
Arnold when he was working on the Grand Ole Opry. Roy Acuff
called me and said 'Why don't you talk to Eddy?' That's how it
started. Back then I was handling the tent show for Harry Stone with
Jam Up and Honey, and Uncle Dave Macon and I used to travel in
the car with his son. Uncle Dave used to carry a ham with him when
we'd leave on a Monday morning, and go into little towns like Hope,
Arkansas, where we played. I booked the dates. Uncle Dave would
bring the ham into the cafes and get the cook to slice it and we'd
have country ham and eggs in those restaurants! I worked with
J. L. Frank, Pee Wee King's father-in-law, and Pee Wee knows all
about me."

I knew that the Colonel was working on a book and didn't want
to be interviewed about Elvis, but I thought that since he'd brought
up the King of Rock 'n' Roll, maybe I could get him started in that
direction. "Did you have Hank Snow when you found Elvis?" I
asked.

"I didn't find Elvis. He found me. I hadn't even heard about
him," the Colonel quickly explained. "I don't want to discuss Elvis
because I have my own book in progress. But I will talk to you about
the Grand Ole Opry, because you are a nice man. You're an institution today, an important man to that company. I watch your show
when I'm home. You're doing a hell of a job. Because you're the
only one in the country that's doing an organized setup that's consistently sticking to the routine that you started with."

I told him how much I appreciated his comments: great compliments coming from a man like Tom Parker. He continued talking about the Opry days, when he first met Hank Snow.

"I was booking the early dates for RCA on Eddy Arnold, then one time I had a tour with Minnie Pearl and Hank Snow. I set the tour up like they do today with all these sponsors. RCA wanted to promote Hank's special album, *I Don't Hurt Anymore*. We went on tour and I had a whole flock of country acts on there. Hank was the headliner. It made him a hit record. We sold records, and if they bought Hank's album, they could see the show for fifty cents. We had Paul Howard and Wally Fowler. Ernest Tubb. I was one of the stump guys who kept the acts working in Florida, Arkansas and all over the country. I booked a couple of hundred dates on Ernest Tubb."

I was interested in the Acuff/Arnold connection, and asked the Colonel to elaborate about Roy, Eddy and the Grand Ole Opry. "When Roy couldn't get enough bookings I'd book whatever was open, so we became good friends. I met Eddy Arnold when he was on the Opry, and I realized Eddy couldn't go nowhere just doing the Opry every Saturday night. They paid scale, and what the hell?"

"You caused Eddy to leave the Opry then," I said.

"I sure did. He did too. He had to want to leave or he wouldn't have left," the Colonel assured me. "But what would you do if you were an artist and you were getting seventy dollars a night or whatever the scale was, and I got him a shot a week later on the Prince Albert segment of the Opry. I was the first guy who ever got a thousand dollars to do the Prince Albert segment. Rod Brassfield, remember him, I took him to New York and paid all his expenses and got him a deal with Prince Albert for so much a week for a year. The Opry and WSM actually made more stars than the station gets credit for, but when they got big and could make more money, they left. But back when we got started we went back to WSM when they needed us, guest appearances. Hank Snow had never been on a big New York show. A week after we got started I got him on *The Perry Como Show* for a thousand dollars. I got Eddy *The Dinah Shore Show* for the summer."

*   *   *

WHEN I FIRST came to town, the Opry was getting a piece of everything from live performances to booking. The Colonel would never let a thing like that get past him. Nor would Eddy. But when Eddy resigned, someone at the Opry warned him, "How can you leave? The Opry is what's making people big stars!" To which Eddy allegedly replied, "If that were true the Fruit Jar Drinkers would be the biggest act in America."

"How long were you with Eddy?" I asked.

"Close to ten years," he said.

I asked him how long he was with Hank Snow, wondering if the antagonistic feeling was just on Hank's part, due to his belief that the Colonel aced him out of 50 percent of Elvis Presley's management.

"I never was with Hank Snow per se, we only had an agency together," the Colonel said. "When the company got involved with Elvis it just didn't work out. See, Bob Neal was handling Elvis Presley in the beginning. I was just the consultant until we made a settlement and split up. I couldn't make the thing work with other people. No way. Then Elvis went to the army for two years and I spent my money keeping Elvis's name alive for the two years until he came out. That's why we only did four television shows."

"Well, there's all those stories about you having Hank Snow on those shows and Hank couldn't follow Elvis," I commented.

"All I know is this, Hank Snow could follow anybody," the Colonel said. "Hank was a great artist. You hear all that crap and I pay no attention to it. There's so many distorted facts. Once my book comes out . . ."

"When is your book coming out?" I asked.

"I don't know. I run out and get new stuff all the time," he said. "We have different people working on it. I'm eighty-four now, and if I don't finish it myself Loanne will finish it."

The Colonel had married Loanne about four years earlier, at age eighty. He was quick to remind me that his first wife, Marie, had been very active in the charitable organizations in Madison, Tennessee.

"I was married for forty-two years to Marie, who lived in Madison and belonged to all the clubs there. You ever hear of the King's

Daughters in Madison? It's an organization in Madison, did you ever hear of Louise Draper or the Draper people in Madison?''

I told him I'd heard of the Drapers.

"They owned those big stores down there," the Colonel said. "Louise Draper—now you're getting an interview that you couldn't get if you paid me for it. Louise was in charge of the King's Daughters. And the King's Daughters in Madison have a big home there and they take care of children of mothers who have to work. I put the kitchen there in that home. Over the years I probably donated fifteen or twenty-five thousand dollars to them. Over the years, I've donated over $300,000 to Davidson County and Madison and Nashville charities. Governor Frank Clement used to handle the fund for me when I was out of town. He's got the whole works. There's a little park in Madison, and I donated the $1,500 to buy the property. That's forty-five years ago or so."

After the Colonel died, I decided to give Louise Draper a call and find out more about the charitable side of the Colonel. So many nasty things had been written about the man, I thought maybe Louise would have a different perspective. Indeed she did. Louise had been reading the same negative stories as I had, and had tried to set at least part of the record straight. In a letter to the Nashville *Tennessean,* she stated:

> With the death of Colonel Tom Parker go many memories for those of us at the King's Daughters Day Home. I felt it was time that others knew a different side of this man who seemed to be a controversial figure in the media and public's eye.
>
> When we broke ground for our day care 30 years ago in Madison, Tennessee, Colonel Parker's wife, Marie, was a member of the International Order of King's Daughters and Sons, a philanthropic organization. The Parkers were the ones who furnished the kitchen for our new day care at that time.
>
> We opened with 5 children, ages 3 to 5 years and a staff of 3 (cook, teacher and director). We are now licensed for 75 children and 20 more for a summer program. This school caters to disadvantaged and single parents. Regardless of resources no child is turned away who has a need.
>
> The continued service this day care renders is due to the fine, caring people like Colonel Parker. His generosity continued even after the illness and death of his first wife, Marie. His gifts contin-

ued year round, whenever a need arose: a refrigerator, a washer and dryer, and checks for special days such as Easter and Christmas.

At the death of Marie Parker, the Colonel requested in lieu of flowers that donations be sent to the day home in her memory. The response was unbelievable. These gifts helped add an additional room to the center which was badly needed.

We are indeed grateful for this special man, who always asked that no mention be made of his gifts. Those of us who knew him will always remember and give thanks.

Sincerely, Louise Draper (Charter Member of the Board, King's Daughters Day Home)

THE COLONEL DID a lot of giving that people didn't know about. And he was very practical about it. The fund that Frank Clement oversaw was earmarked for smaller organizations and charities that didn't get the big publicity and big donations. It was the Colonel who insisted that Elvis's gold Cadillac be donated to the Country Music Hall of Fame. "I've been a lifetime member of the CMA," the Colonel explained. "Elvis and I owned the car together. The estate wanted to sell it, and I wanted to donate it. It was in a hell of a mess, had been stored for four or five years. It would have cost about twenty thousand dollars to fix it all up. We ended up donating it."

Ever the promoter, the Colonel paused, then added: "There's a plaque there with my name on it."

His pragmatic approach to gift-giving is best shown in a story he told me about one of his contemporaries, an old-time booker and agent named Oscar Davis. Oscar Davis, known as the Baron of the Box Office, was a great friend to the Colonel. In his later years, Oscar fell ill, and Buddy Lee decided to throw a fund-raiser for him. The Colonel again responded in typical "cut to the chase" fashion.

"Oscar got broke and in a desperate position and then he got sick. And Buddy Lee had a stag party to make some money for Oscar. They were going to sell tickets and asked me to buy ten tickets at two dollars apiece. I wrote them a letter and said, 'What's twenty dollars going to do for Oscar Davis?'

"Furthermore, I didn't think a stag party was proper to help people out. And from then on, I sent Oscar Davis a hundred dollars a month."

*   *   *

I ASKED THE Colonel what he thought of country music these days, and he had but one criticism: "I'll say this, the only thing that's losing the flavor a little bit is the dressing up, it's getting away from the country atmosphere," he said. "One guy who always stayed with his costumes is Hank Snow."

"You like the rhinestones, then?" I asked.

"Yes. I think they should use that once in a while to retain the early days when they started."

"Porter still does," I reminded him.

"Yes, he does. Like for example, the shows they do in New York would have more impact if they were all in their costumes. Not gaudy, but the country style. They shouldn't dress too modern."

SINCE WHAT I really wanted was to conduct an in-depth interview with the Colonel, I again asked him if I could come to Las Vegas.

"No, this is the best interview I can give you," he said. "I'm saving all that for my book. This is more than I ever give anybody. I've had a lot of offers to do a book on the Opry. Figures you wouldn't believe. I remember right after Elvis died, a couple of people from New York came and offered me a half million bucks to talk about country artists. But they were looking for filth. I turned down two million after Elvis died. See I was going to open my own office as a consultant. Elvis's father asked me to stay with him. I did. When Vernon died, Priscilla asked me to stay with them."

I think it was important to the Colonel that people know he was on good terms with Priscilla Presley. He brought up the Elvis Presley stamp ceremony in January 1993, and even asked his wife, Loanne, to mail me copies of the press clippings. She did, and in an article about the official stamp ceremony, Priscilla was quoted as saying, "I would like to thank Colonel Parker for being a vital and significant force in Elvis's career. I'm sorry that he couldn't be here to help celebrate this very special occasion. He's been very supportive and a very good friend to all of us here at Graceland."

The Colonel made sure I understood why he wasn't present at

Graceland. It was because he was in Las Vegas, taking care of business. "They were going to send a plane for me but I couldn't because we had a special post office at the Hilton and I had to work there with the stamp signing envelopes," he said.

With the Colonel's help, Las Vegas set a postal record with over six thousand fans and stamp collectors lining up to buy the Elvis stamp, with a special hand-cancellation commemorating the event, personally signed by Colonel Tom Parker. The postal service earned over $37,000 in sales that day.

Since the Colonel had brought up his book again, I mentioned that Hubert Long, an old-time manager, had told me that the Colonel was considering titling his memoir *How Much Does It Cost If It's Free?* That got him started first on Hubert, and then on why he was considering that title.

"Hubert was a record salesman in Houston for RCA," he explained. "We played there with Eddy and he came around the show and he was a right-away guy. Hell, I got mail from him, letters when he came to see me before he died. I gave Hubert some good advice once, and it's good advice for any manager or booker or record label executive.

"I said 'Don't never fall in love with your artists. Don't get too close. Don't try to live next door. Let them live their own lives. Otherwise you'll be a slave.' Like Elvis. He always called to see the Colonel. He lived his life and I lived mine. I kept my nose out of his personal business."

Then the Colonel told me a story that in his mind explained not only the title, but how he viewed business deals.

"There's not much that you get for free that doesn't cost you something," he said. "An advertising salesman friend of mine came to see me once. I'd just been out on the road with the Duke of Paducah—I did all the stuff for the Duke. When I got home, my friend was sitting on the porch. He said, 'Gosh I've been waiting for you for two days.' I said, 'What the hell you doing waiting for me for two days here on my porch?' He said, 'I went to the bank in Madison to borrow five thousand dollars. The banker said he'd give me the loan if you co-signed.'

"I was a longtime customer at that bank. I'd gone to them for a loan when I was just starting with Eddy Arnold. I had no money and we needed promotion money, so the banker said, 'What do you have for collateral?'

"I said 'I got an old car out there that I paid a hundred and forty-five dollars for at four dollars a month.'

"He said, 'There's no value there.'

"So I said, 'Even if it was a good car and I welshed on the loan, what difference does it make what the car's worth?'

"So he loaned me the money just on my face. I paid him back in about a year and a half. That's still my bank today.

"So back to the friend who was sitting on my porch wanting me to co-sign a loan. I said, 'Jesus Christ, what the hell's the matter with you? Why do you go to the bank to borrow five thousand dollars? Why didn't you come to me?'

"He said, 'You mean you would lend me five thousand dollars?'

"I said, 'Yeah, you go to the bank and tell them if they sign the note, I'll let you have it.'

"So the banker called me the next day and said the guy had come over there and asked them to sign the note. I said, 'Sure, I'm like you, I want to know I'll get my money back.'

"That's show business."

I asked him what he did with his time. "I read a lot, and I have a lot of friends who call and talk," he said. "I think a lot. I've got plenty to do."

I thanked him for talking with me, and told him I might call again sometime if he didn't mind.

"Right," the Colonel said. "Just don't give my number away."

"MAKE 'EM LAUGH, MAKE 'EM CRY AND SCARE HELL OUT OF 'EM!"

COLONEL TOM PARKER was a big fan of Smiley Burnette, and even dressed up to impersonate him once in a while. And after hearing Porter Wagoner talk about Smiley's philosophy regarding showmanship, it's easy to see why the Colonel admired his style. Smiley's best remembered for being Gene Autry's comic sidekick, but Smiley was an accomplished singer and composer, a member of the Nashville Songwriter Hall of Fame. Smiley first met Gene when he auditioned for a role in one of his western films. They were filming in the Grand Canyon, and Smiley had to sing Gene some original songs as part of his audition. He sang two or three duds, and Gene instructed him to go back to his motel and write a good song. The next morning Smiley showed up with "Riding Down the Canyon," which became a western classic and a huge hit for Gene. Needless to say, Smiley got the job.

In the early days of his career, Porter Wagoner toured with Smiley as a sideman, and Porter says he learned the ropes of show business from him. Smiley and his band played a lot of small-town theaters back then, attracting a wide-ranging audience: kids, teenagers, middle-aged folks and the elderly. "Smiley always said he had to do three things at every show for it to be a success," Porter says. "First, make 'em laugh, then make 'em cry—then scare hell out of 'em. He was a great storyteller, so he had both funny stories and tearjerker tales. But the way he'd scare the audience was with his pistol. Since he was known as a western star, he always carried a gun. He'd come out and give a lecture about gun safety, reminding the kids that they should never, ever mess with a gun unless they made absolutely sure it was unloaded. Then he'd pull out his pistol and point it at the ceiling and pull the trigger: click. Then he'd pause and fire it again. This time there'd be a blank in it and it would sound like a cannon going off. All those kids would jump and scream, and he'd go off the stage happy that he'd scared hell out of them. The kids loved it, of course.''

Smiley also taught Porter to travel light. "I'd go out on a four-day run with seven or eight suitcases." Porter laughs. "Smiley would go with one shirt, one pair of pants and one pair of boots. Every night he'd wash out his clothes and shine his boots. I'd end up waggin' all them suitcases all over and Smiley'd just shake his head. I couldn't travel that way, washing out my clothes every night. But I did learn to cut down on the baggage!''

20

BARBARA MANDRELL:

THE QUEEN OF BLUE-EYED SOUL

REFUSES TO REST ON HER LAURELS

hile I was on vacation in September 1997, I picked up a newspaper and read the headline: COUNTRY STAR CALLS IT QUITS. The article said Barbara Mandrell was going to retire from music and devote her time to an acting career. I first met Barbara in 1968 when Merle Travis brought her to my television show. In the years since we've become close friends, like family, really; Barbara is like a sister to me, so the surprise announcement came as a shock. She later told me that I wasn't the only one in the dark; her mother and father hadn't been a part of the decision-making process. When Barbara told Mary Mandrell, she said, "Oh, so you're going to be unemployed?"

I asked Barbara what plans she had, then, for the future. "Ralph, you sound like me talking to my daughter!" She laughed.

"Why did you do it, Barbara?" I asked.

"It's a matter of time," she said. "I've had to turn down a lot of scripts because of my tour schedule, including a film I really wanted to make. If I'd agreed to do it, I would have had to cancel dates I'd already agreed to, and I couldn't do that."

"I can't believe it was a decision you made overnight."

"No, it took me about two years to come to the conclusion that I wanted to really make a commitment to acting," she said. "I think it was after I guest starred on *The Commish*. My character was a really awful person, and I got a big kick out of playing her!''

I remembered that episode. Barbara played an evil, conniving psychiatrist who tries to murder the Commish and almost succeeds. She was bone-chilling in the part, too. When Reba McEntire saw the show she called Barbara and said, ''Wow, you make a great bitch!'' Barbara's husband Ken said, ''Hmm. This is typecasting.'' I think that's one of the reasons Barbara and Ken have one of the best marriages in show business—they love to rag each other and frequently do.

Barbara explained that playing her recurrent role in Aaron Spelling's *Sunset Beach* had presented problems while she was touring. ''Soaps are all-consuming,'' she said. ''You usually get one night to memorize your script for the next day's shoot. So I'd film all week, then catch a plane for weekend concerts, and be memorizing lines on a redeye flight back to Los Angeles Sunday night.''

Barbara plays Alex Mitchum on the show, a world-renowned photojournalist, a cancer survivor and the mother of a grown son. The character isn't a bit like the evil psychiatrist on *The Commish;* Alex is so nice she left town rather than indulge in an affair with a married man with whom she was smitten. ''I was kind of disappointed,'' Barbara says with a sly grin. ''I thought, 'Darn it, this woman is *too* good!' ''

I asked Barbara if there were any scripts she'd turn down because of the character.

''I don't think I'd want to play a country singer because people would always be thinking 'Barbara Mandrell' instead of the character. I played a bar singer on *Touched By an Angel,* and asked them to rewrite one scene where the character wants to go to Nashville to get a break. I suggested she choose Atlanta so people wouldn't have the Mandrell/country music image.''

''Any other taboos?''

''I wouldn't play anyone who was Satanic,'' she said.

''How about a prostitute?''

''That wouldn't bother me.''

''An alcoholic?''

''Sure.''

"A dope addict?"

"Oh, yeah."

"So basically, you'd rather play the Wicked Witch than the Fairy Princess?"

Barbara laughed. "It's so much easier to be mean! I can't cry on demand."

I asked Barbara if there were any songs that brought her to tears and she named two: "That's What Friends Are For," which she recorded in 1976, and a religious song, "He Grew the Tree." When she cut "That's What Friends Are For," she teared up when she got to the song's tag. She told her producer, Tom Collins, that she would have to re-sing the lines. "Oh no you won't, Barbara," Tom said. "That was perfect." Producers dream of those moments when such powerful emotion is captured. On the other hand, "He Grew the Tree" got out of hand.

"I'd start to sing and immediately start crying," she explained. "And I don't mean tearing up, I mean crying enough that we had to start over! The song is such a powerful one that I really had to hold myself together to finish the session."

Surely, then, I said, she'd be able to bring up that emotion in an acting situation.

"I've pulled off a crying scene twice," she said. "Once I really had to work at it and the other time it came natural. I was supposed to cry on *Sunset Beach* when my character was told her cancer was worsening. I went over in the corner and it took a while to work up to a good cry, but by the time they started shooting tears were falling. Then, wouldn't you know it, I didn't hear them say 'cut' and stood there crying for several more minutes. They thought I was just having an emotional reaction to the scene. I thought, 'Isn't somebody *ever* gonna say "cut"?' "

"The next time was easier—it was when my daughter Jaime and I worked together in an episode of *Diagnosis Murder*. Jaime played the murderer and I played her mother who confesses in a desperate attempt to protect her. That scene called for tears, and it seemed so real that they flowed freely."

Barbara's daughter Jaime has been trying to break into films, and she's learning it isn't a walk in the park. "Her career is starting out like so many others," Barbara said. "You go and read for a part and don't get it. Then you go and read for another part and you don't get it. It's that old L.A. joke:

" 'What do you do?'

" 'I'm an actor.'

" 'Oh, where are you waiting tables?'

"I was worried about her and sat down for a big mother/ daughter talk. I told her I understood how it must hurt to get turned down again and again. 'Talk to me when you are feeling down,' I said. Jaime just smiled and said, 'Oh, it doesn't hurt. That's just the way the business works. I'll know I'll get something eventually.' What a great attitude! So I told her to keep that 'don't take no for an answer' attitude and to never depend on others to do it for you. I also told her to stay modest on the outside, but burst with confidence down inside her spirit. I think that's very important."

Barbara says confidence and attitude are important, and for her there's another part of the success equation: goal setting. "A couple of years before I turned forty I made a list of things I wanted to accomplish before that birthday rolled around," she said. "One of the things I wanted to do was to coordinate an event in Nashville that would bring in celebrities from a variety of fields to raise money for a worthy cause. I wanted to show off our city to public figures—and remind the public that Nashville is a great city, known for more than country music. We have so much here—great hospitals, universities, book publishing companies—many things that make us proud."

Barbara pulled off that goal when she hosted 1988's Barbara Mandrell Celebrity Softball Classic to raise money for Vanderbilt University's Organ Donor/Transplantation Program. It took her a year to carry out the plan, but the game was well worth the time and energy and probably one of the most fun times I've had in my entire career. The event raised over a half million dollars and drew together most of country's big stars as well as people like Bob Hope, Herschel Walker, Oprah Winfrey, L. L. Cool J., Erma Bombeck, Chuck Norris, Lynn Swann, Walter Payton, Betty White, Meat Loaf, Sheena Easton, Dick Clark—too many celebrities to begin to name. Another thing she put on her things-to-do-before-forty list was the writing of her autobiography, something she'd been unwilling to do in years past. *From the Heart,* published in 1990, was a bestseller.

"After years of saying I would never write a book, I realized I had a story to tell that might help someone. That story was about my wreck, my head injuries and all that I went through—and put other people through—on my way to recovery."

She was referring to the 1984 head-on collision on Nashville's Briley Parkway, a crash that nearly killed her. "I became a different person," Barbara admitted. "I stuttered. I didn't want to be around people. I wanted to crawl into a hole, and I most certainly didn't want to perform. My father told me, 'Barbara, don't let some car wreck stop you from performing. If you decide to quit, let it be your decision. Don't let someone else take it out of your hands.' It took three years—three healings—to get completely over the wreck. I guess the best way to describe it is that I felt there were three layers of fabric around me that had to be lifted away to get back to me."

I told Barbara that I had a photo of her—one of many—hanging on my office wall. It's a shot taken after her comeback performance on February 28, 1986, at the Universal Amphitheater in Los Angeles. Standing there with Lee Greenwood, Tammy Wynette and Morgan Fairchild, Barbara looks a little like a whipped puppy.

"I was terrified that night," she reflected. "I'd never had stage fright in my life but after the accident I was afraid of everything. I had cue cards for everything—every song lyric and every word I spoke on stage. When I read lines, I didn't stutter. Gene Miller, who worked for me, gave me some important advice before the show: 'Fear doesn't come from God. Fear comes from Satan, so when you're afraid, don't cry out to God, rail at Satan.' "

One of the oddest sensations occurred when Barbara began listening to her old albums. It was like she was hearing them for the first time. "I really listened with detachment," she now says. "Sometimes I'd say, 'Oh, that was great.' And other times I'd say, 'Holy Moly! Why did I ever let that one go out?' "

Talking about her albums made me wonder if Barbara could be happy unless she was making records, playing concert dates and performing for the huge audiences she attracts.

"The thing I've loved about my career in show business is that it's been exciting," Barbara said. "I knew what I was going for and what I was hungry for. But I didn't know what the future held. That uncertainty made every step interesting. I don't know what's ahead now, but I'm confident that whatever it is, I'm going to be happy."

THAT'S A VERY typical Barbara Mandrell philosophy: charge right ahead and see what happens. If it doesn't happen soon enough, see if you can give it a little shove. ("I always pray for patience," Barbara laughs. "And I ask God if He could do it right away.") But whatever your ultimate goal, or destination, is—enjoy yourself along the way. Barbara has enjoyed each step of her career.

Unlike many of her contemporaries, she never had another kind of job. As a child Barbara was a multi-instrumental whiz playing steel guitar, saxophone, dobro and five-string banjo. Her steel playing so impressed guitarist Joe Maphis that he invited her to join his show at the Showboat Club in Las Vegas. By the time she was fourteen and the Mandrell Family Band was formed, Barbara had already toured with stars including Red Foley, Tex Ritter and Johnny Cash. The Mandrell Family Band played shows in Vegas, military installations in California and benefits—anywhere they could get work. Her father Irby often booked military shows, since the military was exempt from California's strict laws concerning minors performing in nightclubs.

This wasn't the first time Barbara retired from music. She married the family band's drummer, Ken Dudney, in 1967, and when he joined the military she briefly quit performing. But when Ken was shipped overseas, Barbara came to Nashville, where her parents had moved, and attended the Grand Ole Opry.

"It's weird," she told me. "Before that night I never thought about the national recognition side of music. But that night when I sat up in the balcony and watched Dolly Parton onstage, I knew I wanted to be there, too. I loved watching the people's faces—seeing their smiles—as they watched Dolly sing."

She signed with Columbia Records in 1969 and never slowed down. She had solo hits with songs like "Do Right Woman, Do Right Man" (and named her band the Do-Rites) and "The Midnight Oil," as well as a string of duet hits with labelmate David Houston. In 1976 she moved to ABC-Dot (later absorbed into MCA) and continued her string with "Married But Not to Each Other," "Standing Room Only," and the trademark "Sleeping Single in a Double Bed."

Barbara's chart-toppers would take up an entire chapter, for radio and the public quickly warmed to the little blonde whose blues-tinged vocals had the press dubbing her "The Queen of Blue-Eyed Soul."

In 1980 she was named Entertainer of the Year by both the Country Music Association and the Academy of Country Music; when she was given the CMA Entertainer of the Year nod again in 1981 she became the first artist in history to win for two consecutive years. By 1980 she had her own wildly successful network television show, *Barbara Mandrell and the Mandrell Sisters,* a show that probably did as much to heighten country music's visibility as any other artist's show ever did.

Then, in 1984 came the car wreck. I didn't realize just how serious her injuries were in the immediate aftermath of the crash. I remember giving her a book, knowing that she was an avid reader. What I didn't know was that following the wreck she refused to read anything. They were tough times, and as you saw earlier in the chapter, recovery wasn't swift. Now Barbara can look back on those days with objectivity, even humor at times. "If I get into a no-win argument with Ken I'll sometimes say, 'Well, I had a head injury. What's your excuse?' "

She laughs easily, at herself, at society's foibles. When we talked of her new direction I asked how she'd feel, being a novice of sorts in the movie world when she was already such a legend in her own musical setting.

"Hey, I'm an old lady about to turn fifty and it's great to still be learning!" she said with a grin. "I've got three children. Two of them are grown and one is in the sixth grade. And I'm still learning and growing. That's got to make life exciting."

I told her I was glad she could joke about age because getting older bothers me at times. It seems like you become expendable as you grow older. Instead of valuing you for your knowledge and experience, some people would just as soon throw you out with the trash. I don't feel old. I work out and I eat right. So it's sometimes hard to realize society might perceive me as over-the-hill.

Barbara told me something I'm going to remember, because it's an interesting take on the passing of years and youth:

"When I turned twenty-two, I was twenty-two," she said. "Then I turned twenty-three and found that I was still twenty-two. When I turned thirty, I was twenty-two and sure enough, when I turned forty, I was *still* twenty-two. That's how I felt! So Christmas of 1998, when some folks might say I'm turning fifty, you can bet I'll be turning twenty-two again. I don't care what they say."

She does seem young. And maybe it's that unquenchable spirit she has, the one that keeps her from resting on her professional laurels, the one that allows her to take on a whole new world in midlife. I'll bet she conquers it, too.

MEL TILLIS ONCE told me about a classic incident that happened at the deejay convention held here every year. First called the Grand Ole Opry Birthday Party, this was a function dreamed up by the WSM publicity staff to try and romance country deejays. It was held at the Andrew Jackson Hotel during October in the early days, then moved to the Opryland Hotel during February and renamed Country Radio Seminar. I used to set up shop at the Andrew Jackson Hotel and broadcast my daily shows from the convention.

It was freewheeling back then; events used to get out of hand more than they do these days, what with artists, deejays, record label people and the media partying until dawn. Now they're a little more businesslike. But back in the old days, you never knew who you were going to stumble into around the next corner. And you never knew who might crawl in your window.

Mel had taken rooms at the Capitol Park Inn with Wayne Walker, who wrote hits including "Just Before Dawn." Somewhere along the line, the two had hooked up with Billy Swan, who was just getting started in the business, and the good-time king, Johnny Paycheck. Mel says they'd been partying pretty hard when they stumbled back to the Capitol Park Inn. They all went in for a nightcap, and Billy admitted he had no money for a room.

"Well, all right," Mel said. "S-s-stay here. But this room only has two beds. You'll have to s-s-sleep in the bathtub." Mel, of course, often stammers and has made a second career out of joking about it. The only time he has no speech problem is when he sings.

Johnny Paycheck left to find his car and get to his own hotel, and Billy Swan grabbed a pillow and curled up in the tub. Since Nashville was still in the middle of an early fall heat wave, Mel opened a screenless window before he lay down on his bed.

It had been a long day, and Mel told me he was so wound up from all the festivities that he was, in his words, "laying there addled." All of a sudden he heard a noise, and opened his eyes only to see a man crawling in the window he'd left open. Without daring to move, he peered over at Wayne, who was snoring by this time. Mel's stammer becomes very pronounced when he gets excited, and try as he might, he couldn't spit out even one word. Finally he opened his mouth and sang at the top of his lungs: "Oh, Wayne, wake up. Somebody's 'a comin' through the window."

Then Johnny Paycheck's voice whispered from the window. "Stop singin', Mel—it's just me looking for my car keys."

21

IT WAS A VERY
GOOD YEAR

Talking with Barbara Mandrell about aging reminded me of a song I love: "It Was a Very Good Year." I recalled that one of my favorite nights on *Nashville Now* was in 1989 when Richie Havens performed that song on the twentieth anniversary of Woodstock. I didn't even know Woodstock was coming up back in 1969. I was in New York to do a syndicated radio show, and nobody in the office mentioned it until after it was all over. Then, of course, everybody was talking about it.

Richie opened the show the day he performed. He was scheduled to go on fifth in the lineup, but artists were stuck at the hotel, unable to get to the field where they were to play until they could get helicoptered in. Since Richie was the first one there he opened the show and played for three hours. The song he opened with was "Nobody Left to Crown."

"That song is a message that we as a people must learn to do something for ourselves and not wait for somebody larger than life to come along and do it for us," Richie told me.

Listening to his performance of "It Was a Very Good Year" on *Nashville Now* twenty years later made me sorry I'd missed his three-hour set at Woodstock; he was spellbinding. I don't have to recite all the lyrics here; I know you know how the song goes, starting with "When I was seventeen, it was a very good year." (If you've never heard the song, it mentions the ages of seventeen, twenty-one and thirty-five as being pivotal in a man's life.)

I was seventeen years old in 1950, working at the White Way Laundry in Nashville, waiting on music people like Owen Bradley, never dreaming I'd one day have a career in television. In fact, a couple of years earlier, when I picked up a copy of *Mechanics Illustrated* and saw an article about television I wondered if I'd ever live long enough to see this marvel. I couldn't imagine that special programs would be produced strictly for television. It seemed to me that television would be radio shows with pictures; they'd put a camera in the radio studio so you'd be able to tune in to broadcasts of *Fibber McGee and Molly, One Man's Family* or *Ma Perkins*.

The first time I ever saw a television set was in the window of a Western Auto Store on Gallatin Road. I was standing in a crowd of other wide-eyed gawkers watching a North Carolina football game. Then, when I was working my first radio job in Paris, Tennessee, I used to go over to the Graystone Hotel to sit in the lobby and watch snow on their television set. They had antennas, but the reception was terrible anyway. We've come a long way.

I turned twenty-one in 1954 and made my television debut in Nashville; it was a very good year. I was working at WSIX in Nashville, an ABC affiliate and the first station with which I'd worked that had more than a thousand watts of power. There I had my first opportunity to make a mark as a television announcer—for live studio wrestling. What an experience. I was supposed to do play-by-play announcing on a sport I'd never even seen! I studied wrestling books, talked to Jack Simpson, the regular announcer, and, as I mentioned in my first book, researched as though I was preparing to announce at the Olympics. I saw it all during those days; Geraldo Rivera had nothing on me. One woman urinated in excitement on the studio floor; another guy broke a soda bottle across a bleacher and charged at one of the wrestlers. No one was injured in either case. Both situations were, however, as close to reality as television wrestling ever got.

I consider myself fortunate to have lived through such interesting times. Makes you wonder what it would be like to come back in a hundred years. Sometimes, of course, the more things change, the more they stay the same. You do see the view from Nashville chang-ing—and sometimes it comes back around full circle. Thirty-two years ago I went into my friend Fred Carter Jr.'s office and told him I wanted to sing. Fred was heading up ABC Records at the time; and he's a good example of the diversity of music in Nashville, hav-ing played guitar for everybody from Bob Dylan (with whom he toured) to Willie Nelson.

I'd already done a recitation recording called "What Is a Truck Driver" and we even did a big photo spread of Fred and me in an eighteen-wheeler to promote it. Trust me, I wasn't exactly competi-tion for Dave Dudley or C. W. McCall. And when I facetiously com-plained, "All my friends sing—Fred, let me sing . . . ," nobody was more surprised than me when he agreed.

One of the things I'm proud of is that I was one of the first people in Nashville to cut a Kris Kristofferson composition; I recorded "Late Night Morning Sidewalks," which I believe must have been a precursor to "Sunday Morning Coming Down."

I never became a star, but Fred and I became fast friends, so you can imagine how tickled I was when his daughter, Deana Carter, burst onto the country music scene in 1997 to become one of the year's biggest success stories. I guess she almost had to become a singer.

"In our family you either had to sing harmony or wash dishes," she quips. "So naturally I picked a harmony part."

Deana represents both the past and the future: the view goes full circle. Her debut album, a critical success that sold four million cop-ies in about a year, is titled *Did I Shave My Legs for This?* Her label was against the title at first, but she held her ground; she's her father's daughter. She's a character in the way Dolly and Loretta are: candid and charismatic—the very characteristics I sometimes worry are lacking these days. When she won a CMA award in 1997 she ran across the stage and hopped straight up into the startled arms of presenter Ricky Skaggs. It made for great television.

WHEN I WAS thirty-five it was a very good year because after two failed marriages I'd finally found a woman who'd put up with me. Joy must have married me for love, because I didn't have any money and when we met in 1965, she'd never even heard of Ralph Emery. So I didn't have wealth or fame to offer her.

It certainly was not an affluent time. I was working hard doing the all-night radio show on WSM as well as an afternoon television show. I was going out on the road on weekends with a package show that included Hank Williams Jr. and the inimitable Audrey Williams, newcomer Waylon Jennings, Tommy Cash, Merle Travis and Faron Young. And I hosted some shows for the Navy that I recorded at Bradley Barn. All that sounds impressive, but the reality was that it didn't always bring in enough money.

I remember breathing a big sigh of relief that the United States Navy paid me right on time when Joy was in the hospital having Michael. I desperately needed that check to pay the bill and "buy" my wife and son's way out of the hospital! But all those hard years just paved the way to national television shows like *Pop Goes the Country*, *Nashville Now* and *On the Record*. So many shows over the years, and so many nights that made each year a very good one.

There was the night in 1992 that George Bush, then a sitting President, visited the show and we got to talking about television viewing habits.

"Are you one of those people who flips through the channels with a remote control?" I asked.

"I have something worse than that," President Bush said. "I have five screens with one in the middle. If I see something I want to watch I can flip a switch and turn off the others, or set them all on one channel or mute part of them or tape all five channels at once."

He paused, then said, "Barbara gets absolutely livid."

When Arkansas Governor Bill Clinton was campaigning for the presidency in 1992, he and Senator Al Gore came to *Nashville Now*. I don't know how I managed it, but I convinced Bill and Hillary to stand up and demonstrate an Arkansas hog call!

Then there was Halloween of 1986. Faron and I dressed up in costume: Faron as a convict, complete with ball and chain, and me as one of the Three Musketeers, complete with plumed hat.

"You *used* to be a sheriff," I observed.

"Yeah, I used to be a sheriff," Faron said, swinging his ball and chain. "Then I got a divorce and this is all I got left."

I started to laugh. "You mean all you got left is that one little ball?"

"You got that right. One ball, pal. One ball."

We almost had to cut to the commercial because Faron and I and the studio audience were in tears.

Another time I got dressed up was in 1993 when Shotgun Red, *Nashville Now*'s popular puppet, and I appeared as Sonny and Cher singing "I've Got You Babe." I went in drag as Cher, and it was a close call as to who I most resembled: Tiny Tim or Howard Stern.

I remember one of our "Let Minnie Steal Your Joke" episodes when neither Minnie nor I could get through the sketch without collapsing in laughter. The joke was too corny to be funny, but for some reason that made it hilarious. It went like this:

Two nuns were traveling when their van ran out of gas. They walked down the road to a gas station to buy a gallon or two, but the station had no container. So the nuns went down the road to a hospital and asked if they could borrow a container. "Certainly, Sisters," said the attendant. "But the only container available is a bedpan." The nuns accepted the loan, went back to the station and got their gas. When they were pouring it into the tank a car drove by and a guy yelled out the window:

"Now that's *real* faith."

We've had comedians from outside the country community, too. I remember introducing the very young Jay Leno and Jerry Seinfeld to my *Nashville Now* audience. I had to laugh when I recently watched *Seinfeld* in my age-reflective mood. Here was his opening joke: "My parents recently moved to Florida. They didn't want to move to Florida, but they're in their sixties and that's the law."

Earlier in this book I've detailed many favorite moments from my *On the Record* series. One I didn't get into was my interview with Andy Griffith, one of television's most valued icons. Andy told me that he believed the key to the unbelievable success of the *Andy Griffith Show* was Don Knotts's character Barney Fife. Andy said Don Knotts was the funniest actor he's ever met, and the true comic genius of the show. When Don left to make movies for Universal, the genius was gone and it marked the beginning of the end. I thought it took a big man to give his supporting star credit for one of the biggest shows in television history.

Andy shed some light on how actors play certain professions, too. Regarding his portrayal of Matlock, he told me, "I don't know anything about the law. But I know how to entertain."

When we were sitting back in the dressing room, Andy told me about a phone call he once received from an aunt. It was after he'd appeared in a television movie playing a particularly evil man. "This country needs role models," his aunt chided. "And I don't believe we need to see Andy Taylor, the lovable sheriff of Mayberry, as a villain!"

Over the years I've introduced so many stars singing their big hits: Tennessee Ernie Ford's "Sixteen Tons," Conway and Loretta's "After the Fire Is Gone," Tammy Wynette's "Stand by Your Man," Tanya Tucker's "Delta Dawn," Hank Jr.'s "Born to Boogie," Roger Miller's "King of the Road," Johnny Cash's "Folsom Prison Blues," the Judds' "Mama He's Crazy," Willie's "City of New Orleans," Trisha Yearwood's "She's in Love with the Boy," Alan Jackson's "Here in the Real World," Randy Travis's "Pickin' Up Bones," Marty Stuart and Travis Tritt's "The Whiskey Ain't Workin' "—the list goes on.

One of the best nights happened on October 13, 1970, when I introduced my two guests, Marty Robbins and Merle Haggard, on my television show at Channel 4. The show brought out such a huge audience that we had to stop letting people in at the 1,000 attendee mark. The studio had been designed for 250. Roy Rogers and Tex Ritter were in the audience and they caused quite a stir. I've thought about reediting that historic show and asking Merle (who was Hollywood handsome back then, by the way) to cohost a re-airing of it.

Another big night for me was February 26, 1991, when I got to fulfill a lifetime ambition and interview Jimmy Stewart. We were both in Oklahoma City helping raise money for the Cowboy Hall of Fame's Cowboy Crisis Fund, which helps cowboys who've fallen on hard times. I told Mr. Stewart that a woman had once called *Nashville Now* and asked me who I'd want to interview if I could pick anyone in the world, and without hesitation I said "Jimmy Stewart." He seemed pleased about that. I asked him who his favorite western stars were and without hesitation he said, "Duke Wayne would be at the top of the list. And of course my friend Hank Fonda." I mentioned that I'd heard that Henry Fonda was the actor who had shot at Jimmy Stewart more than any other in his career. "I wouldn't be surprised," Mr. Stewart said. "He really got after me." Jimmy Stewart has been in the Cowboy Hall of Fame since 1972. He's another legend we lost in 1997.

So almost fifty years in show business have gone by, and I don't know if turning sixty-five in 1998 means I'm in the autumn of my life or not. I've had reason to contemplate mortality this year, though, because for so many of my friends the winter of 1997 and 1998 was their last: Owen Bradley, piano great Floyd Cramer, Buddy Lee, Cliffie Stone, Grandpa Jones, Carl Perkins, Justin Tubb, Eddie Rabbitt, Helen Carter, Tammy Wynette. Last year I lost Bobby Dyson, the bandleader from my first television show.

Another death hit the Nashville community hard in April of 1998: Otto Kitsinger. Otto was a country music historian who worked as a researcher for me and many others in the business. I worked with him for the *On the Record* shows and so many other projects. He died of heart failure about a week after Tammy Wynette's passing. He, too, will be sorely missed. For those of us who love country music this has been a very hard year.

One thing I do know. I can hear my days and the days of Owen and Grandpa and Carl in the words of the song: "I think of my life as vintage wine from fine old kegs."

I don't know if this will be my last book. When Patsi and I started I assumed it would be, but as it came together I realized that for every story told there were four or five untold. There was no way to put them in and allow the reader to get this book home without a pickup truck to haul it in. I look back through the pages and once again am reminded of the richness and the diversity of the music Nashville makes. And I'm again reminded of those powerful words Ray Charles once said to me:

> We should never let this sound—the sounds of the hills and mountains—slip away, no more than I think we should allow the genuine old-fashioned-type Muddy Waters blues slip away. Why? We Americans don't have nothing else, musically speaking. We don't have Bach and Beethoven or Tchaikovsky or Sibelius. They're other countries' music.
>
> But Muddy Waters, George Jones—we *own* that music! We can go to the bank with *that.*

ACKNOWLEDGMENTS

Though this book is credited to the efforts of Ralph Emery and Patsi Bale Cox, I can assure you that without the help of a lot of people we could not have accomplished our task of writing *A View from Nashville*. It was a team effort.

First of all I am very indebted to Dee Jenkins, the late Conway Twitty's widow. Dee came to my office on perhaps four or five occasions to share her grief-laden memories of Conway and the subsequent relationships with members of the family. She is a nice lady with a keen intellect, a great memory and a wealth of research materials. When I discovered I could not remember all of the details of Conway's memorial service as well as I should have, she provided me with a videotape of the service from Conway's estate. I might add, Dee finds this video too painful to watch.

To try to address the question of why Conway, who had fifty-five #1 records, had surprisingly few awards as a solo artist, I consulted Jim Foglesong, who at one time directed all of the country music activities at MCA Nashville. He was also at various times on the Country Music Association's Television Committee. I discussed Conway with Joe Talbot, a Nashville publisher and music executive, as well as a big fan of Conway's music. Joe has long been a mover and shaker on the CMA Board and his insights were invaluable.

The writing of this book took place roughly from February 1997 to March 1998. Along the way I talked with many people in Nash-ville's music industry, and utilized radio and television interviews I'd done with many of the stars who appear in this book.

I want to thank Merle Kilgore, Hank Williams Jr.'s' manager, for his extensive assistance. Merle holds the distinction of having worked for both Hank Williams and his son, Hank Jr., and numbers among his close friends Johnny Cash and Johnny Horton. It was Merle who told me the eerie story recounted in the chapter titled "The Drummer Is a Rummer and Can't Hold the Beat," which deals with a message Johnny Horton sent to Merle, years after Johnny died.

On May 21, 1997, we were able to tape a story of an angel in the life of Sammy Kershaw for that same chapter. We got another ghost story from Deborah Allen. Here I want to thank Laurens Glass, who helped research this book (for all too short a time). She worked on the "Drummer" chapter as well as the follow-up interview with Theodore Bikel, where she confirmed facts about the Katharine Hepburn story. Laurens is a segment producer for Dick Clark Pro-ductions in the *Prime Time Country* series at The Nashville Network. I was sorry that she was only able to work with us a few months on the book, as her responsibilities increased with the Dick Clark organization. She's good at her job.

Anytime you do a book about country music, you're probably going to consult Bill Ivey, the Executive Director of the Country Music Foundation, and his wonderful staff. I want to thank Kent Henderson, Alan Stoker, Kyle Young and Ronnie Pugh for helping us with many aspects of this book.

A View from Nashville required an enormous amount of transcrib-ing. In addition to my sessions with my collaborator, Patsi, we tran-scribed countless television shows and radio shows dating from the late 1960s to 1998. Julie Breuher helped transcribe and was invalu-able for her fast typing and quick turnarounds.

One of the strangest stories in this book (and there are many strange ones) is the story about Johnny Horton's hit "The Battle of New Orleans." For helping clear up the confusing details, I am indebted to the song's publisher, Don Warden, who now runs Dolly Parton's Nashville office.

In developing the Vince Gill stories, I was able to call on both

Vince and his beautiful mother, Jerene Gill, who lives in Oklahoma City.

Researching the story of Alan Jackson's first years in Nashville sent us to several music executives, in addition to early interviews with Alan: Marty Gamblin, who runs Glen Campbell Enterprises' Nashville office and manages Bryan White; James Stroud, who heads Dreamworks in Nashville; and Shelby Kennedy, A&R exec at Disney's Lyric Street.

Some parts of this book were painful. One example was the Faron Young story about a longtime friend of mine who sadly took his own life. Helping with Faron's story were his son Robyn and long-time friend, country music promoter Jim Case. I also relied on a number of radio interviews I'd done with Faron in the 1970s and 1980s.

As I recount these acknowledgments, I can't help but think about interviewing Carl Perkins on May 12, 1997, and Owen Bradley on September 4, 1997. There was no way to know that it would be the last time I would talk to either of them.

I found the recollections of eighty-seven-year-old Ken Nelson fascinating. Ken ran Capitol Records' country division in the 1960s and 1970s. He now lives in California, is widowed and loves to golf with his grandson and travel with his daughter.

Additional help with the "Four Horsemen" chapter came from Opry star Carol Lee Cooper, who conducted a series of interviews with Owen Bradley, and with A-Team drummer Buddy Harmon.

Another interesting afternoon occurred in February 1998 when I interviewed Fred Foster, the man who gave Roy Orbison, Kris Kristofferson, Dolly Parton, and many others the chance to record on his label, Monument Records. Fred is gifted with a steel trap mind and has made many contributions to this wonderful business of music. Fred told me he was going to write a book one day. If you do, Fred, I'll be first in line to buy a copy.

Rick Blackburn, who now runs the Atlantic Records operation in Nashville, was once in charge of CBS Records here, and he was responsible for my Ray Charles interview. Rick, I want to thank you. It was a great experience that I'll never forget.

I'd always heard the story that Hank Williams got fired from the Opry, so I found it fascinating that the story isn't exactly accurate.

I want to thank Irving Waugh, former president of WSM Radio and Television, for pointing me in the direction of the real story, and Don Helms for telling it to me. Don was Hank's longtime steel player, starting out with the legend when he was sixteen years old and Hank was nineteen.

One day I tracked down Porter Wagoner to check out a story, and since Porter's a natural yarn spinner, I asked him for some funny tales. He came through just like I knew he would, and while we didn't use them all, the ones we did include made a great contribution.

Special thanks to Buck Owens, whom I interviewed, about the days when he and Loretta Lynn were playing music in Washington State, for Loretta's *On the Record* appearance. And thanks to Merle Haggard for his interview on Brooks & Dunn's *On the Record,* and to Rodney Crowell for his satellite appearance on Vince's *On the Record.*

When I interviewed Colonel Tom Parker, he mentioned a woman named Louise Draper, a founder of the King's Daughter's Day Home in Madison, Tennessee. When I called the Home, they put me in touch with Mrs. Draper and she kindly shared a letter she wrote to the Nashville *Tennessean* following the Colonel's death. I think you'll see a side of the Colonel you might not have guessed in that letter.

I'm extremely appreciative of the help TNN's Jim Hagans gave in providing so many photos for the book.

Special thanks to Frank Sutherland at the Nashville *Tennessean* for allowing us to use quotes from a Conway Twitty report copyrighted by the *Tennessean,* June 7, 1997.

The ladies in my office here in Nashville get a big thank-you for a myriad of phone calls, research from books, tapes, disks and whatever else it took to complete this project. I'm speaking of my valuable right arm, B. J. Haas, who runs Ralph Emery Television Productions, and Debbie Sharp, who not only keeps our spirits up, but does every task—dirty or clean—and does it well! And my daughter-in-law, Detra Emery, provided valuable office assistance through the summer of 1997 while on break from from her duties as a high school teacher.

My literary agent, Mel Berger, of the William Morris Agency in

New York, gets a special thank-you for his continued encouragement to write this book. After my first two, I didn't think I had anything left to say. Now I see that I did.

This book also gave me the opportunity to work with a remarkable editor, Henry Ferris of William Morrow. Henry's a Georgia boy now living in New York with his wife and new twin daughters. His regard for and grasp of Nashville and country music was greatly appreciated.

This book has been a labor of love. Thank-yous goes out to all the stars, musicians, writers, producers, directors and management teams that I have had the pleasure of working for and with over the past near-half century.

Finally, I'd like to thank my wife and chief sounding board, Joy, for her patience and understanding, and for her extensive help in the preparation of this book.

I hope I haven't left anyone out.

INDEX